THE JUDICIAL MIND REVISITED

STUDIES IN BEHAVIORAL POLITICAL SCIENCE

Series editor Robert Presthus

Also in the series:

POLITICAL SOCIALIZATION, Kenneth P. Langton
COMPUTER SIMULATIONS OF VOTING BEHAVIOR, William R. Shaffer

THE JUDICIAL MIND REVISITED

*Psychometric Analysis
of Supreme Court Ideology*

Glendon Schubert
University of Hawaii

New York
OXFORD UNIVERSITY PRESS
London 1974 Toronto

Copyright © 1974 by Oxford University Press, Inc.
Library of Congress Catalogue Card Number: 73-90376
Printed in the United States of America

For Robin
a lark on the wing

Foreword

Scientific research has several well-known characteristics, including its "publicness," by which is usually meant the self-conscious attempt to specify exactly how the generalizations derived from one's research are obtained. This drift, in turn, makes possible a second characteristic, replication, the reappraisal of earlier findings using alternative data and methods. But the most vital attribute of scientific research is the quality of mind we usually call objectivity or detachment. Clearly detachment has many faces, but I refer here to the condition that enables one to remain personally disengaged from his hard-won findings to the extent that he can accept another property of scientific inquiry, the fact that knowledge is accretive. In a sense, all generalizations wait to be destroyed.

All these conditions are patent in Glendon Schubert's work, and perhaps most clearly in the present volume which seems to me a model of what any discipline must become if it is to develop the body of verified generalizations that define a science. Conclusions set down earlier in *The Judicial Mind* (1965) are reviewed here in the light of more recent data and more sophisticated methods. A broader theory of ideological structures is offered which permits the application of Schubert's typologies to more comprehensive theories of political coalition-building. In most instances, e.g., the political liberalism scale and certain other factor analytic scales, the findings remain unchanged. As Schubert concludes, "the identification of major scales and their general patterning and interrelationship as reported by the earlier study are strongly confirmed by the present study." Regarding certain subscales such as racial, voting, and civic equality, the evidence is deemed "disappointing," in part because of limited sample sizes.

But even more important than the substantive contributions of this book by one of America's most creative and productive political scientists, is the example and the inspiration it provides for a disinterested scholarship. I believe this volume will have a pervasive influence in the discipline, not only among those concerned with the analysis of judicial behavior but equally among those whose major interest is in the theory and method of social science.

Robert Presthus

Preface

This book presents a theory of political ideology. The theory represents a synthesis and application of the ideas of several leading psychologists rather than of political scientists. The psychologists upon whose work I have particularly relied include Thurstone, Guttman, Eysenck, and Coombs. The theory constitutes an explication of how systems of belief concerning issues of public policy affect choices among decisional alternatives.

But theory without methodology is like bread without wine—or, as some may prefer to put it, like lyrics without music. Hence a second major emphasis in this study is upon the methods by means of which the theory is operationalized and tested. The approach here is to compare the relative efficacy of three multidimensional methods for analyzing interagreement matrices: principal-components factor analysis, oblique factor analysis, and smallest-space analysis. Each of these methods determines the position of a configuration in multidimensional space; the criterion used to appraise the relative goodness-of-fit of these configurational relationships—which model differences in political ideology among the subjects of the study—is provided by linear cumulative scales of decisional choices. So this book is also a study in comparative methodology for multivariate analysis.

Both the theory and the methods used are perfectly general and are potentially applicable to the study of political ideology in a wide variety of cultural, political, and social arenas and for subject populations ranging from mass publics to élite groups. It happens that the subject population for the empirical data examined in this particular application consists of a small political élite who play a critical policy-making role in the American polity: Supreme Court justices. These include the entire population of justices who had been members of the Court during the period of the first quarter of a century following the termination of World War II, but the primary empirical focus is upon the Supreme Court under the Chief Justiceship of Earl Warren (1953–1969). The briefer period of Fred Vinson's Chief Justiceship (1946–1953) also is examined by the same theory and methods, in order to establish a broader context within which to investigate the dynamics of ideological change. The systematic data do not extend to include the recent period of Warren Burger's Chief Justiceship, but the theory is applied, hypothetically, in discussion of post-Warren developments in policy-making by the Court. So, from a substantive point of view, this book provides a case study of policy development by the Supreme Court during an era when the impact of judicial policy—in many fields extending from racial equality to fair procedure and the right to privacy—has been a conspicuous catalyst of political and social change in American society. The emphasis here, however, is not on the description and classification of the Court's policy outputs; rather it is on describing and classifying the continuities, communalities, and differences in the policy choices of the individual justices of the Court, for whom it provides an empirical inventory. In that regard the present work functions also as a sequel to Pritchett's *Roosevelt Court*, in combination with which it provides a profile of political ideology on the Supreme Court over the course of four decades, from the beginning of the thirties through the end of the sixties.

It is perhaps somewhat unusual for an author, at least among political scientists, to be about equally concerned with theory, methodology, and the empirical characteristics of his substantive data, as I believe I have been in the present work. But there are at least two additional respects in which this book is even more unusual. As its title implies, this study is an overlapping replication of an earlier one. Taking advantage of the more sophisticated methods and better data now available, the present study undertakes both a reliability and a validity check on the earlier one. In a field that is still bedeviled by individualistic notions to the effect that every doctoral dissertation should make both an unique contribution to knowledge (instead of contributing to confidence by confirming the findings of others), it is no more customary for writers to exhume their earlier efforts than it is for doctors to exhibit the patients with whom they have been unsuccessful—both political science writers and physicians prefer to bury their dead, let sleeping dogs lie, etcetera. Here, to the contrary, a different conception of the philosophy of behavioral science supplies the premise for my belief that we ought to be at least as willing to re-examine our own possible mistakes as we are eager to expose the failings of others.

The other respect in which this book is unusual is found in its employment of both physical modeling and color photography for objectives that are functionally related to the analysis. Rejecting the traditions that help to keep social scientists in bondage to their colleagues in the physical sciences, I have built physical models of the ideological configurations that I sought to analyze, understand, and explicate. I did this because I found the multidimensional relationships, on which I sought to focus, too difficult to apprehend without such assistance. Then, to discriminate the several categories of ideological type that needed to be tracked through several different series of analogous structures, I used color coding. And next, in order to be able to project at least some sense of these objects into the book, I invoked color photography of one set of the physical structures. Persons who believe that political science should remain at the level of the reprinting of political cartoons and box organization charts will no doubt poke fun at my crude efforts to deal seriously with the problem of visualizing a set of structural relationships that, though extraordinarily systematic and continuous, are also highly abstract and fairly complicated. But the modular structures depicted herein are not Tinkertoys; they are rather an initial, however feeble, step in the direction of developing a political theory that derives from the premises of twentieth-century astronomy instead of those of nineteenth-century biology or sixteenth-century classical physics. As Felix Cohen once remarked, in speaking of the reaction of most law professors to the work of the early legal realists, "The first steps taken are clumsy and evoke smiles of sympathy or roars of laughter from critics of diverse temperaments. The will to walk persists."*

II

Two disclaimers are necessary in order to properly clarify the limits that apply to the scope of the findings supportable by the kind of evidence presented here. In the first place, the book is full of talk about the "attitudes" of Supreme Court justices, but the attitudinal differ-

*"Transcendental Nonsense and the Functional Approach," *Columbia Law Review*, Vol. 35 (1950), p. 834.

ences delineated and denoted obviously are hypothetical rather than empirical constructs, because the data analyzed are based on observations of judicial votes in the decisions of cases—and not even on judicial responses to questionnaire items (which would be the more conventional sort of data to use to measure attitudes) or the protocols of the revelations of judges to their psychoanalysts (which would be less conventional, but certainly beyond reproach—on this score—if available). On the other hand, the categorizations of policy choices described here *are* empirical constructs, and these classifications are premised on an explicit theory of attitudes; but in spite of the excellent fit that the data provide for the model, we can say no more—and yet no less—than that we cannot reject the theory on the basis of these observations. Persons who would expect to be able to *prove* that Supreme Court justices made the policy choices that they did because of their beliefs about the values at stake in the decisions accept such a different concept of scientific method from the outlook that guided my work in this book that nothing I might say or do would be likely to seem persuasive to them. Certainly I would agree that the more, and the more different kinds of, relevant and supporting evidence that can be brought to bear on the hypothesis about judicial attitudes investigated in this book, the more confidence we all are entitled to repose in the probable validity of the theory. Hence I look forward to the possibility of skeptics producing studies of the attitudes of Supreme Court justices, based on interview data (whether survey or psychiatric), and irrespective of whether the evidence thus adduced turns out to be confirming or disconfirming—although one always hopes, of course, for the latter. But in the meantime, the argument that the findings presented here are tautological, *because* attitudinal positions are inferred from decisional choices, is properly addressed not merely to this particular work, but rather to the entire field of modern social psychology. *All* attitudinal studies with which I am familiar attribute attitudinal positions to respondents on the basis of their decisions in regard to stimuli—whether those are questionnaire items, oral probes in an interview, pictures projected on a screen, observations of nonverbal behaviors in experimental small-group settings, or problems (of public policy) that confront a small group for conjoint decision. Variations in responses and co-variation in stimuli are investigated, not with the objective of determining invariant causal relationships, but rather for the purpose of understanding how the respondent himself is a major intervening variable whose "response set" in the form of his beliefs and expectations makes a critical difference in how he will act in response to the stimuli. Nothing could be more different from operant conditioning and behaviorist psychology; and loose talk about Clark Hull and B. F. Skinner is a red herring, and I have been a good listener to it long enough. I have acknowledged in the first paragraph of this preface, and in greater detail in the introductory chapter that follows, my intellectual debts to certain other psychologists, and to the kind of psychology that they stand for—and to any person sufficiently well-informed to understand the difference, factor psychology and psychometric theory generally, to say nothing of political behavioralism, are about as far removed from operant conditioning and Skinnerian behaviorism as Earl Warren is from Warren Burger in their respective attitudes toward the proper role of the Supreme Court in contemporary American life.

The second disclaimer concerns the assertion, frequently advanced by friend and foe alike of my previous work during the past decade, that attitudes are not everything, either in life or on the Supreme Court. Let us join in burying that straw man; I have never thought or said anything that could reasonably have been construed to imply that I thought that scarecrow to be alive and well and pre-empting the judicial mind. As anything and everything that I have written surely will attest (and I forbear from citing here the dozens of explicit references that come readily to mind, including several that propose quite elaborate models combining many other classes of variables than attitudinal ones), the attitudes of judges like, I presume, those of other persons have an important bearing upon their choices in regard to certain types of decisions. So also do social relationships and interaction, the quantity and quality of information relied upon to define the decisional issues, estimates of the probable implications of outcome alternatives, beliefs about one's institutional role obligations, concern for the cultural image that one will leave as his judicial trace, a host of largely unexplored biological variables (ranging from temporary but acute physical illness to senescence), and a variety of environmental and cultural variables. It is not impossible, I believe, that the day may come (although I do not anticipate it in the present century) when an operationalized dynamic causal model of human decision-making, capable of being applied to the policy choices of Supreme Court justices, will be available to political scientists (or whatever may then be called persons who do such work). But in the meantime, while more modest operations seem feasible and appropriate to our limited competence as behavioral scientists, it may not be inapposite to proceed incrementally, to see what can be learned about individual classes of the variables that seem relevant to the ultimate definition of a more adequate (and complicated) model. While applauding the efforts of those who may choose to work with social, cybernetic, institutional, cultural, biological, and other classes of variables, I present here a book that focuses upon a specific kind of socio-psychological—attitudinal—variables. I do so not because I think that nothing else matters or that nothing else of importance can be said about Supreme Court policy-making or decision-making; I do so because I hope that I may have something of relevance (and possibly, of importance) to say about how the personal beliefs of the justices are related to their voting behavior on the Court. To the extent that any of the findings of this book turn out to be true (or accepted as such), such truth will, of course, be partial, relative, and temporary. Persons who expect to find some other kind of validity, about either the Supreme Court or anything else in life, are not likely to find themselves in agreement with much that I say. And naturally, they will misunderstand and tend therefore to misrepresent, in their own recasting of it, my point of view.

III

This book was begun over half a dozen years ago, barely a year or two after its prototype had appeared. Inevitably I have incurred many obligations and received much help in the process of writing it. No doubt my most immediate debt is to those persons who convinced me of the importance of undertaking this research replication; and the most articulate and persuasive of these were my longtime friend and sometime colleague, Robert Presthus, and my present friend and colleague, Yasumasa Kuroda. A great debt is owed another friend, David Danelski, who not only provided similar encouragement, but also read through the entire manuscript and offered helpful advice in other respects as well. My own long-standing interest in physical modeling of political relationships received important reinforcement and tutelage from my colleague James Dator. My understanding of certain aspects of factor analysis has been enhanced by the writings of, and by conversations with, my colleague R. J. Rummel.

For aid in data processing and access to the necessary facilities, I am indebted for the assistance provided by my former colleagues, James Prothro (in his capacity as Director of the Institute for Social Research at the University of North Carolina, Chapel Hill), and Fred Schindeler (formerly Director) and Kurt Danziger (formerly Acting Director) of the Institute for Behavioural Research at York University, Toronto. I was helped in data coding by Edward Weissman, then a graduate student in political science at U.N.C., and Mark Lerner, a graduate student in political science at York; and in data processing by Jacqueline Damgaard, a graduate student in psychology at Duke University, and Frank Nutch, a graduate student in sociology at York. The draft of the manuscript was typed by Mary Grayson, my former secretary here at the University of Hawaii. In making and in photographing the physical models presented herein, I received indispensable help from two of my offspring—it hardly seems appropriate to speak of them as "children" any more: Sue, who is an undergraduate majoring in art and psychology, and Jim, who is a doctoral candidate in political science (but in peace rather than judicial research). The book is dedicated to my youngest daughter, who is already far better educated in the basics of modern science than her father is likely ever to become.

G.S.

Lanikai, Oahu,
October 1973

Contents

LIST OF FIGURES

* = in color

LIST OF TABLES

THE JUDICIAL MIND REVISITED

1 Introduction

Pilgrimages, including those of the mind, are perhaps best viewed as an index of the aging of the pilgrim; the young in heart are too full of life and too preoccupied with their involvement in new experiences to be concerned with the truth value of their remembrance of things past. It is from this universal—and therefore charitable—perspective that one ought, perhaps, to appraise the apparent disinterest of our era in the cumulation and replication of social science knowledge. The notoriously much more rigid posture of the natural sciences toward questions of empirical reliability and validity as the basis for theory has been dismissed as irrelevant to the contemporary needs and interests of social science by several generations of academic pioneers who have tended to define social science as a kind of neuter gender, practised by men of good will who are neither real scientists nor real artists. And now we face a prevailing climate of opinion that results in an academic ideology encouraging social scientists to be ruled even more by their hearts and less by their heads than has been the case heretofore. Under these circumstances a special need may be fulfilled by a book that rejects the premise that "Knowledge for what?" is the only relevant question, and that focuses instead upon a question that underlies any kind of scientific inquiry (whether natural or social): "What knowledge?"

The argument above, which satisfies me now as a justification for my taking the time and energy to write this book (as well as for imposing it upon others), is of course a rationalization and not the real reason why I agreed to do it. I agreed to write it because three personal friends independently asked me to do so, and having turned them all down, I eventually yielded to a combination of the persistence of Vance Presthus and the reinforcement provided by ties that were then developing between me and both York University and Oxford University Press. A major idea underlying the book, as I understood it then, was to present a case study of the "logic-in-use"[1] that explains my own role in the design, execution, and reporting of what was (at least, for me) a major research project, of which the principal discussion is found in my book *The Judicial Mind.*[2] Certainly there might be some virtue in a frank exploration of the mistakes that were made in design, execution, and reporting—the aspects of social science research that usually seem too unimportant to warrant their being discussed—together with a retrospective review of the claimed successes of an earlier research undertaking. On the other hand, the social science of the late sixties was blessed with what some might consider to have been a surfeit of personal documents about the growing pains of behavioralism, and it would take a bolder and more grizzled veteran than I to dare to augment that literature. But two counterpoint themes to a narrative based at least in part on the personal journalism of "telling it how it was" occurred to me: why not compare what was then possible with what can be done now? And why not take advantage of the opportunity to re-evaluate the substantive findings about Supreme Court policy-making throughout the period of both the Vinson and the Warren Courts?

One major weakness of the earlier study was the relative crudity of the techniques for data analysis then available, even at the avant-garde establishment where my work was done. This situation had begun to change dramatically by the mid-sixties, within the space of the few years that it took to get the book written and published; and by the late sixties much more sophisticated computer programs were at least accessible, if not readily available, at all four of the North American universities—which would all have to be reckoned as about average in their computer facilities competence—at which I worked during that period. So the task became redefined and reformulated as follows: to recode and audit the original data and to update them by half a dozen years; to retain the original theory, model, methodology, and basic design; to take advantage of the several alternative computer programs for multivariate analysis, all of which are in principle much superior to the single primitive program employed for the original data analysis; and to seek to ascertain what differences in substantive interpretation one ought to feel compelled to make between the original findings and those now feasible, taking full advantage of hindsight, a decade of experience, awareness of research by others, and similar matters. Such a statement of goals necessarily implies not only a shift in focus away from research history and in the direction of telling it as it is, but it also involves a substantially overlapping replication of the original study and a retest of the original theory together with an audit and reconsideration of the substantive findings reported in *The Judicial Mind.*

Perhaps I should point out that once I made the decision to replicate, accepting the design (including theory, model, and methodology) of the original study, I exhausted most of the discretion open to me in the execution of the replication. This was by no means the case in the original study, because (for reasons that I shall detail below) in making it my discretion as an analyst was continuously being brought to bear upon what became the substantive findings, from the earliest to the latest stages of the work. But the combined effect of a design that is fixed (as now) rather than unfolding (as it was originally) plus the sophistication of modern computer programs, has transformed my own role. A creative manipulator in the original study, I have been reduced to functioning much more as office manager and technician in the replication. No doubt that consequence is bad, from the point of view of my personal aesthetic gratifications; but from the point of view of making a substantially independent examination of the reliability and validity of the original research project, my affective losses all reappear on the plus side of the objectivity ledger.

So the re-visiting with which this book is concerned may be a kind of intellectual pilgrimage, but if so it is of a very special sort. It is really not at all interested in the past as such. It does focus upon how, and the extent to which, what we accept as knowledge (in this instance, about the behavior of Supreme Court justices) is influenced—for better or for worse—by the processes through which that knowledge is acquired. Thus the book directs attention continuously to questions of research theory, as a function of questions about research methodology.

In the remainder of this chapter, I should like to explain how and why the original study was done, and what appear to be its major substantive findings. The research would probably never have been undertaken except for the circumstance that I was invited to spend the academic year 1960-61 as a Fellow at the Center for Advanced Study in the Behavioral Sciences on the campus of Stanford University. During several preceding years, various of my students and colleagues and I had experimented in both teaching and research with what were then (and are mostly still) conceptualized as unidimensional models of attitudinal constructs that we hypothesized to bear upon judicial behavior. It seemed obvious to me that these unidimensional models would have to be combined in some way in order to make possible a better fit with the evident empirical multivariance of Supreme Court decision-making. So I went to the Center with a quite specific goal in mind: to learn what was necessary about behavioral theory and methodology in order to construct a multidimensional model of the Court.

Political scientists who did their graduate work in the late forties were not trained in the use of such psychometric methods as factor analysis and cumulative scaling. Even in the late fifties the state of the art was such that when cumulative judicial scaling was introduced, the procedures employed were manual.[3] I learned factor analysis in the autumn of 1960 at the Center by sitting down with a copy of Fruchter[4] and a desk calculator, working through the exercises in the book. There was a complete centroid computer program for factor analysis available to me at the Center through the Stanford University Computing Laboratory;[5] this was very similar to the program that Louis Thurstone had used a decade earlier at the University of Chicago Psychometric Laboratory in the pioneering factor analytic study of judicial behavior[6] and also to the procedures for manual factor analysis described even earlier in Thurstone's pathbreaking book on the subject.[7] But there had been only a slight advance, in terms of procedures for computation, from the mid-thirties and the discussion in Thurstone's *The Vectors of Mind*, through and including the Stanford University complete centroid program that I employed a quarter of a century later. Indeed, the criterion used by John Gilbert, now of the Computing Center at Harvard University but then the statistical consultant of the Center, to determine acceptability of the factorial output of the centroid program, was replication of the results that I had produced for a sample of the data by means of the desk calculator. It then became quicker, more convenient, and more accurate to process the remainder of the data through the computer instead of through the calculator; but the point is that there was otherwise no qualitative difference in the results produced by computer methods as compared with manual methods. Of course it is probably true that a better educated analyst (*i.e.*, a psychologist or possibly a sociologist) confronted with the same problem at the same time and in the same place might have obtained access to one of the several principal components or principal axes computer programs for factor analysis then in the process of development elsewhere in the country. But no such person would have been interested in my substantive research problem, and in any case such doors were not readily open to me as a political scientist—even in the context of the interdisciplinary setting par excellence where I was conducting my inquiry.

Part of the difficulty with the use of the centroid program was not technical but stemmed from lack of theoretical sophistication. Gilbert had had no previous encounter with factor analysis, so part of our joint learning experience was to spend hours discussing the classic problems that had emerged historically in the development of the method and that were still discussed as problems in texts published during the fifties. The "problem of communalities" is a good example: it now seems obvious—but it didn't then, either to Gilbert or to me—that a Supreme Court justice's self-correlation, especially when what was supposedly being measured was attitudinal homogeneity, should be defined as unity. In the event, I made what I now think was the erroneous but then conventional decision to use each justice's highest empirical correlation with any of the others as the estimate of his communality. In general, the result was that different levels of self-correlation were attributed to the several justices, and none was assumed to be in complete agreement with himself! An example of a technical defect of the centroid computer program was its lack of an iteration procedure, which meant that only an initial and rough approximation could be made of each factor.

A third difficulty, which probably resulted both from my lack of training and of experience in the management of a research project involving extensive and interrelated data transformations and analyses, was a premature drive on my part to attain closure in the graphic representation and presentation of the results of the data analyses. Faced for the first (and really, only) time in my professional career with an adequate and readily accessible supply of supporting research services in terms of research assistance, typing assistance, art, drafting, and photographic services, I was seduced by the temptation to exploit these amenities by getting things done that I well knew would be much more difficult to accomplish in both economic and administrative terms once I returned to Michigan State University. So I drove hard to get all of the manual cumulative scales typed up and all of the two-dimensional perspectives of the three-dimensional factorial spaces drawn by a mathematical draftsman and photographed prior to my departure from the Center. At least in part I was also attempting, with all the rigor as well as the vigor of my Calvinist indoctrination as a child, to play the role of the Good Fellow at a research center, as I then defined such a role: to conceive, design, carry out, and so far as humanly possible wrap up and write up a research project as tangible evidence of the good work that one had done during his fellowship tenure. The inevitable consequence was, of course, that I was thereafter saddled with a host of minor errors which, when they did become apparent, were unnecessarily difficult and expensive to correct. Some, indeed, proved impossible to correct: a single typographical error in the citation of a case on a scale (1958E) wound up as an error *in the errata* two years after it was detected and became the straw that broke the back of my friendship with the director of the press that published the book. More important, however, is the question, to what extent did premature closure in graphics lead to insufficient and ill-considered substantive interpretations? This is the sort of question that, though usually neither asked nor answered, the re-analysis here should elucidate.

I turn now to the inherent weakness of the centroid factor analysis. The goal of factor analysis, for the purpose that I was using it, was to transform a correlation matrix (*i.e.*, a statistical statement about the relative similarity of pairs of points drawn from the same set) into a specification of the homologous point-configuration in multidimensional space (*i.e.*, a statistical statement of subsets of correlations between the points and each of the reference dimensions that together define the space). From a geometric point of view, the point configuration is a set of vectors, and in the vernacular of educational psychology, of "test vectors," imbedded in the space. These vectors can be described by an infinite number of frames of reference (*i.e.*, sets of reference axes). From a mathematical point of view, the most parsimonious frame of reference is that provided by the set of principal axes or components, of which the first will account for the largest proportion of variance among the vectors (or alternatively, in the correlation matrix); the second principal axis will account for the next largest amount of variance, and so on. Furthermore, the principal-axes frame of reference is unique in that it is the only set of axes that is best in the least-squares sense of maximizing the squares of vectorial correlations with axes.

This much mathematicians, statisticians, and psychologists seem to be agreed upon. There is less agreement concerning what psychological meaning if any ought to be attributed to any (including a principal-axes) reference frame and whether a psychologically meaningful frame is likely to consist of correlated axes, which are oblique rather than orthogonal. I shall return to these then disputed subjects presently.

As Thurstone and many other commentators have pointed out, a set of centroid factors provides a crude estimate of the principal-axes solution for any given matrix. Moreover, the best approximation is for the first centroid and the first principal axis; the estimates generally become successively poorer for higher order (*viz.*, for weaker) factors. Relying on the centroid analysis when and where I did would probably not have been possible even a year later; my work came at the very end of the classical period in factor analysis, an era that is conveniently demarked by the publication of the first edition of Harman's *Modern Factor Analysis*, a book that appeared in 1960[8] but remained unknown to me until after I had left the Center. I have already referred to the deleterious effects of my premature closure on graphics and a most ironic example of this, to which I have previously confessed but without an adequate appreciation of its irony,[9] is the circumstance that when I decided to update the analysis a couple of years later as the book neared publication, I had to perform manual calculations for the two additional matrices: by 1963 Michigan State University no longer had an operational centroid program, although a principal-axes computer program was readily available. So I was stuck, even before I managed to get my book into print, with the realization that what I was discussing was a myopic and astigmatic view of the configurations of variables that I was trying to interpret.

In the original research there were seventeen different and chronologically successive sets of centroid factors. In analyzing these data, I usually was pretty confident about the first factor, and for a majority of the sets I was reasonably confident about the second factor as well. But I attempted to make a consistent three-dimensional interpretation across all seventeen terms of the Court; and for the third centroid factor, it was only in my most euphoric moments that I could shake off the gnawing conviction that what I was really doing was much about nothing: that I was superimposing substantive "meaning" upon patterns of error variance. I was torn, I guess, between equally strong but opposing convictions: that there really was a consistent third factor in the correlations, and that I had failed to observe it through the instrumentality of these centroid constructs. Certainly, I never seriously entertained the idea of attempting to interpret the fourth centroids, although these were calculated by the program, because it was abundantly clear that my measurements—to the extent of my confidence in them—could readily be accommodated within the confines of Euclidean space. It seemed logical to assume, however, that if one had the principal axes available for interpretation, much of the fuzziness that had bedeviled my earlier efforts would disappear. All of the first three axes would be sharply delineated and perhaps even a fourth might then be amenable to a consistent and valid interpretation. If one could determine precisely the hyperellipsoidal reference space, then he could also get a much more accurate fix on the structure of the configuration of variables; but with only a crude estimate of the parameters of the space itself, at best only a rough guess of the structure of the configuration was possible. Or, if one prefers analogies, moving from centroid to principal-axes analysis would be an experience akin to that of a nearsighted motorist who, after having struggled to survive with only his natural vision on a busy ten-lane freeway, retravels the same route with his glasses on.

The major substantive findings of the earlier study can be briefly described. I shall discuss first the structure of the factorial configurations and the principal scale differences. Then I shall compare the clusters of ideological types and scale types that are generated in two-dimensional space, by the cumulative scales and their factorial analogues (*i.e.*, the rotated oblique factors). Finally I shall discuss the ideological parameters which define the position of the configurations in three-dimensional factorial space, and we shall hypothetically consider the possible content of a fourth ideological parameter.

It is convenient as well as conventional to discriminate between the periods of the Vinson and the Warren Courts,[10] and we can further subdivide the Vinson Court period into early (1946-48) and later (1949-52) subperiods. The unit of analysis of *The Judicial Mind* for both scaling and factorial measurements was the term of the Supreme Court extending from October of one year through June of the next. There was no good statistical or psychological reason for aggregating the voting data in such units, but a decade ago I was still bound in intellectual servitude to the conventions of public law research to such an extent that for me at that time, what was an adequate legal justification sufficed, irrespective of its statistical or psychological rationality. I had defined my task as being, among other things, to articulate with Pritchett's *Roosevelt Court*,[11] and the better to do that I organized on a term basis as Pritchett had, and I deliberately overlapped with him for one (the 1946) term. But having once accepted that premise, I never really was open to, nor did I consciously consider, what alternative grounds there might be for grouping the data.[11a]

For present purposes I shall attempt to generalize about what *The Judicial Mind* data show when several terms are grouped, because this treatment corresponds better to the basis on which I have carried out the re-analysis, which is by "natural" Courts in which a new period is defined whenever, but only when, a change occurs in the personnel of the Court.

During the early period of the Vinson Court, the configuration of points in three-dimensional factorial space shows one cluster consisting of Murphy, Rutledge, Douglas, and Black, all of whom have high positive loadings on the first factor and low correlations with the other two factors. The remaining five justices all have negative loadings on the first factor; but they are divided by at least one of the two remaining factors into two clusters, with Frankfurter and Jackson in one and Vinson, Reed, and Burton in the other. On the basis of the factorial data alone, there is of course no ground for defining the substantive differences that these three clusters of justices represent; but one clearly can say, on the basis of the factorial data alone, that the configurations for the early Vinson Court do consist of these three distinct clusters.

During the next four terms of the later Vinson Court, Murphy and Rutledge had been replaced by Clark and Minton. The consequence was still three clusters but with the first now consisting only of Black and Douglas, the second unchanged (Frankfurter and Jackson), and the third now consisting of Vinson, Reed, and Burton augmented by Clark and Minton. Evidently there had been a shift away from whatever was represented by the Black cluster to whatever the Vinson cluster stood for. The 1953 term was Warren's first, but his position in the configuration for that term is no different from what one would have expected for Vinson. There was one change, however: Burton and Minton are closer in this term to Frankfurter and Jackson than to Warren, Clark, and Reed. In Warren's second term (1954), both he *and Clark*[12] formed a cluster with Black and Douglas; Harlan replaced Jackson both as a justice and in configurational position, clustering with Frankfurter; and Burton and Minton returned to a position closer to Reed, with whom they formed the third cluster in the 1954 term. The same three clusters occur in the 1955 term, except that Warren is now even closer to Black than is Douglas; and Clark, who refused to go so far, is in an independent position, not close enough to be considered part of any of the three clusters. Thus the first three terms of the Warren Court were transitional, with Warren changing from a position in what had been the Vinson cluster to a modal position in the Black cluster. Clark accompanied Warren about halfway before returning to a place in Clark's initial cluster of affiliation when he joined the Court. Warren's movement, incidentally, is the only change in configurational position beyond what might be attributed to measurement and other error variance, that I originally denoted for the entire seventeen-term period of the original study. And Warren's change set the basic pattern that can be observed for the remaining thirteen terms of the Warren Court, although the *Judicial Mind* study covers only the first half (seven terms, 1956-62) of that period.

In 1956 Brennan (replacing Minton) joined what I shall henceforth refer to as the Warren (rather than the Black) cluster, and Whittaker, replacing Reed, took up a position near Harlan and Frankfurter, leaving only Burton and Clark left to form the third cluster during this and the following term. From then through the next five terms, the changes in the composition of the three clusters were slight. Goldberg became the fifth member of the Warren cluster during the 1962 term; Stewart became and remained a part of the Harlan cluster beginning in the 1958 term; and Whittaker and Frankfurter both were removed from that cluster by their respective resignations in the spring and summer of 1962. Clark alone remained of the former third cluster after the 1957 term until White joined with him to reform the third cluster in the later part of the 1961 term. If we link together the structures that have just been described, the overall pattern is as follows: the largest and—though not brought out above—also the most cohesive cluster was the first one, which included Murphy, Rutledge, Black, Douglas, Warren (except during his first two terms), Brennan, and Goldberg. The first cluster included a plurality of the Court during 1946-48, 1956-57, and again from the middle of the 1961 term through the 1962 term; from the 1958 through the first half of the 1961 term, the four-justice first cluster was balanced by a second cluster of equal size consisting of Harlan, Frankfurter, Whittaker, and Stewart. Prior to Harlan's appointment, Jackson could be observed in the second cluster, which at any given time included only two or three justices, except for the three-and-one-half terms specified above when both the first and second clusters each included four justices. The third cluster included five justices during the four terms 1949-52, and four during the 1953-55 terms; overall it included Vinson, Reed, Burton, Minton, Clark, Warren (during his first term only), and White. The first cluster was a plurality group for a total of six-and-one-half terms, and it was balanced by the second cluster for an additional three-and-one-half terms; the third cluster was the plurality group during the remaining seven terms. Douglas was in the first cluster throughout sixteen of the seventeen terms covered by *The Judicial Mind*, and Black was also there during fifteen of those terms; and these two were the only justices who were members of the Court throughout the entire period of the analysis.

Certain gross substantive observations can be made concerning the relative size and influence of the three clusters and the Court's policy outputs. The times when the first cluster constituted at least a plurality of the Court (1946-48, 1956-57, and latter 1961-62) were eras of conspicuously progressive policy-making in regard to civil libertarian, social, and economic values alike. The brief renaissance of "the libertarian four," as Pritchett has called them[13] during the post-World War II years falsely promised to be the beginning of the judicial revolution in civil liberties policy that came, in fact, a decade and a half later, beginning only in the last term under present consideration (1962). The influence of the four civil libertarians was cut short by the deaths of two of them during the summer of 1949. When a new resurgence in civil libertarianism began in 1956 and 1957 as the consequence of the reconstitution of the first cluster as a group of four (due to Warren's conversion and Brennan's appointment), there was a reaction in the form of a political movement to restrain and reform the Court.[14] The upshot was that the second cluster became both more widely separated from the first cluster in the configuration as well as sufficiently large enough (through the appointments of Whittaker and Stewart in place of third-cluster members Reed and Burton) that it not only could and did cut off further innovation by the first cluster but also brought about explicit reversals of then recent civil libertarian decisions in several policy sectors. The third and concluding period of first-cluster plurality in the late 1961 and the 1962 terms was in fact the beginning of the sweeping judicial reforms sponsored by the Warren Court during the rest of the sixties, which clearly has been the most liberal period of Supreme Court policy-making in American experience. On the other hand, the seven terms that constitute the period of third-cluster predominance (1949-55) are explicitly the era of McCarthyism; and although the major decision in the school segregation case did come near the end of this period, the time was predominantly one of conservatism and even reaction in Supreme Court policy-making.

In summary, the first cluster seems to be associated with libertarian activism; and both the second and third clusters, although distinct from each other, functioned as a conservative check on the first cluster. But at this gross level of analysis, no causal relationships have been proven; and the observed patterning of co-relationships between cluster predominance in the structure of the Court's configuration and the direction of Court policy-making might be spurious. To adduce the required evidence of causation we must examine individual voting behavior in regard to explicit policy dimensions.

With the data classified in time units as small as Court terms, only two major attitudinal scales were consistently observed: a C scale of political liberalism and an E scale of economic liberalism. The major content of the C scale consists of civil liberties claims, including the claims to fair procedure of criminal defendants in either federal or state courts. The major content of the E scale includes the upholding of governmental regulation of business, the upholding of union claims in labor disputes, and the upholding of underdog fiscal claims against relatively affluent defendants. Although term scales also are reported in *The Judicial Mind,* [15] it was of course possible to combine these term scales in a general C scale for the entire period of seventeen terms, and similarly a general E scale was constructed. Were it not possible to construct such general scales from the term scales, we ought to have such slight confidence in the substantive findings of the term scales that we would not want to use them as a measure of judicial attitudes for these justices.

Each general scale defines a rank order of all eighteen justices in the sample; and by calculating the averages of the term scale scores, we can subdivide each scale into three segments: pro (strongly positive), neutral (moderately positive through moderately negative), and con (strongly negative). Using such cutting points, we can observe[16] from this general civil liberties scale that seven justices are pro political liberalism (Murphy, Rutledge, Douglas, Black, Warren, Brennan, and Goldberg); six are neutral (White, Stewart, Jackson, Frankfurter, Harlan, and Whittaker); and five are negative on political liberalism (Burton, Clark, Vinson, Minton, and Reed). For the corresponding E scale, there are six pro (Murphy, Black, Douglas, Rutledge, Warren, and Brennan); eight are neutral (Vinson, Clark, White, Goldberg, Minton, Reed, Stewart, and Burton); and only four negative (Frankfurter, Harlan, Jackson, and Whittaker). Comparison of the two scales indicates that there are six justices who are pro on scales of both political and economic liberalism: Murphy, Rutledge, Douglas, Black, Warren, and Brennan. It seems justifiable to classify these half-dozen consistent supporters of liberal values as "liberals." Another four persons are neutral toward political liberalism but negative on economic liberalism: (Frankfurter, Harlan, Jackson, and Whittaker): they can appropriately be classified as "economic conservatives." A third group of five justices (Burton, Clark, Vinson, Minton, and Reed) is neutral toward economic liberalism but negative on political liberalism: this group can, with symmetry, be classified as "political conservatives." Of course, it is immediately obvious that the six liberals previously have been identified as members of the first factorial cluster; similarly, the four economic conservatives were all observed in the second factorial cluster; and the five political conservatives, in the third factorial cluster.

Because we know, to whatever degree of detail one might wish to examine, precisely what is the substantive content of the decisions and issues measured by the cumulative scales and therefore also, of course, of any typology constructed by co-relating the scales, we are now entitled to identify the three factorial clusters. Clearly, the scales confirm, but make more specific, the interpretation that we had ventured on the basis of gross trends in the Court's policy-making. The first cluster consists of the liberals who have sponsored change in the Court's policy-making in the direction of support for both civil liberties and greater economic egalitarianism. The second cluster consists of the economic conservatives whose support of civil liberties was sufficiently unzealous that, when the Court itself came under political attack in 1956 and 1957 because of its emerging zeal for political liberalism, they readily supported the third cluster justices in checking the liberals. And the third cluster, the political conservatives, consists of the Trumanites—four of the five were the justices whom Truman appointed to the Supreme Court—who closed ranks on the Court when Joe McCarthy blustered "Boo!" The Supreme Court's major structural differences, in so far as these reflect differences in voting behavior, are a direct result of the relative strength from time to time of representation among the justices of three major ideological perspectives: liberalism, economic conservatism, and political conservatism.

But the three scale types account for only fifteen of the eighteen justices in the sample. Not as yet apportioned among the three scale types discussed above are Goldberg, White, and Stewart. It is of at least incidental interest to observe that these are also the last three, of the justices in the present sample, to be appointed: Stewart was Eisenhower's fifth and final appointee, in 1958; and White and Goldberg became, in 1962, John Kennedy's only appointees to the Court. Goldberg's combination of support for political liberalism but moderation toward economic liberalism defined what for this earlier sample seemed to be an otherwise unique type that we might, isomorphically, call "political liberalism." White and Stewart, with neutral positions and average scores on both scales, were called "moderates." So the last three justices to be added to our sample seemed to fit least well the groupings defined on the basis of the differences among their fifteen predecessors.

An even more explicit measure of the relationship between the two cumulative scales and the factorial configurations is provided by a rotation of the factorial reference axes to oblique positions for which the criteria are supplied by the cumulative scales. The details of the procedure for this transformation have been discussed in *The Judicial Mind*,[17] but we can note here that the effect is to identify analogue scale vectors upon which the projections from points in the configuration correspond in rank order at average correlation levels of .92 or higher with the cumulative scale rankings of the same justices. The points on the scale vectors at which the projections from the configurational points fall can alternatively be described as "loadings" on these analogue scales. Because they are positively correlated, these scale (*viz.*, rotated factorial) vectors are in an oblique relationship to each other. By plotting the projections of the points on the plane defined by the scale vectors in the three-dimensional factorial space, I denoted the ellipse which I termed a "radex" in *The Judicial Mind*.[18] This was in effect a joint construction of the cumulative scales and the factorial point configuration. That elliptical space clearly denotes the same three factorial clusters and scale types that we have discussed above.

But there are one or two minor differences in interpretation implied by the radex. There is no change for the six liberals of the first cluster; nor is there any change for the four economic conservatives of the second cluster, except that Stewart, who measured as moderate on both scales, is clearly positioned in the economic conservative group (and he *was* included in the second factorial cluster). Similarly, White, who was moderate on both scales, is positioned as the least extreme point in, but nevertheless in, the political conservative cluster, which otherwise is unchanged except that Clark is positioned independently in the bottom sector for which the C− and E+ axis segments constitute the parameters. Goldberg is directly above Clark but alone in the opposite sector enclosed by the E− and C+ axis segments. (The six liberals are in the sector between the C+ and E+ axis segments, while economic and political conservatives all are in the C−/E− sector; the liberals lie almost precisely on the abscissal reference axis, while the economic conservatives are all above and the political conservatives all below that axis.) But Goldberg's position implies no difference in classification; he can still be called a "political liberal." The only change beyond the partitioning of Stewart and White out of the moderate category is for Clark, whom we should now have to consider to be an "economic liberal," isomorphic with our designation for Goldberg.

All of the evidence that we have examined strongly supports the finding that there were three major groupings of the justices: the half-dozen consistent liberals; the five economic conservatives, plus Goldberg who differs from them primarily in his stronger support for political liberalism; and the five political conservatives, plus Clark who differs from them primarily in his stronger support for economic liberalism. Some of the detailed evidence, to which I have not previously directed attention, indicates that perhaps Burton, whose opposition to both scale values was in better overall balance than that of any of the other non-liberals, might well be considered to constitute the Court's only consistent conservative during this period (and therefore, a separate type, all by himself).

Notes to Chapter One

1. Abraham Kaplan, *The Conduct of Inquiry: Methodology for Behavioral Science* (San Francisco: Chandler, 1964), p. 3.

2. Glendon Schubert, *The Judicial Mind: Attitudes and Ideologies of Supreme Court Justices, 1946-1963* (Evanston: Northwestern University Press, 1965).

3. Glendon Schubert, *Quantitative Analysis of Judicial Behavior* (Glencoe: The Free Press, 1959), chapter 5.

4. Benjamin Fruchter, *Introduction to Factor Analysis* (Princeton: Van Nostrand, 1954).

5. *The Judicial Mind*, p. 70.

6. Louis L. Thurstone and James W. Degan, "A Factorial Study of the Supreme Court" (University of Chicago, Psychometric Laboratory *Report No. 64*, March 1951).

7. Louis L. Thurstone, *Multiple-Factor Analysis: A Development and Expansion of The Vectors of Mind* (Chicago: University of Chicago Press, 1947).

8. Harry H. Harman, *Modern Factor Analysis* (Chicago: University of Chicago Press, 1960).

9. *The Judicial Mind*, pp. 69-70.

10. C. Herman Pritchett, *Civil Liberties and the Vinson Court* (Chicago: University of Chicago Press, 1954); Harold J. Spaeth, *The Warren Court: Cases and Commentary* (San Francisco: Chandler, 1966).

11. C. Herman Pritchett, *The Roosevelt Court: A Study in Judicial Politics and Values, 1937-1947* (New York: Macmillan, 1948: reprinted in a paperback edition by Quadrangle Books, 1969).

11a. The use of "natural" court periods instead of the traditional term periods was first suggested by sociologist Eloise C. Snyder in her "The Supreme Court as a Small Group," *Social Forces 36* (March 1958), 232-38.

12. See *The Judicial Mind*, pp. 118-19, 232.

13. Pritchett, *Civil Liberties and the Vinson Court*, chapter 10.

14. See Clifford M. Lytle, *The Warren Court and Its Critics* (Tucson: University of Arizona Press, 1968); C. Herman Pritchett, *Congress versus the Supreme Court, 1957-1960* (Minneapolis: University of Minnesota Press, 1961); Walter F. Murphy, *Congress and the Court: A Case Study in the American Political Process* (Chicago: University of Chicago Press, 1962); and Glendon Schubert, *The Constitutional Polity* (Boston: Boston University Press, 1970), chapter 3.

15. At pp. 104-12, 130-38.

16. *The Judicial Mind*, pp. 125, 145.

17. *Ibid.*, pp. 70-75.

18. *Ibid.*, p. 271.

2 *Theory*

The theory of the judicial mind presented in the earlier study is a psychometric theory based directly and primarily upon the work of four men, all of whom are internationally distinguished for their contributions to psychological measurement theory and methodology. Louis Thurstone was the American discoverer of multiple factor analysis.[1] His student, Clyde Coombs, has been a leading contributor both personally and through his own students to the development of non-metric methods of multidimensional scaling.[2] Louis Guttman of Israel has for over a quarter of a century been associated with linear cumulative scaling[3] and more recently, he has been the co-sponsor of a family of non-metric multidimensional scaling computer programs, among which is the smallest space analysis employed in the present study. Hans Eysenck is an outstanding exponent in England of the relationship between factor theory and ideology, and of factor analysis of survey data on attitudes toward issues of political, social, and economic policy.[4]

The model to be presented here is a synthesis of concepts drawn from all of these principal sources. It is certainly a factorial model and can readily be assimilated to factor theory as that subject recently has been explicated by, for example, my colleague R. J. Rummel.[5] But it does not employ factor analysis or factor theory in a conventional, to say nothing of routine way. The model also is one of multidimensional non-metric scaling, and as such is much indebted to the prior work of Louis Guttman and James Lingoes—and, at an earlier stage of the development of the model, to the work of Lingoes' teacher and my own former colleague at Michigan State University, Louis McQuitty. As

I acknowledged in *The Judicial Mind*, the model was constructed at a time and under circumstances such that I was directly and personally influenced by Clyde Coombs, who was at that time engaged in the writing of his *Theory of Data*, in which he explicates the relationships (at the level of psychological measurement theory) between cumulative scaling and factor analysis, and the differing implications of dominance as distinguished from proximity decision functions. And not least, my understanding of the relationship between attitudinal measurement, ideological constructs, and the interpretation of them owes a great deal to the writings of Hans Eysenck, as I have taken pains to point out in one of several discussions of attitudinal/ideological theory that have intervened between the publication of *The Judicial Mind* and the present study.[6]

My own concern in *The Judicial Mind* was not to attempt to make any contribution to psychometric theory or methods; rather, I viewed myself strictly as a kind of engineer, applying to my own particular substantive problem a cluster of theories and methods that had originated in quite another context, but which I deemed useful to my own purposes.[7] It was, therefore, strictly coincidental that so far as I was concerned, I happened to be among the relatively early political scientist users of factor analysis as a theory and method for empirical political inquiry. My principal interest was then the substantive question of the effect of judicial ideology upon judicial decision- and policy-making; or, to define it in more general terms, in the relationship between political belief systems and political behavior. Indeed, my title for the original book was originally, and remained until the book was in an advanced stage of publication, *The Liberal Mind*. I believed then as I think now that the question of patterning of attitudes toward questions of political and economic policy in the ideological combination that conventionally has been designated as that of "liberalism/conservatism" is a phenomenon of the American political culture during the middle decades of the twentieth century and has neither a necessary nor a peculiar relationship to the role of judges, to say nothing of the rarefied arena of the United States Supreme Court. Consequently, in studying what my publisher, emphasizing the empirical setting rather than its theoretical implications, convinced me to call "the judicial mind," we are not studying the mind of everyman, but we are examining an aspect of political ideology which is much more general in its implications than may seem apparent in its explication.[8]

A Psychometric Model of Supreme Court Decision-Making

The model presented in *The Judicial Mind* is the same one that has guided the present study. The model states that, whatever their degrees

of complexity, it is possible to represent symbolically the ideological
positions of the justices comprising the Supreme Court at any particular
time as a configuration of ideal points in a psychological space of some
specifiable dimensionality. The distance separating the ideal points of
the configuration is a direct function and measure of their ideological
differences in terms of the relevant parameters that define the psychological space. Two justices with exactly the same point of view toward
all issues decided by the Supreme Court during a particular period of
analysis could, and would have to, be represented by one and the same
ideal point. There is, according to the model,[9] complete isomorphism
between the configuration of ideal-points in the psychological (called in
the present study joint scalar, factorial, or smallest) space and the belief
systems of the justices that motivate their voting in Supreme Court
decisions. Differences in ideology (which are differences in their attitudes toward particular issue aggregates) cause the justices to vote
differently in decisions of the Court in which such issues are at stake;
and the votes of Supreme Court justices are therefore articulations of
ideological differences. By observing the frequencies of voting agreement and disagreement across all issues by pairs of the justices, a
correlation index of ideological homogeneity can be constructed; and a
matrix of such correlations can then be transformed by some appropriate method of multivariate mathematical analysis into an ideal-point
configuration in one of the psychological spaces referred to above.
Alternatively, the votes of the justices can be observed individually in
relation to a clustering of decisions concerning a single issue, in which
case an index can be constructed which arrays the justices in terms of
their degree of relative support for that issue; and of course, each of
several other issues can be examined in a similar manner. The dimensionality of the psychological space containing the ideal-point configuration is a function of the number and interrelatedness of the issues
involved. If there is only a single issue that divides Supreme Court
justices in all of their decisional behavior, then a cumulative scale of all
of their votes will *be* the space-defining parameter; and the configuration will take the form of the set of ideal points arrayed in sequence
along that single line. If there are two issues of importance, then the
space will be a plane surface; and the configuration of ideal points will
be arrayed in some manner around the origin of that space, just as each
of the two issues can be represented as a vector which transects the
space in some determinate relationship to the ideal-point configuration.
With three major issues or sets of highly intercorrelated issues the space
will be three-dimensional and still Euclidean. Spaces of a dimensionality
of four or higher cannot be physically modeled, but the statement
made about two-space, concerning the determinate relationship be-

tween issue-vectors and configurational ideal-points, still obtains for
spaces of a higher dimensionality than two. Indeed, if one's interest lies
in a particular pair of issue-vectors—let us say, for example, that two
issues predominate both qualitatively and quantitatively in the content
of Supreme Court decision-making—then the pair of vectors for these
two issues defines a plane that transects in a determinate manner the
space of three or higher dimensionality. In such a case, of course, it will
be only coincidental that any of the ideal-points of the configuration
will also lie in that plane; but we can observe the relationship between
those ideal-points, however complex the space defining their configuration may be, and the transecting plane, including the issue-vectors that
define it.

Consequently, by investigating the relationships between and among
issue-vectors and ideal-points in the space of the model, we can learn
about ideological relationships within, between, and among the minds
of the justices who, in an empirical sense, comprise our set of respondents.

The model postulates a decisional function for respondents analogous to that of survey attitudinal research but with the difference that
the precise questions, to which justices provide answers in their votes,
are left largely implicit for the purposes of the present analysis. The
case records are examined for the purpose of observing individual
voting positions in relation to decisional majorities and for the purpose
of classifying the substance of the decisions according to the relatively
small set of issue variables that have been pre-selected to guide the
analysis. Of course, it is possible but neither necessary nor parsimonious
from the point of view of allocating research resources, to content-
analyze either the pre-decisional or the post-decisional[10] parts of the
case record with a considerably greater degree of precision; and of
course opinions written after decisions have been made in order to
justify them are rationalizations—but that does not mean that the
classification of judicial votes for purposes of issue-scale analysis is a
meaninglessly tautological enterprise, as one critic of this method has
suggested.[11] *If* it could be demonstrated that the issue(s), as defined
and discussed in judicial opinions, show negative, or zero, or even low or
merely moderately high-positive correlations with the issues presented
for decision by the Court, then we should have to take the claim of
tautology more seriously and define issue-scales on the basis of cer-
tiorari papers or appeals briefs or the like; in the absence of any such
evidence, to say nothing of demonstration, it seems reasonable to rely
upon what are conventional observations of the content of decisions for
our purposes of macro- rather than micro-classification of that content.

A second criticism that has been made of the model is that its utility is limited to description because it guides the selection and organization of data about historical events—decisions that already have been made. Such a statement is a perfectly valid remark about how the model can be, and frequently has been used; but it is quite wrong to allege that the model cannot be, or has not been used for predictive purposes. I had thought that I had dealt adequately with this point in previous writings;[12] but one certainly can, and should be willing to, predict that changes in judicial attitudinal and ideological positions generally will occur so gradually that, in forecasting dispositions of issues expected to arise before the Court, the highest probability values attach to the presumption that each justice will vote consistently with his *own*—not necessarily the Court's—previous voting positions on the same issue. Issues are variables that attract, in the form of alternative solutions to empirical problems, varying degrees of support, isomorphically with the definition and conceptualization of a cumulative scale.[13] Hence one assumes that there is indeed a kind of *stare decisis* underlying the Supreme Court's decisions but that it is based on *personal* rather than institutional precedents.[14] Certainly I have myself used the model to make what were explicitly advertised to be *pre*dictions at the time the statements were published or set in type in advance of the decisions to which they related.[15] And my entire posture in *The Judicial Mind* was such that we can consider both the scales published therein, and the multidimensional space that it proffers as a delineation of the judicial mind of the Warren Court,[16] to be my prediction that the individual justices who remained on the Court would continue to implement their respective ideologies by (1) retaining their relative positions on the scales, and (2) projecting ideal-points that would remain in the same basic configurational pattern in subsequent observations of them in multidimensional space. The earlier study overlaps with the present one to the extent of all of the first seven periods and through the first half of the eighth period. This is the equivalent of about 75 per cent of the present study. Hence, we can quite appropriately view the era of the Warren Court during the sixties, from September 1963 through June 1969 (the later half of the eighth period plus the ninth and tenth periods, the last quarter of the time and data analyzed herein), to be a test of the hypothesis that attitudinal and ideological positions of Warren Court justices as measured and stated in *The Judicial Mind* will be confirmed by the new and additional data that became available for examination only after the earlier book had become committed to publication in its present form. And so I believe that it is not too much of an exaggeration to state that in a fundamental way much of the present analysis constitutes a test of my prediction of the judicial mind of the Warren Court.

The Meaning of Dimensions in Complex Psychological Space

There are various ways in which we can generalize about the structure of any point configuration. Such a configuration can be defined by sets of reference factorial axes; but these factorial "reference" axes do *not* constitute (as many factor psychologists have argued) an "arbitrary" frame of reference so that, although they determine the configuration, they have no substantive meaning of their own. Certainly, such an argument makes no sense from a statistical point of view because, as I explained in detail in the earlier study,[17] the first factor, which accounts in either centroid or principal-component factor analysis for a larger proportion of the matrix variance than any other factor (with the second factor accounting for the next largest proportion, etc.) scales the points in the configuration along a dimension *which stands for whatever they agree and disagree about most often and most consistently*. Similarly, the second factor scales the justices as points in the configuration along the second most important dimension in the defined sense of why they agree and disagree, and a symmetrical explanation obtains for the third and successive factors. Whatever the accepted dimensionality of the space, the point configuration is strictly determined by the point correlations with the set of reference factors. Evidently, if the configuration itself has substantive meaning, so must the reference frame that absolutely determines it. What psychologists mean when they say that the reference frame is "arbitrary" is that only coincidentally will the reference dimensions correspond to (*viz.*, be perfectly correlated with) the scale variables in terms of which they are able to measure the substance of whatever the configuration points represent. For most educational psychologists, at least during the classical period of factor analysis, points were verbal or other skill tests which consisted of putatively homogeneous items clustered on the basis of their imputed content to define human mental traits such as "number recognition"; and particularly under the simple structure criterion posited by Thurstone, rotated factors were axes with which the tests generally had *either* maximal *or* minimal correlations. The content of such rotated factors was defined by observing the content of the tests showing large correlations; and the factors performed the function of denoting how the set of tests could be related to a set of dimensions smaller than the number of variables in the correlation matrix. But our objectives here are quite different. We know what our rotated factors are (the cumulative scales), or we can know before we ever undertake factor analysis; and we have, therefore, a pre-determined criterion for rotation of factorial reference axes. We deal with persons rather than with tests (*i.e.*, with respondents rather than stimuli), and we have scaled them according to their array along linearly measured attitudinal variables. What we seek from the factor analysis is a multidimensional frame of reference that will denote for us how the set of scales is correlated from the standpoints of these particular persons. Therefore, by observing how the cumulative scales correlate with the point configuration which factor analysis determines, we learn how the cumulative scales—the attitudinal variables—are interrelated. Or put otherwise, by rotating the reference axes to positions, whether oblique or orthogonal, that correspond best—providing the correspondence is acceptably close—to the criteria provided by the cumulative scales, we observe the interrelationships among the attitudes of the set of respondents. This observation is made, of course, in the rotated frame, within which the point configuration has remained invariant from what it was determined to be by the initial reference frame, whether centroid or principal components. Rotation changes the perspective from which we perceive the point configuration, but it has no effect on the configuration itself.

Granting the above, the question of the meaning of the factorial reference frame is strictly an empirical one: having determined the rotational frame, the substance of which is known, and having observed the relation between the two frames, is it possible to infer any consistent meaning for the set of factors that comprise the reference frame? I thought so at the time I wrote *The Judicial Mind*, and I still think so for reasons that I have subsequently detailed,[18] although I should now prefer to state the case somewhat differently than I did then. First I shall summarize the earlier presentation; then I shall venture a reformulation that is in closer accord with my present thinking.

Except during the half-dozen terms that were dominated by the third factorial (*viz.*, the "Truman") cluster (of those discussed in the first chapter) when the first cluster included less than four justices, the first reference factor distinguishes between the liberals (all of whom have positive correlations with it) and the other justices (whose correlations with it are negative). Furthermore, both of the analogue vectors for the cumulative scales (C' and E') are maximally correlated with the first factor in all of the dozen terms in which it does distinguish between the liberals and the others. It seems appropriate, therefore, to assume that (1) this factor can be observed only when the liberal cluster is large enough—four or more—so that the primary division in voting behavior is between liberals and others; and (2) that the factor is one of general liberalism, at least in the sense in which liberalism is understood in Western societies during the twentieth century; earlier liberalism was understood to connote a different combination of attitudes toward C and E.[19]

But because so much of the thrust of the policies advocated by the Supreme Court liberals during the period under analysis here was in the direction of social egalitarianism, I called it that in *The Judicial Mind*,[20] although "general liberalism" would have done just as well. Each of the cumulative scales tended to be highly correlated with either the second or the third factor in those terms when the first factor was recognized to be general liberalism; and in those half-dozen terms when the general liberalism factor did not appear, then each of the cumulative scales was highly correlated with either the first or the second factor, leaving the third uninterpretable during these terms. I assumed that these second and third factors each represented a combination of primarily one of the cumulative scales, plus several of the minor scale variables that have not been mentioned heretofore in this discussion; and I assumed further that if correlations, between either the second or third factor and one or the other of the major cumulative scales, were both perfect and exclusive, then such a factor would be identical to (*viz.*, congruent with) the cumulative scale.

I called "Libertarianism" the factor, other than the first, that correlated more highly with C than with E; the other, which correlated more highly with E than with C, I called "Individualism." It will be recalled that "Egalitarianism" was observed only as the first factor and only in twelve out of the eighteen terms. Libertarianism and Individualism were each observed in all eighteen terms but as differing factors. Libertarianism was the first factor four times (during 1950-53), the second factor eight, and the third factor five times; Individualism was the first factor twice (in 1949 and 1954), the second factor nine times, and the third factor six times. In ten of the eighteen terms, Libertarianism was a higher order factor (*viz.*, the first or second when the other was second or third) than Individualism; but this almost equal priority of precedence seems quite consistent with the empirical knowledge that the average size of the C and E samples is almost identical (.35 and .34 respectively, of the total of 1643 observed decisions that comprise the universe). So my interpretation was that if at least four liberal justices were in a given term sample, the first factor would be Equalitarianism; the second would be either Libertarianism or Individualism, depending upon whether there were more decisions on the C than on the E scale in the particular term; and the third factor would be whichever (as between Libertarianism or Individualism) was not second. Lacking any consistent empirical information about the minor scales, I was unable to proffer an operational specification of how they were related to the non-primary factors of Libertarianism and Individualism, but I did hypothesize that they were correlated with them.

I assumed also, on the basis of inference from Guttman's theoretical writing on the relationships among cumulative scales in two- and three-dimensional space[21] and on the basis of discussions with Gutt- man, that in addition to the substantive (semantic) content of the attitudes measured by the cumulative scales there is a psychological content which consists of such psychological components of the atti- tudes as *intensity* and *closure*.[22] The non-primary factors were measur- ing, I assumed, such psychological content in addition to the substance of the C and E scales respectively. I then discussed a hypothetical procedure—it was not performed empirically—for rotating the second and third factors, Libertarianism and Individualism, so that they coin- cided to form the ordinal axis—the abscissa remained the first factor of general liberalism—of the plane defined by the C and E scale axes and imbedded in the three-dimensional space. Of course, any two intersecting lines in three-dimensional space define a plane, so there is no doubt about the legitimacy of the geometry of the transformation that I described. The doubt arises concerning the substantive interpretation that I proposed, a matter concerning which I felt considerably less than certitude when I wrote the earlier book and about which I now suspect that I was mistaken. I argued that the result of the rotation was to eliminate the non-liberalism content (which is true by definition) but I should also have added that the excised *non*-liberalism semantic content included the *psychological* content that I had attributed to Libertarian- ism and to Individualism. Instead, I added to the complexity by proposing that psychological labels ("Pragmatism/Dogmatism") be as- signed to the ordinal axis of the liberalism plane.[23] What I should now prefer to do, but did not learn until later through subsequent research in a different empirical setting,[24] is to make a simpler and more intuitively plausible interpretation of the content of this plane on the manifest level. When scales of political and economic liberalism are co-aligned, in the positive direction they define the ideology of modern, twentieth-century liberalism; and the negative direction is, of course, that of modern conservatism. When the two scales are aligned oppo- sitely (E− with C+), the direction is that of the ideology of classical liberalism; and E+ aligned with C− defines the direction of classical conservatism. If C and E are assumed to be independent of each other, then the plane is that of a circumplex, such as the one presented in *The Judicial Mind*,[25] and if C+ and E+ are correlated, then we should expect in a study of contemporary judges to find the correlation to be positive, in which event the two correlated scales would define an ellipse such as the one that is presented in the same work, but as I now think mislabeled there as a "radex."[26]

Where the earlier interpretation may be in error is in referring to

"Pragmatism" and to "Dogmatism" in (and in discussions of) both the circumplex and the elliptical figures, instead of to the more prosaic "Classical Liberalism" and "Classical Conservatism." (Substantively, the figures discuss relationships among clusters of the configuration that we have already considered, above. This does not mean, of course, that it is inappropriate to investigate the hypothesis that the content of the three-dimensional space, beyond that relatively small field of it which lies *within* the liberalism plane, consists of non-liberalism, semantic-plus-psychological content of sufficient relative importance that it would be appropriate to name and describe the factor on the basis of psychological concepts. It is even possible that Pragmatism/Dogmatism is the most appropriate designation for such a third (rotated) factor. In three-dimensional space and in relation to the liberalism plane, the rotated third factor would be perpendicular to that plane at its origin *if* the space were an ellipsoid; but if anything other than that special case obtained and the third factor were correlated with either—or, more likely, with both—of the C and E scales, as the theoretical argument of the earlier work, drawn from Guttman, explicitly assumes that it will be correlated, then a more complex space of three oblique axes will be defined. There may have been a rotated third psychological factor, of pragmatism, but it could not be observed in the plane *defined by* the two liberalism scales, as I purported to portray it.

Subdivisions of, and Alternatives to
the Major Dimensions of Political and Economic Liberalism

The initial research design carried out at the Center defined only the two major scales of political liberalism and economic liberalism, respectively, plus four minor scales: federal fiscal interests (F+), federal centralization (N+), judicial supremacy (A+), and judicial centralization (J+). These scales were considered to be minor because, at least when data are grouped on a term basis, empirical samples for them are much too small to satisfy the technical canons for cumulative scalability. In fact, F scaled in four out of seventeen terms, N in only one, and A or J not at all.

One chapter of *The Judicial Mind* is devoted to the discussion of subcomponent scales of C and E. All of that discussion is based on research that came, after the initial design and was carried out, in a series of graduate seminars, the first two of which convened in the interval between the Center experience and the publication of the book. The first seminar focused on the E scale, and out of it was generated the hypothesis that there are five E subscales: (1) pro underdog fiscal claims; (2) pro governmental regulation of business; (3) pro union in labor disputes; (4) pro economically inferior litigants; and (5) pro the constitutionality, on federal grounds, of state taxation.

Attempts were made to identify empirical samples for each of these subscales for a period of five terms, for which the data were pooled because it was recognized from the experience with the minor scales that subsets of data drawn from term samples would rarely be adequate to support analysis; but even so, sufficient samples were obtained only for the first three. It was also discovered that the correlation between (1) and (2) was so high that they should be dealt with as a single composite subscale. Consequently, only two subscales of the E scale were tentatively confirmed by the limited empirical evidence that was examined: fiscal claims/pro regulation of business, and pro union. The second seminar made a similar investigation of the C scale. This led to the hypothesizing of five subscales: (1) pro political equality; (2) pro political freedom; (3) pro religious freedom; (4) pro claims of fair procedure; and (5) pro privacy. The sample of religious freedom decisions was too small to test, but the other four were empirically confirmed. Political freedom and fair procedure were so highly correlated that they could be combined as a composite subscale, at least for the sample of respondents who comprised the Supreme Court during 1956-60.

These first two seminars were held in the spring of 1962 and that of 1963. The third seminar met in the spring of 1966 after the book had been published. The work of this third seminar, which was experimental in several senses, has been reported in some detail,[27] but it is relevant here to note that by this time, it seemed desirable to subdivide the political equality subscale further into three components: civic equality, racial equality, and voting equality. No doubt, this decision constituted an overly sanguine estimate of the enduring importance of the Supreme Court's then contemporary involvement in legislative reapportionment policy-making. The 1966 seminar also collected part of the data (for the period 1963-66) that are incorporated in the present re-analysis, although it grouped them somewhat differently than I shall do in the chapters below. These data were factor-analyzed for purposes of the seminar, using a principal-components computer program; and the output was interpreted to include four significant factors.

The first three were the same ones that we have considered above— general liberalism, libertarianism, and individualism—but the fourth component was novel. It was identified as a dimension of radicalism/ reactionism in terms of receptivity to change. The more novel civil liberties subcomponents of voting equality, racial equality, and privacy all were highly correlated with this factor, while such more traditional subcomponents of liberalism as fair procedure, political freedom, and governmental regulation of business all had negative correlations with the fourth factor.

A subsequent study of the attitudes of American judges toward liberal values[28] showed that this same dimension appeared in a smallest-space analysis. (Smallest-space solutions, of intercorrelations between persons [Q-analysis], usually are at least one lower in dimensionality than corresponding factorial solutions; and in this instance, what appeared as the *fourth* principal component in the 1966 seminar study discussed above was the *third* smallest-space dimension, distinguishing among issues according to whether they were perceived to be relatively novel or traditional from the point of view of social change. It should be noted, however, that in the [earlier] factor analysis the variables were persons, whereas in the subsequent smallest-space analysis the variables were questionnaire items—for which factor analysis also would probably have produced a three-dimensional solution with corresponding dimensions.)[29] Internationalism and political freedom were consensually perceived to be relatively traditional issues; ethnic equality, sexual equality, and humanitarianism were viewed as relatively less traditional; while economic equality, sexual freedom, and religious freedom were considered to be the most radical issues.

The seminars and other post-Center research laid the groundwork for some changes that now seem desirable in thinking about the factorial structure. Of course, the work on subscales indicated that an attempt should be made to scale the data systematically in terms of the subscales of the major scales, as well as the C and E scales themselves and the four minor scales. One might anticipate two advantages from having such information concerning the subscales: this might make possible an operational test of the structure of both consistency and error in the major scales; and one might hypothesize that if major scales load on several different factorial dimensions, this is because different components (subscales) of the major scales load on certain factorial dimensions while other subscales load on other factorial dimensions. Hence, the subscales might provide an operational basis for delineating much more precisely the substantive structure of the factors (*viz.*, the ideological dimensions.)

But given the better technology now available, we ought also to be able to push ahead on several other fronts of theoretical interest. For one thing, the plane of liberalism that was left at the hypothetical level in the earlier study should be studied empirically, both in regard to the relationships within it and in regard to its placement in three- or four-dimensional space. We should also be able to ascertain how well the primary oblique factors of an oblimin factor analysis coincide with our criterion (major) cumulative scales. A comparison of principal-component factor and smallest-space solutions of the same correlation matrices should permit us to test the hypothesis that the smallest-space approach makes possible, as its proponents claim, a simpler and more parsimonious interpretation of complex multi-variate relationships. And the availability of an option within the smallest-space computer program permitting the choice of series of solution sets at specified levels of dimensionality allows us to call for one-, two-, three-, and four-dimensional solutions for each correlation matrix. Thereby we can select the most satisficing solution within each such set, which will be the smallest space in which the variance of the matrix can satisfactorily be contained; and we can also undertake to model certain of these solutions both to aid in our analysis and to aid in the comprehension of it. The graphic portrayal of the one-dimensional solutions is of course possible albeit perhaps too limited; for the four-dimensional space it is impossible. But the two-dimensional smallest spaces can be graphed, and the corresponding three-dimensional spaces can be physically constructed. I shall do both in an endeavor to explicate and clarify as many as possible of the theoretical questions and relationships that have been raised in this chapter.

Notes to Chapter Two

1. Louis L. Thurstone, *The Vectors of Mind* (Chicago: University of Chicago Press, 1935).

2. Clyde H. Coombs, *A Theory of Data* (New York: Wiley, 1964).

3. Louis Guttman, chapters 2 and 3 on "The Problem of Attitude and Opinion Measurement" and "The Basis for Scalogram Analysis," in Samuel Stouffer *et al., The American Soldier: Studies in Social Psychology in World War II,* Vol. 4 of *Measurement and Prediction* (Princeton: Princeton University Press, 1950).

4. Hans J. Eysenck, *The Psychology of Politics* (London: Routledge and Kegan Paul, 1954).

5. Rudolph J. Rummel, *Applied Factor Analysis* (Evanston: Northwestern University Press, 1970), chapter 2: "Philosophy of Factor Analysis."

6. See my "Ideologies and Attitudes, Academic and Judicial," *Journal of Politics,* Vol. 29 (1967), pp. 3-40, especially at pp. 26-28.

7. It is apparently from this perspective that psychologists have tended to view my factor analytic work: for instance, Australian John Ross' "Multidimensional Scaling of Attitudes," ch. 17 in Gene F. Summers, ed., *Attitude Measurement* (Chicago: Rand McNally, 1970), p. 289.

8. For example, my article on "Ideological Distance: A Smallest Space Analysis Across Three Cultures," originally published in *Comparative Political Studies*, Vol. 1 (October 1968), pp. 319-49, has been reprinted in John C. Pierce and Richard A. Pride, eds., *Cross-National Micro-Analysis* (Beverly Hills: Sage Publications, 1972), as an example of cross-cultural ideological analysis in a book that otherwise has nothing to do with judges, to say nothing of courts and law *per se*. That particular study is a secondary analysis which compares the political orientations of British political party members (Eysenck's data) with those of American state supreme court judges (Stuart Nagel's data) and Japanese high court judges (James Dator's data).

9. Previous comments by others concerning similar remarks of mine, in which I have purported to make statements about the logic of a model as distinguished from whatever I personally may happen to believe to be empirically valid, impel me to emphasize this caveat: that I am describing the model at this point in the text and not attempting to discuss my beliefs about empirical multi-causality in Supreme Court decision-making.

10. See my "Jackson's Political Philosophy: An Exploration in Value Analysis," *American Political Science Review*, Vol. 59 (1965), pp. 940-63; and Fred Kort, "Content Analysis of Judicial Opinions and Rules of Law," chapter 6 in Schubert, ed., *Judicial Decision-Making* (New York: The Free Press of Glencoe, 1963).

11. Theodore L. Becker, "Inquiry into a School of Thought in the Judicial Behavior Movement," *Midwest Journal of Political Science*, Vol. 7 (1963), pp. 259-60.

12. For instance, "Prediction in Law and Judicial Behavior" and "Predictions for the 1962 Term," pp. 102-108, 137-42, in my article, "Judicial Attitudes and Voting Behavior: The 1961 Term of the United States Supreme Court," *Law and Contemporary Problems*, Vol. 28 (1963); and "Appendix: Report and Analysis of the 1962 Term Predictions," pp. 575-87 in my *Judicial Behavior: A Reader in Theory and Research* (Chicago: Rand McNally, 1964); and my *The Judicial Mind*, pp. 42-43.

13. See *The Judicial Mind*, p. 29.

14. See Reed C. Lawlor, "Personal *Stare Decisis*," *Southern California Law Review*, Vol. 41 (1967), pp. 73-118; and my "Civilian Control and *Stare Decisis* in the Warren Court," chapter 3 in my *Judicial Decision-Making*.

15. In addition to the references cited in note 12 above, see my *The Future of the Nixon Court* (Honolulu: University of Hawaii Foundation, 1972), pp. 39-51; and Reed C. Lawlor, "What Computers Can Do: Analysis and Prediction of Judicial Decisions," *American Bar Association Journal*, Vol. 49 (1963), pp. 337-44.

16. *The Judicial Mind*, pp. 124, 145, 266, and 271.

17. *Ibid.*, pp. 186-90.

18. *Ibid.*, pp. 191-95; and my "Ideologies and Attitudes, Academic and Judicial," *Journal of Politics*, Vol. 29 (1967), pp. 3-40.

19. See Kenneth R. Minogue, *The Liberal Mind* (New York: Random House, 1964).

20. *The Judicial Mind*, p. 224, table 34.

21. Louis Guttman, "The Principal Components of Scalable Attitudes," and "A New Approach to Factor Analysis: The Radex," chapters 5 and 6 in Paul F. Lazarsfeld, ed., *Mathematical Thinking in the Social Sciences* (New York: The Free Press of Glencoe, 1954), pp. 216-348.

22. *The Judicial Mind*, chapter 8.

23. *Ibid.*, p. 266, Figure 15, and p. 271, Figure 16.

24. See my "Political Ideology on the High Court," *Politics, The Journal of the Australasian Political Studies Association*, Vol. 3 (1968), pp. 30-34.

25. *The Judicial Mind*, p. 266, Figure 15.

26. *Ibid.*, p. 271, Figure 16.

27. See my "Simulating the Supreme Court: An Extension of the Tenth Man Game," *Case Western Reserve Law Review*, Vol. 23 (1972), pp. 451-500.

28. See *op. cit.* ftn. 8, *supra*, at Figure 2c.

29. Cf. Figures 1 and 2 with Figures 3 and 4 of my "Political Culture and Political Ideology: Some Cross and Sub-Cultural Comparisons," paper presented at the third meeting of Specialist Group No. 3 of the Ninth World Congress of the International Political Science Association, in Montreal, Quebec, Canada (August 24, 1973); submitted for publication.

3
Empirical Data and Methodology

In *The Judicial Mind*, I described in some detail the empirical data of that study. It seemed necessary to do that, in part so that it would be possible for interested readers to determine precisely the extent to which my work did in fact articulate with Pritchett's *The Roosevelt Court*; in part so as to "leave the clear trail" that I assume it to be the obligation of every researcher, who purports to accept the ethic of modern science, to blaze; and in part because the data archival facilities and nationally standardized computer programs, which now abound, did not exist even a decade ago. Furthermore, I felt obliged to describe my methodology in considerable detail, not only because I could be certain that it would be quite beyond the experience of most persons who could be expected, on substantive grounds, to be likely to read my book; but also partly (no doubt) because the methods were then unfamiliar to me too. Relatively little Q factor analysis had been ventured up to then, particularly in the United States; and my procedures and reasons for utilizing cumulative scales in conjunction with factor analysis were—and indeed, remain today—quite novel. But apart from the latter consideration, it seems to me that the situation in general is very different now, a dozen years later.

My empirical data have been for several years completely archived, and they are readily and inexpensively available in full to any reader who might wish to explore or check them.[1] The standard computer programs that I employed were available at all four North American universities where I worked on the present book, and they certainly are accessible to any reader who can also get access to my data. Consequently any reader can at little cost of either time or money completely replicate any transformation of the data that underlies any finding that I discuss herein, and similarly he can also undertake, if he chooses, a wide variety of variations on my own selected themes here, including having classes study the data for pedagogical purposes, as I myself did, with a graduate seminar at the University of North Carolina, Chapel Hill, a few years ago. Beyond these considerations of convenience, there is the additional matter that for the earlier book all of the cumulative scaling data were, and all of the factorial data could have been, produced by hand; while none of them have been manually produced for the present study, and I am (as I write) almost overwhelmed by stacks of computer output. It is inconceivable in any case that more than a minute distillation from this vast array of data could ever be published; but it is also quite unnecessary to do so because of the ease with which anyone can retrieve any part of it that might be particularly desired. Consequently I shall report here only very selected and summary data configurations that bear directly upon what I shall discuss, which should have the dual effect of helping to keep the book both more manageable and more readable.

The most succinct and objective way to describe the data is to present the coding manual that is filed with them in the data archives, so I reprint that manual here as Appendix A. The data to which the manual relates consists of some 4578 decisions of the United States Supreme Court that were announced over a period of twenty-three years (and Court terms), extending from October 1946 through June 1969. This period coincides with the Chief Justiceships of Fred Vinson and Earl Warren. The decisions purport to include all cases that the Supreme Court decided on the merits of the substantive issues raised during the denoted time period. Almost exactly half of these decisions—some 2359, or 51.5 per cent of the total—entailed dissent from at least one member of the Court; and the present study is confined to this subset of non-unanimous decisions, although the corresponding unanimous decisions are equally readily available to anyone who might wish to examine them for purposes of comparative analysis along certain common parameters that are necessarily shared by both split and consensual decisions. The manual describes both the non-unanimous and the unanimous subsets and indicates that they are characterized by three principal coding categories. Each decision (actually, each individual case that is the basis for a decision, whether the latter be individual or for a cluster of cases) is identified both uniquely and (deliberately) redundantly. The vote of each justice who is a member of the Court at the time the case is decided is specified in relation to the variable of participation in the majority, or any of several modes of not doing so; and the policy-decisional outcome of the case is denoted as a function of one of a defined subset of scale variables. Instead of dividing the data, as was done in *The Judicial Mind*, into traditional subsets that correspond to the annual term cycle of the Court, here the data are partitioned into a new subset each time a change in the membership of the Court occurs. A total of twenty justices—two chiefs and eighteen associates—served from the appointment of Fred Vinson through the retirement of Earl Warren; and in view of the circumstance that the maximum size of the Supreme Court is nine justices, one might logically anticipate that these data are divided into a dozen chronologically distinct subsets. In fact, however, it proved possible to generate as few as ten decks because there were double vacancies on two different occasions. The apportionment of justices by decks, and the frequencies of data cards by decks (but separately for the non-unanimous and unanimous deck subsets), are reported in Appendix A.

Two of the justices, Black and Douglas, served throughout the period of this study, both having been appointed in the late thirties among the initial members of the Roosevelt Court and both continuing on under Warren Burger.[2] On the other hand, four justices—Murphy, Rutledge, Goldberg, and Marshall—each served for only a single "natural court" (deck) period of this analysis. It is of course possible to speak with somewhat greater assurance in characterizing, as we shall do, the behavior of justices for whom we have available ten observations instead of only a single one. The average number of observations is of four-and-one-half data decks or natural courts for all twenty justices included in the present sample. Hence, observations of their voting behavior in more than a thousand decisions each are the basis for the findings concerning a majority of the justices, in the present study.

Descriptive Parameters for Dyadic Associations

A very simple initial type of computer analysis consisted of the compilation of the marginal frequency distribution totals for every possible pair-wise association of the variables. For each deck and each card of each deck there are nine variables (coding assent-dissent behavior) for the justices, plus three variables (coding subscale, scale, and decisional outcome) for the cases. Contingency tables listing interaction frequencies, plus the corresponding percentage tables (both horizontal and vertical) and chi squares, were calculated for each variable in association with each of the other eleven substantive variables for each card (decision). Included as a part of such contingency frequency tables are, of course, the fourfold tables that correspond to the phi correlation coefficients, to measure the voting association between each pair of justices, that in matrix form provide the basis for the multidimensional scaling analyses. As a possible convenience to readers, the phi correlation matrices are reported in Appendix B.

The contingency table for columns 78/79 shows the partitioning of scales into subscales, subject to a caveat noted below concerning the redundancy of zero punches and blanks for column 78. The column 78/80 and 79/80 contingency tables give, for each deck, the marginal frequencies for decisions supportive of (pro) and non-supportive of (con) the subscale and scale variables. The marginal frequencies for each justice, in terms of the voting participation categories, also were reported by this program; and these data include, of course, the frequencies of assenting and dissenting, as well as of non-participation, for each justice.

Table 3.1 summarizes the frequencies of decisions supportive and non-supportive of each scale and subscale, by decks. As the note to the table explains, combined frequencies (pro plus con) totaling ten or more decisions are italicized in the cell entries of this table, directing attention to the *potentially* scalable data sets. Of course, not all such samples produce acceptable scales, because other criteria must be met, but samples totaling less than ten can be rejected prima facie as inadequate for testing. This table supplies the data for half a dozen figures which will be discussed in the following chapter, but certain findings are manifest even on superficial examination of this table.

One particularly sharp change occurs, both qualitatively and quantitatively, in the apportionment of decisions to the scales and subscales of Deck 8 in comparison with all of the first seven decks; and although the peaks of Deck 8 drop off to some extent in Deck 9, they are at least partially reaffirmed in Deck 10. In the earlier study, I had classified C and E as major scales; F, A, N, and J as minor scales; $\overline{\text{B}}$ and W as subscales of E; and the remaining seven variables as subscales of C. This table raises serious doubts concerning several of the earlier hypotheses—which were presented as that because of my recognition of the inadequacy of term samples as a basis for testing either the minor or the subscale variables. Evidently, J is not a sufficiently important issue to be included in the analysis at all; it appears to be of even marginal importance during the first two periods only. Of the other three hypothesized minor scales, F is twice as important as either A or N; but all three are of only sporadic rather than continuous interest, and in any event none achieves an average magnitude different from what is typical of the *sub*scales of C and E. Hence, although we may discrimi-

TABLE 3.1
Apportionment of Decisions Pro and Con Scales and Subscales

Scales and Sub-Scales	Deck 1	2	3	4	5	6	7	8	9	10	Avg.	% Pro
C	28-68	39-89	15-20	18-17	04-07	48-42	51-81	161-36	73-44	129-32	57-44	56
FP	09-30	21-41	12-08	10-12	02-05	15-21	27-39	59-16	28-15	51-14	23-20	53
RP	10-21	07-18	01-04	05-03	01-01	09-10	11-19	21-12	07-10	38-07	11-10	52
PF	04-06	04-20	00-03	01-00	00-01	19-09	09-14	19-03	19-08	22-07	10-07	59
RE	00-01	04-04	00-01	00-02	00-00	00-00	03-02	22-02	05-06	08-03	04-02	67
VE	00-01	00-01	00-00	00-00	00-00	00-00	01-00	29-01	06-02	09-00	04-00	90
CE	03-02	01-04	00-02	00-00	00-00	02-02	00-03	07-02	08-03	00-00	02-02	54
RF	02-04	01-01	02-01	01-00	00-00	03-00	00-04	04-00	00-00	00-01	01-01	54
E	66-53	46-62	12-19	37-08	11-02	50-19	80-36	80-39	60-12	40-23	48-27	64
B	51-39	32-48	10-09	23-02	10-01	43-07	52-23	62-31	45-04	32-19	36-18	67
W	06-11	05-08	00-06	06-04	01-00	06-12	19-09	16-06	11-07	06-03	08-07	54
F	42-27	25-33	07-03	10-04	03-04	09-08	29-08	18-03	08-06	05-00	16-10	62
A	02-07	09-33	07-05	01-03	02-02	12-01	11-09	05-02	02-05	07-26	06-09	40
N	18-07	16-15	06-02	04-04	01-02	08-07	06-05	07-01	00-01	07-01	07-05	59
J	14-04	08-06	00-01	00-03	01-00	02-00	03-05	03-00	00-01	03-03	03-02	60

Note: Only scales or subscales with frequencies in bold-face type, which indicates that the combined total of pro-con decisions is ten or more, can—although even these do not necessarily—meet the minimum requirements for scalability. For an evaluation of scale/subscale acceptability, see the quantitative and qualitative descriptors of Appendix C.

nate between [F, A, and N] and the liberalism subscales on qualitative grounds, we certainly cannot do so on a quantitative basis.[3] Both of the economic subscales appear relatively adequate, although the anti-business samples are considerably and consistently much larger than the pro-union samples. Analogously, the fair procedure variable is much the largest and most consistent of the civil liberties subscales. The right-to-privacy and the political freedom subscales are not much bigger than W, and there is a large question whether any of the four remaining subscales ought to be recognized as a relevant variable for the period of this study, on the basis of the evidence of this table. Notwithstanding the amount of national attention that has focused on the Supreme Court's role in regard to racial equality and voting equality, these appear, in the context of the full sweep of the first two decades or so after the end of World War II, as of quantitative importance in the Court's decision-making only during the sixties, and then mostly during the early years of that decade, which are encompassed by Deck 8. Civic equality seems to have been strictly an issue of the mid-sixties; and religious freedom (mostly school prayer and Bible-reading) must be categorized as a non-issue—Madalyn Murray O'Hair notwithstanding—from either a quantitative or a scaling point of view.

Linear (cumulative) scaling was initially performed by means of the BMD Guttman scaling computer program.[4] As Appendix C indicates, six major scales were coded for each period; and in addition, the two scales that on the basis of prior work were hypothesized to be both quantitatively and qualitatively most important were further partitioned into subscales, of which seven relate to civil liberties issues and two to economic issues. A tenth subscale (that for "national government fiscal claims") is redundantly coded identically both as a subscale and also as one of the six major scales: evidently, this reflects an error in categorization (e.g., judgment) on my part; it would have been better to have coded this variable as a major scale only. The latter practice would have made it possible to avoid another type of redundancy that became evident—to me, at least—only long after the computer runs had been completed and I was pretty effectively committed to the data in their present format: the zero punch for the column (78), in which subscale variables were coded, included not only one of the civil liberties subscales (civic equality), as I had intended, but it included also the non-subscale (but scale) and the non-scale cases which were coded as blanks in columns 78, or 78 and 79. (The computer does not distinguish between zero punches and blanks; the problem was not serious, and could be and was resolved by extra manual work, but it could also have been avoided by better foresight.) So the avoidance of the redundancy in categorization would also with certainty have avoided the redundancy in counting, because I would have assigned the civic equality subscale to the #1 punch (if that had been available) rather than to the zero punch, thereby assuring that blank would mean blank alone.

As I mentioned in the introductory section of this chapter, the computer solutions output by the BMD Guttman scaling program are rarely optimal because the program orders the data strictly in terms of row and column marginal frequency totals. This would not necessarily be the optimal solution even if there were no missing data,[5] and with data sets defined to correspond with "natural courts," there is sufficient non-participation so that it is necessary for that reason also to undertake manual adjustments of the computer scales in order to achieve the optimal solutions of maximal reproducibility (i.e., consistency in the patterning of voting behavior.) If the scale and subscale data subsets had been uniformly adequate, a total of 150 scales and subscales would have been produced; empirically there were 84 potentially adequate samples, including 100 per cent of the two major scales, 50 per cent of the possible subscales and 48 per cent of the possible minor scales, as indicated in Table 3.1. Appendix C shows that there are 76 acceptable scales, so that 90 per cent of the 84 potentially adequate samples do meet other criteria of scalability. Only 32 of the 60 hypothesized major and minor scales are found empirically; most (20) of these are C scales or E scales. Similarly, 44 of the 90 possible subscales can be identified, but virtually all of these relate to five of the subscales (B̄, RP, FP, PF, and W). Of the remaining subscales RE scales only in the three last periods, VE and CE are observed only once each, and RF not at all. There are also a few marginal scales which fail to manifest sufficient consistency to be acceptable, plus almost a dozen quasi-scales for which consistency is high enough but sample size is inadequate. This leaves some 56 samples remaining whose size is so small that there was no point in even examining them. The chapters below will discuss only the 76 empirical scales—about half of the total of 150 that had been hypothesized to be observable in this study.

Multidimensional Scaling Analysis

Centroid factor analysis alone, without iteration and with communality estimates of less than unity, was the basis for the multidimensional scaling work in *The Judicial Mind.* Consequently there was only a single set of seventeen term phi correlation matrices together with the corresponding fourfold tables as the basis for the factor analysis of the earlier study. Typically the first factor was much the largest in terms of apportionment of the common variance, and the rapidly decreasing size of the eigenvalues for subsequent factors induced the decision to limit the analysis to spaces defined by the first three reference (and hence, orthogonal) factors. The cumulative scales and subscales (as described in Chapter 1, infra) were then used as criteria for rotation of the factorial axes to oblique positions.

In the present study, three different types of multidimensional scaling have been employed: principal-component factor analysis, oblimin oblique factor analysis, and smallest-space. The principal-component program, which included a missing data correlation option, was the version of the BMD series[6] then standard in the winter of 1970; the oblimin solution employed utilized the biquartimin option of a program originally written by John B. Carroll;[7] and the smallest-space program was the then current SSA-1 edition of the Lingoes version of the Guttman-Lingoes series.[8] The principal-component program did select an iterated solution; I did use unities as the estimates of self-correlation (communality); and it did produce in addition to the initial principal-component solution a varimax (orthogonally rotated) solution, although I do not discuss the latter for purposes of the present study because of my assumption, based on the earlier centroid analysis of almost three-fourths of the data and confirmed by the evidence to be presented here, that the relevant dimensions would be correlated analogues of the cumulative scales and therefore in oblique relation to each other. In order to test the hypothesis suggested by the earlier study that larger data samples for cumulative scaling purposes might require four-dimensional space for their mutual accommodation, the first four principal components for each deck were selected for examination and possible further analysis. Averaging factor eigenvalues across the ten deck periods, the first principal component has a mean value of 3.11, the second of 1.51, the third of 1.08, and the fourth of 0.89; together the first four components account, on the average, for 73 per cent and the remaining five components for an average of 27 per cent of the total common variance. Both the first and second component eigenvalues exceeded unity in all ten periods; that for the third did so in seven periods; and that for the fourth in only two periods. These statistical indices suggest that we should be able to observe any consistently important cumulative scales (*i.e.,* obliquely rotated factorial dimensions of substantive importance) within the confines of no greater than four-space; that the fourth component is, generally speaking, very marginally important at best; and that a three-dimensional or even two-dimensional solution might prove to be, at least for certain purposes, not only parsimonious but also optimal.

The oblimin program takes as its input whatever factors may be selected from an orthogonal factor program output. But the number of orthogonal factors to be obliquely rotated must be specified, and an independent operation of the program—a separate computer run—is necessary for each change in the size of the dimensionality. For the present study, two-dimensional and four-dimensional solutions were obtained from the oblimin program for all ten periods; and after that output had been examined, I decided that the likelihood of obtaining sufficiently different information from a three-dimensional solution was too low to justify the expense of making the additional computer run.

For the smallest-space program, it was possible to specify that solutions for one dimension, then two dimensions, next three dimensions, and finally four dimensions be output successively in a single computer run for each data deck (*i.e.*, for each of the ten periods); and therefore I have been able to examine on a comparative basis the adequacy and optimality of solutions of varying degrees of complexity ranging from linear to four-dimensional, non-Euclidean space for all ten periods of the analysis.

So the multidimensional scaling output consists of the following alternatives for each data deck: an unrotated four-dimensional, orthogonal principal-component solution; both two- and four-dimensional oblique oblimin solutions; and smallest-space solutions at the levels of one, two, three, and four dimensions. There are, therefore, seven different space alternatives for each of the ten periods, or a total of seventy spaces (of which sixty are multidimensional) that provide the basis for the substantive discussion of this study.

The procedure for fitting cumulative scales to their analogues in multidimensional space can be briefly described as follows. The factor loadings (or smallest-space coefficients, or whatever the scores of variables might be upon the reference parameters that define the position of the configuration of variables in the space) are reordered in the sequence of the cumulative scale that is being fitted. This procedure results in an asymetrical matrix with rows in the order of scale rank, and columns identified by dimension numbers. If a plotting subprogram has been appended to the multivariate analysis program, then that two-dimensional output should be visually inspected as the basis for initial estimates of the weights to be attached to (and to which) dimensions. The sequence of columns (dimensional scores) should at this point be resequenced so that the dimension comes first that is presumed to have the greatest influence upon the scale rankings—for example, the dimension with which the scale is most highly correlated—and so on, with dimensions that are presumed to have little or no influence upon the scale coming later or last in the order of the columns of the matrix. In practice, it is easier to work with weights than with correlation coefficients, although at a later stage of the calculation it is necessary to normalize the weights (by an operation described below) so that the vectors for both ideal-points and the scale analogue can be transformed back to the scale of unit radius that determines the metric of the space. The estimated trial weight for the dimension first in the resequenced order of columns of the matrix is then multiplied by all of the scores in that column; and because the weight will be $\leqslant \pm 1.00$, the effect mathematically will be either to reproduce the column unchanged or else to lessen, by a constant proportion, the size of the loadings or scores. The ordinality of the column is then compared with the (apart from possible ties, natural) sequence in which the rows have been placed, so that attention can focus on the intransitivities that deviate most from that natural sequence. (I emphasize that these intransitivities are of differences in *rank*, not in metric amount; consequently a difference of several ranks but of very little metric amount would be deemed more important than a very large metric difference which has the effect of merely transposing adjacent ranks.)

Attention is then directed to the remaining columns, with the objective of estimating what weight(s) on which one(s) will have the effect of most reducing the rank order differences that were denoted in the first column without introducing more new or larger intransitivities than were apparent in it, so that the result will be to *increase* the rank correlation between the ranking of the row *sums* and the natural order that has been supplied by the criterion scale. Evidently the effect of multiplying the column by some weight other than +1.00 is to specify what, after normalization, becomes the directional cosine for the rotation of the dimension in relation to the criterion provided by its orthogonal position as a reference dimension; so a trial weight is the algebraic equivalent of what is geometrically the rotation of the dimension in the space of whatever dimensionality is under examination.

Analysis proceeds by this process of approximation, including the re-examination of the weights of dimensions of higher (in the sequence of the matrix) order in the light of changes in the row sums sequence brought about by the subsequent weighting of what are, in the same sense, lower order dimensions. Or from a geometric point of view, each of the several reference dimensions is rotated to a position that uniquely defines a vector in the multidimensional space. It is of course possible to make a poor initial estimate, in which event one is forced sooner or later to abandon the premise concerning the weighting of whatever dimension has been placed in the first column because it does not lead to an acceptably high correlation between the sequence of row sums and the natural order. It is also possible to conclude, after having investigated all such premises that appear reasonable, that a particular scale cannot be accommodated in a particular space, as evidenced by an insufficiently high rank correlation under all such hypotheses that were tested. Otherwise, manipulation continues with what are increasingly smaller marginal rank differences, until either a perfect solution, with a rho = +1.00, is achieved or else it is apparent that further changes on any dimension will entail negative effects upon the ranking either by introducing further intransitivities or else by magnifying those that already exist. At that point the rank order correlation, whether rho or tau, is confirmed by recalculation, and both the dimensional weights and the matrix entries for the variables are normalized.

Normalization is accomplished as follows: all columnar weights and matrix scores are divided by the square root of the sum of the squares of the columnar weights. This process assures that the communality or variance of each dimension is reduced to 1.00 within the limits of rounding error and that the matrix scores of the variables are measures of the projections from the ideal points of the configuration in the multidimensional space upon (*i.e.*, that they are the structural correlations with) the rotated vector for which the directional cosines are now supplied by the normalized columnar weights. In short, we now have not only the scale order of the ideal points upon the analogue scale vector, but we have also a measure of their relative metric differences upon that vector, as a function of their latent ideological differences as determined by the ideal-point configuration.

As Rummel has correctly observed, this is a form of what the vernacular of factor analysis calls target (oblique) rotation, to a criterion supplied by a cumulative scale.[9] It would of course be advantageous if this rather tedious manual procedure for scale-fitting were programmed for computer analysis. Unfortunately, this has not yet been done, for reasons that we will consider in Chapter 5.

Notes to Chapter 3

1. The data described in Appendix A, together with the codebook reprinted therein, are available on magnetic tape or punch cards from the Survey Research Archives of the Inter-University Consortium for Political Research, P.O. Box 1248, Ann Arbor, Michigan, 48106. The data are classified by the archive as a Class III project under the rubric "Schubert, THE JUDICIAL MIND." See *A Guide to Resources and Services of the Inter-University Consortium for Political Research, 1971-1972*, pp. 76-77.

2. For a discussion of the subsequent behavior of Black and Douglas as well as that of Burger, see my *The Future of the Nixon Court* (Honolulu: University of Hawaii Foundation, 1972).

3. The combined frequency totals F + A + N = 52 are virtually indistinguishable from the corresponding totals W + RP + PF = 53.

4. W. J. Dixon, ed., *BMD, Biomedical Computer Programs* (University of California, Los Angeles: Health Sciences Computing Facility, Department of Preventive Medicine and Public Health, School of Medicine, January 1, 1964), Program BMD05S (Guttman Scale #1), pp. 77-87.

5. The rows are ordered strictly by row sums, and the columns by the number of affirmative (numeral seven) responses. Any columns with homogeneous response patterns (e.g., all 7's or else all 1's) are dropped from the analysis—which means in regard to these data that if any justice responds with perfect consistency, either in complete support of or in invariant opposition to a scale variable during a particular period, his relationship to the scale must be determined manually because the program ignores him. Of course, such indices as R and MMR are always miscalculated by the program for any scale for which one or more columns have been thus deleted. Consequently the program only incidentally produces a scale with a pattern that reflects maximal voting consistency (*i.e.*, maximal elimination of inconsistent responses to the extent that this can be achieved by transforming the sequences of rows and columns). Therefore some realignment of rows and/or columns as these have been patterned by the program is usually required based on human visual perceptions which augment, in their sensitivity to the objective of scaling, the simplistic arithmetical instructions that this program has given to the computer. Like centroid in relation to principal-component factor analysis, the BMD05 scaling program does some useful preliminary ordering of the data and makes available an initial first approximation of the solution desired.

6. BMD3M (Principal-Component Factor Analysis); cf. Dixon, *BMD*, pp. 159-84.

7. The York University Institute for Behavioural Research obtained for me from the Dimensionality of Nations Project at the University of Hawaii the version, revised in 1963 at Northwestern University, of the "Program for Generalized Analytic Rotation Solution in Factor Analysis" that Carroll had originated at Harvard University, as revised by Carroll in March 1960. The program used at York was written in Fortran IV G.

8. Similarly, York's I.B.R. obtained from the Survey Research Center at the University of Michigan the Guttman-Lingoes package, a series of programs for non-metric factor analysis and for multidimensional scaling, including SSA1; the version employed is one, revised by James Lingoes, that the Survey Research Center was distributing in the early winter of 1970. See James C. Lingoes, *The Guttman-Lingoes Nonmetric Program Series* (Ann Arbor, Michigan: Mathesis Press, 1973), chapter 2, for further details.

9. Rudolph J. Rummel, *Applied Factor Analysis* (Evanston: Northwestern University Press, 1970), pp. 552-53.

4
Scales

The results of the Guttman scaling are described in Appendix C. That appendix reports all of the acceptable scales and subscales, plus certain others that were tested but found to be deficient in one respect or another. The decisions on scalability were based partly on the scale statistics, including Menzel's S; Guttman's Coefficient of Reproducibility as determined both manually by me [R] and by the BMD program [R']; the coefficient of Minimal Marginal Reproducibility as determined both by me [M] and by the computer [M']; the extent to which the scale pattern improves upon the worst pattern possible given the empirical marginal frequency distributions of the scale [M−R]; and the sample size [N]. The evaluation was also based on the discriminatory power of the scales and subscales as evidenced in their delineation of discrete sequences in the ranking of each natural court; hence, the more and larger the ties in rank, the poorer the discriminatory power of the scale. In order to characterize the scales, I posited criteria for their evaluation, combining with discriminatory power the coefficients of scalability and of reproducibility, plus the extent of improvement upon minimal marginal reproducibility. These criteria and the ascriptions that they determine are defined in the legend to Table 4.1. The individual scale descriptions of Appendix C include also rho (rank) correlation coefficients which measure, mostly for contiguous periods, the similarity between scale patterns. Because the periods were defined to coincide with personnel changes in the composition of the Court, the maximal size of the rankings upon which such correlations were computed is 8, and in two instances drops to 7, even for contiguous scales. In a few instances where I thought it desirable to compare scales for non-adjacent periods, the size of the rankings drops as low as 5, and a correlation for rankings of the latter size must reflect very little inconsistency if it is to remain statistically significant. In the case of certain variables that scale only intermittently, the possibility of calculating interscale rank correlations is correspondingly attenuated. Those correlations that could and needed to be calculated are given in matrix form below the quantitative indices for each scale, and a table showing the size of rankings for correlations between particular pairs of periods appears as the lower half of the matrix of part 3 of the initial (the C) scale.

There is a high positive correlation of over .80 between deck size and the percentage of scales and subscales accepted for the corresponding period, and similarly, of course, a correlation of over .70 between deck size and the evaluation score totals that are reported, by deck, in Table 4.2. It is also notable that there is a 50 per cent improvement in scalability during the latter portion of the data, with the proportion of acceptable scales increasing from 41 per cent, or 2 out of 5, for Decks 1–5 to 59 per cent, or 3 out of 5, for Decks 6–10. Largely, however, this increase in scalability can be explained by the circumstance that the deck sample sizes are larger during the later periods, increasing from a proportion of what is again 41 per cent of the total decisions for Decks 1–5, to 59 per cent for Decks 6–10. Similarly, the proportion of acceptable scales and subscales is substantially lower for Decks 3–5, for which the sample sizes also are lowest—less than 100 decisions for two of these decks and averaging 82 for all three of them—whereas for each of the other seven decks the sample size exceeds 200 decisions. Also relevant, however, is the circumstance that the average proportion of liberals on the Court increases from 36 per cent during the earlier period to 49 per cent during the later period. Such a difference in percentages is equivalent, of course, to only a very small correlation of .16, but even this modest differential is important because the adequacy of scale/subscale sample sizes, both qualitatively and quantitatively, is dependent upon the presence on the Court of a critical mass of at least four strong liberals to control jurisdictional decision-making and thereby to define and to push issues before the Court. The subscales RE, VE, and CE, for example, are scalable only during the last three periods of the Warren Court (Decks 8–10), and three other subscales, PF and RP and W, all scale for every one of Decks 6–10, but only one, two, and three times, respectively, for Decks 1–5.

Table 4.1 shows that the two best scales are C and E. This confirms a major finding of the earlier study. Both C and E are scalable even during the period of the three smallest decks and at an overall level of

TABLE 4.1
Evaluations of Scalability

Scales/Subscales	Number Acceptable	Average Characterization*	Evaluation*	Inter-scale Consistency**
$\overline{\text{B}}$	10	F+	4.3	.88
RP	7	F+	4.0	.81
C	10	F+	3.9	.92
E	10	F+	3.9	.96
FP	9	F	3.4	.87
W	7	F	3.3	.79
PF	6	F	2.7	.73
RE	3	P+	1.7	.80
F	6	P	1.3	.75
N	3	P	0.6	.34
J	2	P	0.6	.67
VE	1	$\overline{\text{A}}$	0.4	.94
A	1	$\overline{\text{A}}$	0.2	—
CE	1	$\overline{\text{A}}$	0.1	—
RF	0	$\overline{\text{A}}$	0.0	—

Total 76

*0.0–0.5 = $\overline{\text{A}}$; 0.6–1.5 = P;
 1.6–2.5 = P+; 2.6–3.5 = F;
 3.6–4.5 = F+; 4.6–5.5 = G;
 5.6–6.5 = G+; 6.6–7.0 = E.

**Average rho correlation for pairs of adjacent scales.

Legend	Ascription	Character- ization	Score	N	S	R	R–M	Discrimination
	(Excellent	E	7	≥ 10	≥ 75	≥ 95	≥ 15	≤ 1 pair
A =	(Very Good	G+	6	≥ 10	[3 out of 4 E-level criteria]			
Acceptable	(Good	G	5	≥ 10	≥ 70	≥ 92	≥ 12	$\leq$ (2 pairs or 1 triple)
	(Average	F+	4	≥ 10	[3 out of 4 G-level criteria]			
	(Fair	F	3	≥ 10	≥ 65	≥ 90	≥ 11	$\leq$ (1 pair + 1 triple, or 1 quadruple)
	(Poor	P+	2	≥ 10	≥ 65	< 90	≥ 11	$\leq$ (1 pair + 1 triple, or 3 pairs)
	(Very Poor	P	1	≥ 10	< 65	≥ 90	≥ 11	$\leq$ (″ ″ ″ ″ ″)
$\overline{\text{A}}$ = Not	(Marginal	M	0	≥ 10	< 65	< 90		
	(Quasi	Q	0	< 10	> 65	> 90	≥ 11	[at least 2 out of last 3]
Acceptable	(Inadequate Sample Size	I	0	< 10	< 65	< 90	< 11	[at least 2 out of last 3]

quality that is strictly modal in terms of the evaluation system employed in the present study. To achieve their average rating, the C and E scales had to be consistently either above .70 in scalability or above .92 in reproducibility, with an improvement range of at least .12 and

TABLE 4.2
Scale Evaluations (by Periods)

Evaluation	1	2	3	4	5	6	7	8	9	10	1-5	6-10	Scales	Subscales	Total
											Periods			Number accepted	
E	2	0	0	0	0	4	1	1	1	0	2	7	2	7	9
G+	1	0	0	1	0	1	1	2	2	3	2	9	1	10	11
G	0	2	0	1	1	1	3	3	1	0	4	8	6	6	12
F+	1	1	1	1	0	1	1	2	0	3	4	7	4	7	11
F	2	1	3	1	0	0	1	0	2	0	7	3	4	6	10
P+	1	5	1	1	0	1	3	1	1	1	8	7	12	3	15
P	1	0	0	1	2	0	0	0	3	0	4	3	3	4	7
No. Scales Accepted	8	9	5	6	3	8	10	9	10	7	31	44	32	43	75
M	1	2	1	0	0	1	0	1	0	0	4	2	5	1	6
Q	2	0	1	1	2	0	1	1	2	2	6	6	7	5	12
I	4	4	8	8	10	6	4	4	3	6	34	23	16	41	57
Number Scaled Not Acceptable	7	6	10	9	12	7	5	6	5	8	44	31	28	47	75
% Accepted	53	60	33	40	20	53	67	60	67	47	41	59	53	48	50
Evaluation Score Totals	33	27	15	21	07	45	41	44	35	32	103	197	105	195	300
Deck Size (No. of decisions)	342	384	098	110	039	206	324	364	215	277	973	1386			2359

with no greater tying than that of two pairs or a triple. In fact, these scales tend to be substantially higher than what these cut-off criteria demand. The only significant differences between these two scales—other than, of course, in their content—appear to be that the data samples for C average about a third larger than do those for E, while the reliability as measured by between-scales correlations is, though high for C, particularly high for E.

If what I have hypothesized to be subscales of C and E are empirically that, then we ought to expect that certain of these subscales will show, for each scale, higher consistency than their parent scale, while other subscales may show less consistency, with the scale itself necessarily picking up some additional inconsistency as a consequence of the mixture of content from what are substantively at least two more discrete subscales.[1] Certainly Table 4.1 supports such expectations: one subscale for each of C and E evinces slightly better scalability than its parent scale; while other subscales have lower evaluation scores, but without exception this seems to be because of the inadequacy of their sample sizes in those periods for which they are not scalable. The anti-business subscale is not only the best but also the largest subscale with its average deck frequency of 53 decisions; and it is notable that the evaluation score for E (3.9) is approximately the mean (4.1) of the scores for its two principal subscales, $\overline{B}$ (4.3) and W (3.2), corrected of course for their relative sample sizes and also allowing for the additional inconsistency introduced by their having become combined into E. On the other hand, the best of its subscales (RP, at 4.0) is hardly higher than C at 3.9; and the other acceptable C subscales (FP, 3.4; PF, 2.7; and RE, 1.7) are substantially lower, with corresponding ascriptive evaluations of "fair" to "poor."

Three remaining hypothesized C subscales must be evaluated as not acceptable, due to their small average subsample sizes, aggregating less than a dozen decisions per deck for all three of these variables together. Thus their joint influence on the empirical scalability of the C scale, although clearly negative in effect, remains small.

Three of the four minor scales are minimally acceptable, but only as "very poor" scales. This means that operationally they were consistently able to exceed the floors for only one, not both, of the two indices S and R; that their discriminatory power typically was low; that their frequency of appearance was low (six times for F, but only three times for N and twice for J). It is notable, too, that these three minor scales seem to be functions of the Court's more conservative, rather than of its more liberal mood: the extent to which F, J, and N are either products of or hangovers from the Vinson Court[2] is indicated by noting that J can be observed only for the first two decks and that four of the six F scales are in the first four decks; while N is evaluated (seriatim) as marginal, as a poor but acceptable scale, and as a quasi-scale for the periods of the first three decks. Furthermore, the overall evaluations of J and N as scalable are as tenuous as such an appraisal can possibly be, reflecting both my own feeling of obligation to apply my criteria consistently, and the observation of arithmetic mean scores slightly above the 0.5 level—if they had averaged 0.4, like VE, instead of 0.6, I would of course have classified both J and N as not acceptable. But J and N did scale several times each, and VE did not; so the results of the table are not illogical, however they may deviate in some details from what one might conclude on the basis of his less manifestly structured intuitions about these data. The remaining subscale, A, is acceptable only once, notwithstanding the seeming anomaly that its sample size is adequate for half of the periods. The explanation is found in the observation that the subsamples for A tended to be of unusually poor quality when appraised by other of the technical criteria for scalability and reproducibility: during the last period (Deck 10), for example, 33 decisions are apportioned to this scale, but of these only three can be used for purposes of scale construction. The remainder have solitary dissents, of which twenty-three are by Douglas.

I turn now to certain more particular aspects of the scale variable summaries, which are reported in Appendix C. Only one of the C scales is of excellent quality (that for Deck 6), but four are good, and only one—the first, notwithstanding the co-participation of Murphy and Rutledge with Black and Douglas—is very poor. And the scale for the last period, packed with the Court's largest critical mass of liberals (Douglas, Fortas, Marshall, Warren, and Brennan) would have scored much higher except for the fact that Hugo Black, who had ranked consistently second during the period of Decks 2—7, now ranks last in his overall support of civil liberties—but not without his casting many inconsistent votes, which account for the reduced S and R scores.[3] The overall discrimination of these scales is excellent, as we shall see in somewhat greater detail presently when we consider the dominance scale for this variable. The rho correlations between the scales for adjacent periods are all high, averaging .92 and exceeding .90 in seven of the nine observable relationships.

Although it has a lower evaluative score than RP, FP is probably the best of the C subscales when consideration is based on all of the available evidence. Fair procedure scales in nine periods and fails to do so for the fifth deck only because its sample size of seven is too small to meet one of the technical criteria for cumulative scaling—otherwise the scale for even that period is evident and is clearly of good quality, and it correlates quite satisfactorily (at .89 and .97) with the scales (for

Decks 4 and 6) adjacent to it. The average correlation between adjacent scales is somewhat lower for FP (.87) than the .92 that we observed for the C scale, but examination of the individual correlations reveals why. The scale for the second period has so much inconsistency that it barely attains the minimal criterion levels for either S or R; and the pattern produced is evidently not very reliable because the correlations of this scale with its two adjacents drops below .80 in both instances, whereas the correlation between the scales for Decks 1 and 3 jumps to .94, clearly demonstrating that it is the scale for Deck 2 that is deviant. The only other conspicuously low correlation between adjacent scales is that for Decks 8 and 9, where again it drops below .80, but then for the obvious reason that Black's rank on fair procedure drops from a tie with Douglas for the 1½th rank for Deck 8, to the fifth rank for Deck 9, and the seventh for Deck 10. The difference between fifth and seventh is not so great as to keep the correlation between Decks 8 and 9 below .90, but the difference between 1½th and seventh is such that the correlation between Decks 7 and 9 drops to .649, confirming that it is Black's increasing conservatism on fair-procedure issues during the middle and latter part of the sixties that accounts for most of the difference between the subscale rankings for these three periods.

When we examine the right-to-privacy variable, what is most apparent is the sharp rise in the quality of its subscales during the latter five periods of the analysis, when three of these subscales rate as excellent, another as very good, and the one for Deck 8 also as very good—and the latter one would have been better except for the circumstance that Hugo Black (who alone contributes more than half of the inconsistent votes denoted on this scale) had begun his back-sliding into conservatism on this, as on most other, civil liberties issues. Similarly, Robert Jackson contributed half of the inconsistent votes to the first scale, on which he ranked *second* and ahead of Hugo Black, William Douglas, and Wiley Rutledge alike—a posture that is not nearly so out of place from his overall orientation as one might think at first blush.[4] But his rank had slipped to a three-way tie for sixth in the subscale for Deck 2, and that difference is quite enough to explain the between-scales correlation of only .522. Black's descent necessarily was arrested by his arrival in the bottom rank for Deck 10, and his drop of four ranks from his position in Decks 8 and 9 is the major cause for the drop in correlation to .691 between Decks 9 and 10. Because the sample sizes were too small for scales to have been produced for the third and fifth decks, and the subscale for Deck 4 shows perfect consistency even though it is for a sample of 8 decisions, I have included the quasi-scale ranking in the set of between-scales correlations that are listed for RP. But even at that, the average for the seven then-possible pairings of scales (of which only five are, of course, adjacent pairs) is only .81 (as compared to .87 for FP), reflecting, I believe, the fact that the sizes of the subscale samples available for the analysis of RP, averaging 21, are only half as good as those for FP, which average 42.

The only other C subscale of fair overall quality is political freedom; and for PF the problem of subsample size is even more acute, being adequate only for the last five periods (for which the average ascriptive evaluation is 4.6 or "good") and for the second one (which is characterized as F+ or "average"). It is the Q for Deck 1 and the I's for Decks 3-5, which contribute nothing to the numerator while adding substantially to the weight of the denominator of the fraction, which determine the average ratio and bring the overall ascription of PF down to the level of a low "fair" rating of 2.7. On the other hand, the drop in the average value of the between-scales correlation to .732 for PF is not attributable to the missing scales for Decks 3-5, with the consequent necessity of correlating Deck 2 with Deck 6; nor to the ranking of only (and inescapably, given our definition of the natural courts to which the decks correspond) five respondents, thereby magnifying the effect of even small inconsistencies in rankings. Whatever the merits of the logic underlying these presumptions, the empirical value of the rho for Decks 2 and 6 is .974, the highest of all in this set of correlations. Neither can we invoke Hugo Black as an explanation, because in regard to political freedom, Black remained true to his proclaimed constitutional faith[5] and despite certain evident problems (which hang, ultimately, upon the thread of the discriminatory power of only two decisions) provoked by the Deck 8 subscale, he remains in Deck 9 and 10 in the same second rank in which we can observe him in Deck 2 (and also the same relative position for which we observe him in Deck 1, after making allowance for the presence then of Murphy and Rutledge). There is generally less consistency between the rankings for PF than for RP and FP, which may in turn reflect greater heterogeneity and variation in policy content for PF than for the other two subscales.

The only other aspect of civil liberties policy-making that appears important from a scaling point of view is that of racial equality. But *Brown* v. *Board*[6] was decided during the third period, for which it supplies the entire frequency—of one, which is the subsample size of the RE variable for Deck 3; and clearly we cannot scale such a sample cumulatively. As Table 3.1 indicates, the total frequency of the Supreme Court's decisions concerning racial equality for Decks 1-7 is only 17; and it is only during the last three of the Warren Court periods that this variable is scalable—and barely so then during the Deck 9 and Deck 10 periods, for which the sample size is in each instance eleven decisions. The ascription for the RE subscale during the only period (that of Deck 8) for which it is based on the more adequate sample size of 25, is excellent; and the scalability indices also are very high, averaging (for the three terms) over .90 for S and over .98 for R, with a good average improvement of .21 shown for R—M. But the two between-scales rho correlations are only fair at .807 and .801; nor can we in this instance blame these values on Hugo Black: he had already, on *this* issue, changed his mind[7] soon enough so that that effect could only have been upon the between-scales correlation for Deck 7 (if there were such a subscale) and Deck 8.

Reapportionment (VE) appears to have been a policy of strictly transitory concern to the Supreme Court, in keeping with its apparently barely marginal visibility to the mass American public.[8] There is a total of three relevant decisions for the first seven periods; then came *Baker v. Carr*[9] and a sudden ballooning of the VE sample to thirty decisions for Deck 8 (of which this decision is a part) to be followed by a drop-off to deck frequencies of eight and nine—which could support, of course, only quasi-scales at best—during the last two periods.

So we can observe only one, and that a highly internally consistent, voting equality scale for Deck 8, with exceptionally high S and R indices of .96 and .99, respectively, but marred by a poor improvement range (with R—M = .086) and inadequate discriminatory power (with a quadruple tie for 3½th place, among Warren, Brennan, Black, and White). Consequently this situation was not one, as most were, that could be resolved by simply applying the defined criteria. There was evident tension between the excellent index levels, the fair discrimination, and the insufficient improvement. The poor improvement was inherent in the marginal distributions of the sample, because too many of the decisions had been determined by a very few stereotyped voting patterns. I attributed an evaluation of F+ (average) to this subscale—but it is average only in the sense of mediation between extremes, not in the sense of modality. The quasi-scale for Deck 9 evinces perfect internal consistency but unacceptably poor discrimination with four tied pairs; it is nevertheless correlated at a high .942 with the Deck 8 subscale. For Deck 10 the sample is inadequate, both in size and in diversity of voting patterns, to make possible the determination of the subscale. There is also only a single subscale for civic equality, but with the difference that this one is produced by Deck 9 (for which the sample size is 11, to be followed by a sample of zero decisions in Deck 10). Clearly CE also must be viewed as a sporadic (if not a one-shot) policy issue, so far as concerns its treatment by at least the Vinson and the Warren Courts. At that it is a very poor scale ascriptively, with a barely acceptable R of .909 and an unacceptable S of .609, but quite acceptable improvement of .141, and excellent discrimination. Justice

Black, incidentally, remained associated with the liberals on this issue, although not very enthusiastically so, since his rank of fifth placed him in the dead center of the Court as the least committed in relation to the other liberals of this period, Douglas, Fortas, Brennan, and Warren.

The other major variable, economic liberalism, scales at least as well and just as consistently as does the political liberalism variable, although the deck subsample sizes tend to be smaller, as previously noted, and discrimination is not quite as good with eight tied pairs in all for E versus one pair and one triple tie for C. But the between-scales correlation average for E is a very high .955, showing excellent consistency in the denoted scale sequence throughout the ten periods. Indeed, the rho for Decks 7 and 9 is an extraordinarily high .993 and that between 9 and 10 is .994. Clearly E scales reliably and at generally quite acceptable levels of evaluation.

The anti-business variable scales the best of all of those discussed in this chapter when evaluated in terms of the scalability criteria, and it is the only subscale observable throughout all ten periods. However, several of the individual $\overline{B}$ subscales discriminate less well than do the discrete scales of E, or of C, or the principal subscales of C. Also, the between-scales correlation average for $\overline{B}$ is .880, which is .075 less than that for E. This drop is accounted for by inconsistent rankings among the conservatives during the first four periods. The only other subscale of economic liberalism, pro-union (W), has an average sample size of only 14, which is about a fourth that of $\overline{B}$; and therefore it is not surprising to note that W results in four unacceptable scales: two for which the sample sizes are just too low, one that is marginal with too much internal inconsistency, and another that is quasi in the sense that all of the indices evince acceptable scalability (at the P+ evaluation level) except that of sample size, which is nine. The six scales that W does produce are, however, of high quality: one excellent, three very good, one good, and only one poor. The average for these six subscales alone would be 5.3 or "good"; but of course the summary evaluation scores reported in Appendix C and in Table 4.1 are averages for the totals for all ten decks, with the consequence that the 32 total evaluation points for W must be divided by ten rather than six, thereby yielding an average score of only 3.2, or "fair" rather than "good." This result certainly is logical in relation to our objective, which is to be able to describe in consistent and objective terms the scalability of these variables throughout the entire period of our analysis; a scale that "isn't there" cannot very well make a positive contribution to such a description.

The W scales do tend to show poorer discrimination than either $\overline{B}$ or E, but again this is probably another consequence of sample size. I have included the quasi-scale for Deck 10 in the between-scales rho correlations reported for the W variable in Appendix C, and in general the effect of including quasi and marginal scales will be to reduce the average between-scales correlation for any variable. But the rho correlations among pairs of three of the last four subscales are rather lower, and for this the explanation is found in the dramatic changes that can be observed to have occurred during the waning years of the Warren Court for *both* Black and Douglas in their sharply reduced willingness to continue to give their support to the kinds of claims then reaching the Supreme Court in behalf of organized labor. It was one thing for the unions of three decades earlier to champion the causes of masses of workers oppressed by their employers; it was quite another matter, evidently, for entrenched union management hierarchies to oppress their own members, oppose both racial and sexual equality in hiring practices, and function as the satrapies of organized crime (including, but by no means limited to, the Mafia)—a development which Robert Jackson had clearly anticipated and opposed a full two decades before a somewhat similar awakening arrived for Black and Douglas.[10] Douglas changed first: examination of the W subscales shows that, disregarding Murphy and Rutledge in the first period, Douglas either ranked first or in a tie with Black for the 1½th rank throughout the period of the first seven decks. But his position is completely inverted in Deck 8, as his rank drops from first to ninth, and he remains in the ninth rank for the last two periods as well. Similarly, Black ranks either second or in a tie with Douglas for 1½th, throughout the period of the first seven decks (with the same caveat for the first one); and in addition, Black, with Douglas now in ninth place, ranks first for Deck 8, which demonstrates conclusively that although Douglas had changed his mind on this issue by the early sixties, Black had not done so—yet. For Deck 9, however, Black appears in a three-way tie for the next-to-bottom rank on W, and for Deck 10 he is tied with Marshall for the equivalent penultimate rank. Of course, this puts Black in his accustomed relationship in the sense that he is once again next to Douglas in the ranking, but at the opposite end of the subscale for Decks 9 and 10 than had been the case for Decks 1, 2, 4, 6, and 7. Indubitably, Deck 8 marks the transition, but with Douglas changing first.

From the point of view of between-scales correlations, the only possible effect of comparing two scales, which are similar except that the second portrays Douglas at the opposite end of the scale from the first, is to produce a greatly reduced rho, which in the case of Decks 7 and 8 turns out to be a drop from .927 (for Decks 6 and 7) to .406. And when we compare Decks 8 and 9, the problem is no longer Douglas—he is now in the same (bottom) rank on both of these scales—but Black, who is first on 8 and seventh on 9; so again we observe a low rho of .593, but a higher one than that preceding it in the sequence because the difference *squared* between ranks 1 and 7 (36) is only slightly more than half as large, both manifestly and in its effect upon the rho, as is that between ranks 1 and 9 (64). And then when we compare Decks 9 and 10, with both Black and Douglas in stable positions on both subscales, the rho climbs to .882, a value that would doubtless have been higher if we were dealing with an acceptable scale for Deck 10 instead of with a quasi-scale which shows both low internal consistency and poor discrimination.

A comparison of the E scale with its two subscales informs us about the more general relationship between *consistency in ranking* as measured by the between-scales correlations, *consistency in response* as measured by the S and R indices, the overall *quality* of scales as measured by the evaluation scores, and sample *size*. There is first of all a direct linear relationship between sample size and the reliability of scales, as demonstrated by the high average rho for E (.955), next that for the larger subscale $\overline{B}$ (.880), and then the much smaller subscale W (.753). On the other hand, both of the two subscales, which are by definition more homogeneous in their substantive content than is the E scale which combines them both, evince slightly higher internal consistency than does E, although the differences here are much smaller than those between the rhos and are in any event not statistically significant. In regard to the relationship between evaluative characterizations of these scales and sample size, it is necessary to make a somewhat tautological statement: in fact there is no consistent relationship because E is 3.9, $\overline{B}$ is 4.3, and W is 3.2. But this is because the score of W includes four ciphers which are averaged in for the decks in which W does not scale, and at that because its sample size is too small. Otherwise, if the size of W samples had been adequate for all ten decks, then both subscales would have been denoted as higher in overall quality than their parent scale. So the more homogeneous (sub)scales do tend to scale better, but they are also harder to observe because samples adequate to produce them are more difficult to come by.

We turn now to the four remaining and, on the basis of the earlier study, putatively minor scales: F, N, J, and A. The best of these clearly is the fiscal (F) variable, which does produce acceptable scales for six periods, but uniformly of poor quality except for Deck 9 when the scale is of barely fair quality. All of the F scales show a considerable amount of internal inconsistency, as reflected in the fact that none of the R scores exceeds, indeed attains, .900, and the discrimination of the scales is not particularly good. The between-scales correlations are moderately high, averaging .746 for the six scales plus the quasi-scale that can be compared. But reference to Table 4.1 shows that F does more poorly than at least five of the subscales, to say nothing of the C and E scales proper. Similarly, N (the federalism variable) scales acceptably only three times, and then only poorly. The two best N scales appear in Decks 6 and 7; but the sample sizes for both are small, and although both do show an unusually large degree of improvement over minimal marginal reproducibility, neither attains an acceptable R. And most deflating is the observation of the *negative* rho between these two rankings—and I do *not* have the directionality of one of these scales reversed by mistake.

The judicial centralization variable (J) scales with average acceptability only for the initial period. It scales somewhat less well in Deck 2, and the rho between these two acceptable scales is .67. Otherwise J yields only a quasi-scale with dubiously low criterion values in Deck 7. Clearly not much can be said on the basis of such data; and the same comment applies to the A (for judicial review of administrative decision-making) scale, which is acceptable only once, and then for Deck 7. It generates several quasi-scales with conspicuously poor discrimination, plus two marginal scales which are correlated at .04—thereby confirming my previous remark (in regard to the non-scalable set of 33 decisions for Deck 10) about how decidedly skewed are the sample of data upon which these marginal scales are based.

It is necessary to conclude, I believe, that the present data, even though based on considerably larger samples than those of the original study and extending over a substantially longer period of analysis, confirm the conclusions of *The Judicial Mind:* that there are two, and only two, reliable scales of good quality, C and E; that the two or three principal subscales of each of these two major scales each also represents an important, recurring, and relatively homogeneous constellation of policy issues; and that with the exception of F, the samples of data for the minor scales are inadequate to support a clear-cut decision concerning their scalability. In the instance of F, I think that the present data do support such a positive decision, which the earlier study had left open because of the inadequacy of the smaller, term data samples to support a decision on the matter.

Scale and Subscale Rankings

Although it is better to employ the rank sequences for the individual periods for certain of the analyses that will follow in subsequent chapters, it is also of interest to consider the composite ranking of all twenty justices for at least those of the variables that scale acceptably in a majority of the periods. In the earlier study, I constructed such composite sequences only for the C and E scales, and for them by using the arithmetic means of scale scores to establish scale positions, thus fabricating what was admittedly a pseudo-interval scale because the level of measurement of the term scales themselves was ordinal. For present purposes I have attempted a different, and I believe a conceptually better justified approach. The underlying psychometric model of the scale defines a dominance relationship between each successive pair in a series of points. So what should be sought empirically is a way of measuring the extent to which each point of a scale dominates those points of lesser rank than itself and the extent to which each is in turn dominated by all points of higher rank. Naturally a certain amount of intransitivity in empirical observations of such rank relationships can be anticipated, and so some criterion of error tolerance should be posited.

The formula that I constructed in order to make this measurement is an index of dominance, which I define formally as

$$D_{ij} = \frac{(>) - (<)}{\Sigma\,(>, <, =)}$$

that is, the algebraic sum of positive minus negative rank-order relationships between any pair of ordered points, divided by the total of common rankings. Negative scores denote either empirical errors in the ranking for a particular period or else valid but inconsistent rankings which result in either instance in apparent intransitivities in the sequence that determines the matrix of dominance index scores. The most important relationships are those between adjacent pairs, which appear in the cells of the major diagonal of the matrix. The off-diagonal cells are of equal weight in the calculation of the dominance index, but of lesser importance than the cells of the major diagonal in the sense that the matrix sequence is determined operationally by (1) selecting the highest positive index values possible for inclusion in the major diagonal cells,[11] to the extent that such choices (2) do not entail avoidable intransitivities in the off-diagonal cells. For any set of twenty points, there are a maximum of 185 different pairings possible; and empirically, given my grouping of the data in partially non-overlapping subsets, the maximum number of dominance relationships between pairs of judges in the present study is 122 for any of these scales or subscales. Matrices based upon sets of rankings for less than the full ten periods will, of course, include a smaller total of dominance pairings.

D can vary from +1.00 to −1.00, but our confidence in its reliability necessarily will depend upon both the quality of the individual period rankings (as measured by such criteria as evaluation scores) and the number of such observations available. In Table 4.3 I have not attempted to include qualitative information concerning discrete scales but I have included quantitative data by listing in the lower half of each matrix the number of periods for which each dominance score is based. The larger the number of observations, the greater the confidence we should have in any particular cell value; and the larger the average number of observations for each matrix, the greater the confidence we should have in the sequence defining that matrix. The range of average number of observations per cell, for each of the matrices whose dominance scales is reported in Table 4.4, is 2.25-2.98, and the mean average is 2.70.

Table 4.3 shows a highly internally consistent matrix for ordering the C scale. The most supportive segment of the scale includes, in the sequence of their sympathy for political liberalism, Murphy, Rutledge, Douglas, Fortas, Marshall, Warren, Brennan, Goldberg, and—as a consequence of his increasing conservatism during the last three periods of the Warren Court—Black, who ranks ninth among the twenty judges in this sample on this variable. Then comes a middle-of-the-scale sequence including White, Stewart, Frankfurter, Jackson tied with Harlan, and Whittaker. The remaining (and most conservative) segment includes all four of Harry Truman's choices for the Court (Burton, Vinson, Clark, and Minton) while Stanley Reed (Roosevelt's second appointment and one who was certainly intended to constitute some sort of gain over Fourth Horseman Sutherland) is the anchor man of the Vinson and Warren Courts, on the C scale. The ratio of intransitivities is certainly acceptably low (.024),[12] and the average number of observations supporting the dominance index values is 2.94. The three intransitivities include Burton's negative dominance of Clark, which is another way of saying that Clark in fact tends to dominate Burton, notwithstanding the circumstance that given the general patterning of their repective dominance relationships with their colleagues, one ought to predict that Burton should dominate Clark if their behavior vis-à-vis each other is to be consistent with their behavior vis-à-vis their colleagues.

In the case of Burton and Clark, what happened in fact was that Burton's ranking was higher than Clark's in two periods, but Clark was of higher rank than Burton in the other three of the five periods during which they served together on the Supreme Court. But Burton dominates Vinson in both of the periods that they were together, while Vinson dominates Clark during those same periods. Otherwise Burton, Vinson, and Clark are all without exception dominated by the first fifteen judges on this scale, just as Burton, Vinson, and Clark all dominate the remaining two judges, Minton and Reed, who occupy the 19th and 20th ranks on this scale. Consequently, Burton ought, at least

TABLE 4.3
Composite C Scale and Dominance Matrix*

Scale Rank →	1	2	3	4	5	6	7	8	9	10	11	12½	12½	14½	14½	16	17	18	19	20
Justices ↓	Mu	Ru	Do	Fo	Ma	Wa	Br	Go	Bl	BW	St	Wh	Fr	Ja	Ha	Bu	Vi	Cl	Mi	Re
Mu	—	100	100	X	X	X	X	X	100	X	X	X	100	100	X	100	100	X	X	100
Ru	1	—	100	X	X	X	X	X	100	X	X	X	100	100	X	100	100	X	X	100
Do	1	1	—	100	100	88	100	100	90	100	100	100	X	100	100	X	100	100	100	100
Fo	0	0	2	—	100	100	100	X	100	100	100	100	X	X	100	X	X	100	X	X
Ma	0	0	1	1	—	100	100	100	100	100	100	100	X	100	100	X	X	X	X	X
Wa	0	0	8	1	1	—	100	100	-10	100	100	100	60	-100	100	100	X	90	100	100
Br	0	0	6	1	1	6	—	100	0	100	100	100	100	100	100	100	X	100	X	100
Go	0	0	1	1	1	1	1	—	100	100	100	100	100	100	100	X	X	100	100	X
Bl	1	1	10	2	1	8	6	1	—	33	50	100	100	100	86	100	100	90	X	100
BW	0	0	3	2	1	3	3	1	3	—	33	100	100	100	100	100	X	100	X	X
St	0	0	4	2	1	4	4	1	1	0	—	100	100	100	100	100	X	100	100	X
Wh	0	0	2	0	0	2	2	0	2	0	0	—	00	100	100	100	X	100	X	100
Fr	1	1	7	0	0	5	3	1	3	3	1	3	—	100	100	100	100	100	X	100
Ja	1	1	3	0	1	1	0	0	0	0	0	0	4	—	50	100	100	100	X	X
Ha	0	0	7	2	1	7	6	1	1	3	4	2	6	3	—	100	X	100	100	100
Bu	1	1	6	0	0	4	2	1	2	0	4	2	6	3	3	—	100	-20	100	100
Vi	1	1	2	0	0	0	0	0	2	0	0	1	2	2	0	2	—	100	100	60
Cl	0	0	8	1	0	7	5	1	8	2	3	2	6	2	6	3	1	—	33	00
Mi	0	0	3	0	0	2	0	0	3	0	0	0	3	2	1	3	1	3	—	100
Re	1	1	5	0	0	3	1	0	5	0	0	0	5	3	2	5	2	4	3	—

Note: For the upper half of the matrix, numbers represent two-place decimals, and the X cells signify no relationship; the cell entries for the lower half of the matrix are observation frequencies. The dominance index is defined in the accompanying text.

predominately, to dominate Clark. The negative score is our signal that he failed to do so. The other two intransitivities both involve Warren and, like the Burton-Clark instance just discussed, rest upon a difference of only a single observation, in each case. The Warren-Jackson case clearly reflects Warren's conservative behavior during his initial term on the Court, which I discussed in some detail in the earlier study. [13] And as Appendix C shows, the Warren-Black intransitivity reflects the fact that Black dominated Warren in four of their first five periods together and tied with him in the other one, but Warren dominated Black only during the last three periods because Black's demarche toward political conservatism did not occur until the eighth period.

The E scale, for which the dominance matrix is not reproduced here although the scale itself is reported in Table 4.4, is slightly more consistent than C, with only two intransitivities, for an error ratio of .016. The sequence most supportive of economic liberalism includes Rutledge, Black, Murphy, Douglas, Warren, and Brennan tied with Minton. It is notable that six of these—all except Minton—are also included among the nine judges most favorable to political liberalism. The middle-of-the-scale sequence on E contains Reed, Vinson, Clark, White, Goldberg tied with Fortas, and Marshall—and it is perhaps worth noting that all four of the Democratic judges appointed by Democratic Presidents during the sixties are included in this group that gave only moderate support to economic liberalism. The economic conservatives, ranking lowest on the E scale, include Stewart tied with Burton, Harlan, Whittaker, Frankfurter, and Jackson. There is perhaps some slight irony in the circumstance that the judge, who as Attorney General and an aspirant for the Presidency only a decade and a half earlier had been described by a journalist as "The Man Who Has Always Been a New Dealer,"[14] should have ended his political career[15] (as Table 4.4 demonstrates) as the most extreme conservative on issues of economic policy to serve on the Supreme Court for the quarter of a century from the end of World War II until Nixon was able to begin building the Burger Court. The average number of observations (2.90) supporting the dominance index values of this scale is almost identical to that for the C scale; and of the two intransitivities, the Black-Douglas reversal is due, I am sure, to minor variations in specific issue content from period to period. Black tended to dominate Douglas in the early periods, while the situation was opposite in the later periods; but what is important is that their average positions over the ten periods are very close, with Black dominating Douglas in four, Douglas dominating Black in five, and the pair tied in the other period. The other intransitivity, Reed-Clark, also rests upon the difference of a single period; and like the

TABLE 4.4
Composite Rankings for Scales and Subscales

Respondents	Scales:							
	C	FP	PF	RP	E	$\bar{B}$	W	F
Mu	1	1	2	1	3	3	1	2
Ru	2	2	2	11½	1	1	2½	3
Do	3	3	2	2½	4	4	9	19
Fo	4	5	10	4½	12½	13	2½	17½
Ma	5	4	6½	7½	14	13	16½	—
Wa	6	8	8	4½	5	5	6	6½
Br	7	9	6½	6	6½	6½	7½	13
Go	8	7	4	7½	12½	13	5	17½
Bl	9	6	5	9	2	2	4	1
BW	10	10	12	10	11	11	7½	11½
St	11	11	9	11½	15½	15½	15	16
Wh	12½	16½	12	15	17½	17½	18½	15
Fr	12½	12	12	14	19	19	18½	10
Ja	14½	13½	14½	2½	20	20	20	11½
Ha	14½	13½	14½	13	17½	17½	13½	14
Bu	16	15	16½	17	15½	15½	12	8
Vi	17	16½	20	19½	9	8½	13½	6½
Cl	18	18	18½	16	10	10	16½	9
Mi	19	19	16½	18	6½	6½	10½	5
Re	20	20	18½	19½	8	8½	10½	4
No. of Scales	10	10*	7*	8*	10	10	8*	7*
Intransitivities	3	3	1	0	2	0	3	4
	Wa/Ja	Wa/Ja	Ha/Cl		Do/Bl		Do/Ma	Wa/Cl
	Bu/Cl	Bu/Cl			Cl/Re		Do/St	Go/Bl
	Wa/Bl	Bu/Mi					Bl/BW	Bl/Re
								Vi/Re
Discrimination	good	good	poor	poor	fair	poor	poor	fair
pairs	2	2	4	5	4	4	6	3
triples	0	0	1	0	0	1	0	0

*Includes one quasi-scale.

Clark-Burton instance on the C scale, involves a triangular relationship with Vinson.

Because one of my objectives in writing the present book is to appraise the reliability of the findings of *The Judicial Mind* in the light of the more complete and better quality data available here, it is entirely appropriate that we should re-examine the general scales for C and for E denoted in the earlier study by comparing them to the two dominance scales that have just been discussed here. Actually, the earlier study reported alternative versions of each of the two general scales, one based on the more objective criterion provided by mean scale scores and the other, in which I placed more confidence, derived from my somewhat more subjective analysis of the consistency of rankings across term scales. The rho correlation of the C scale reported in Table 4.3, with the two earlier versions of the "General Scale of Political Liberalism,"[16] are .969 with the mean scale scores ranking and .986 with the more subjective criterion. The corresponding correlations for E (Table 4.4) with the "General Scale of Economic Liberalism" [17] are .913 and .919. All of these correlations, but especially those for the C scale, are very high and statistically significant at far less than the .01 probability level. Evidently, the relatively cruder data and methods of general scale construction employed in the earlier study did not result in any important distortion of the substantive conclusions reported concerning the policy positions of the justices of the Vinson and Warren Courts in regard to political and economic liberalism.

Three of the C subscales (FP, PF, and RP) produced scales frequently enough to be included in the dominance index analysis; but RE, VE, and CE did not. The objective of this analysis was to include as many of the justices as possible in a single ranking for each variable; and furthermore, the correlation of such variables would be limited to the number of justices included in the shorter of each pair of rankings. Therefore, I included not only the 65 acceptable scales for these eight variables that did scale acceptably in over half of the periods, but I added also the five best quasi-scales, four of which meet at least half of the criteria for ascription as "Excellent" (although their discrimination tended to be poor and their inadequate sample sizes ranged from seven to nine.)

This made it possible to rank all twenty judges on seven of these variables. Only nineteen can be ranked on F because its sample for Deck 10 contains only five decisions, thereby precluding the possibility of obtaining an observation for Marshall on this variable. Both of the E subscales ($\overline{\text{B}}$ and W) are included in Table 4.4, but F is the only minor scale that it was possible to consider; N scaled in only three of the periods, and J and A in even fewer. The maximum number of intransitivities in any of the dominance matrices underlying the eight scales of Table 4.4 is four (for F), which also has, therefore, the highest error ratio at .035—but even that is well below the conventional criterion level of .05 that I had posited. Indeed, it seems to me that the overall level of consistency is extraordinarily high, with two completely transitive matrices (RP and $\overline{\text{B}}$) and an average of only two intransitivities each

TABLE 4.5

Correlations among Scales and Subscales*

	C	FP	PF	W	E	$\overline{\text{B}}$	F
RP	803	790	733	307	184	183	−266
C		970	930	606	408	414	−152
FP			912	618	417	425	−087
PF				584	454	456	−119
W					754	734	257
E						998	539
$\overline{\text{B}}$							537

*Note: All matrix values are three-place decimals representing rank order (rho) correlation coefficients.

for a set of 20 x 20 matrices, even if each does include a proportion of about one-third null cells—which cannot produce intransitivities because they denote pairs of justices that could not empirically form. From the point of view of discrimination among the respondents ranked, however, only two of the composite scales (C and FP) are rated good (with only two pairs of tied rankings), while two others (F and E) have three and four tied pairs respectively. The remaining four subscales (RP, W, PF, and $\overline{\text{B}}$) show poor discrimination, with either five or six tied pairs or else four such pairs plus a triple tie.

The relationships among these eight scales are difficult to perceive in Table 4.4, but they become much clearer in the light of the matrix of their correlations reported in Table 4.5. Evidently E is virtually indistinguishable from its principal subscale, $\overline{\text{B}}$, on the basis of their respective composite scales: the rho is within rounding distance of 1.00, which states that they *are* identical. Similarly, FP and PF form the core content of the C scale, although RP is highly and positively enough correlated with all three of these variables (at +.73 or better) to be clustered with them, just as W must be clustered with E and $\overline{\text{B}}$ for the same reason. At the same time W correlates more highly and positively with the C cluster than do E or $\overline{\text{B}}$, so that it is appropriately positioned in the matrix in the position that we observe it, between the C cluster and the other variables in the E cluster. F clearly falls in a position of independence from either group of variables but closer to the E cluster, with which it is positively correlated, than to the C cluster, with which it is negatively correlated. This matrix is what Guttman calls a quasi-simplex because it denotes what is primarily but not strictly a linear sequence: RP, C, FP, PF, W, E, $\overline{\text{B}}$, and F.

To proceed further with an analysis of relationships among these

variables, we require a means of inquiring into the dimensions underlying the matrix, so we shall return to this subject in the following
chapters. But attention should be directed to one correlation in particular between variables in the different clusters: that between the major
scales C and E is .408, signifying a moderate degree of positive relationship. Of course, our correlation is a rho coefficient, and we can hardly
expect it to be more than a rough estimate of the relationship that we
might be able to observe between two vectors representing the C and E
variables in some form of multidimensional space, whether factorial or
smallest-space. After making full allowance for the nature of our
statistic, the kind of incomplete data upon which it is based, and the
probability of substantial associated measurement error, we can nevertheless note that a correlation of .408 is the cosine for an angle of 65°
55′; and in view of the fact that this is the best estimate that we can
make, we ought to predict this as our expectation for the angle
separating vectors of political liberalism and of economic liberalism in
multidimensional space.[18]

Support for Scale and Subscale Values

In addition to the question of differences among individual respondents
in the extent to which they support in their voting behavior the various
scale and subscale values, there is the even more important question
from a public-policy point of view of the extent to which the Supreme
Court supports particular scale values in its decisions. To facilitate
examination of this matter, Table 4.6 lists the percentage of decisions
favorable to the positive value of each variable for each of the ten
periods and also the size of the related samples as a percentage of the
pertinent deck sizes. This table reports also the average percentages of
support and average sample size for each variable. We already have
some familiarity with the differences among sample sizes, but the
percentages suggest somewhat different insights. Disregarding two
of the minor scales (A and N), for which the sample sizes are too small
for us to pay much attention to average percentages, the range of
support for the other variables is confined to the range 52-67 per cent.
E at 64 per cent is slightly higher than C at 56 per cent, and of the two
E subscales, the support given to B̄ (67 per cent) is somewhat better than
that given to W (53 per cent), whereas the differences among the three
C subscales are smaller. The previously noted observation that the
average size of the C scale is about one-third larger than that for the E
scale constitutes a correction to the counterpart finding of the earlier
study, which concluded with the 1962 term, halfway through the
eighth period of the present study. At that time the average sample
sizes for C and E were equivalent. The fact that this no longer is true

TABLE 4.6

Major Scales and Selected Minor Scales and Subscales, Degree
of Support and Sample Sizes (in Percentages, by Periods)

			1	2	3	4	5	6	7	8	9	10	Avg.
I. *Major*	C	% Pro	29	30	43	51	36	53	39	82	62	80	56
		% Σ	28	33	36	32	28	44	41	54	54	58	43
	E		55	43	39	82	85	72	69	67	83	63	64
			35	28	32	41	33	33	35	33	33	23	32
II. *C Subscales*	FP	% Pro	23	34	60	45	29	42	41	79	65	78	53
		% Σ	11	16	20	20	21	17	20	21	20	23	18
	RP		32	28	20	62	50	47	37	63	41	84	52
			09	07	05	07	05	09	09	09	08	16	09
	PF		40	17	00	100	00	68	39	86	70	72	59
			03	06	03	01	03	14	07	06	13	10	07
III. *E Subscales*	B̄	% Pro	57	40	53	92	91	86	69	67	92	63	.67
		% Σ	26	21	19	23	28	24	23	26	23	18	23
	W		35	38	00	60	100	33	68	73	61	67	53
			05	03	06	09	03	09	09	06	08	03	06
IV. *Minor*	F	% Pro	61	43	70	71	43	53	78	86	57	100	62
		% Σ	20	15	10	13	18	08	11	06	07	02	11
	A		22	21	58	25	50	92	55	71	29	21	40
			03	11	12	04	10	06	06	02	03	12	06
	N		72	52	75	50	33	53	55	88	00	88	64
			07	08	08	07	08	07	03	02	00	03	05

Note: Σ = total sample for period

emphasizes the extent to which the Warren Court placed quantitative as
well as qualitative stress upon civil liberties by increasing the number of
such decisions that it made during the middle and late sixties. This
point is made perhaps more dramatically by Figure 4.1, which demonstrates that the Warren Court's posture, like that of the Vinson Court,
was ambivalent toward political and economic liberalism in the matter
of *quantitative* emphasis during the first five periods. But beginning
with the sixth period, there occurred a steady and rising trend in the
direction of deciding more civil liberties cases, and particularly in the
tenth period at the expense of deciding economic policy issues. The
qualitative picture is different: here (Figure 4.2) the Vinson Court quite

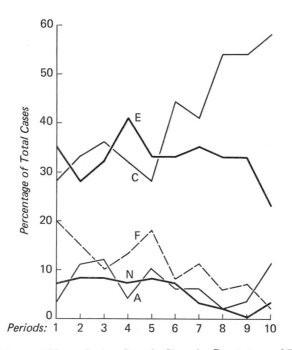

Figure 4.1 Major and Minor Scales, Sample Sizes (as Percentage of Total Cases, by Periods)

clearly favored economic over political liberalism, a trend that began to change as soon as Warren was appointed, although the impact of Warren's Court was different according to whether we speak of the earlier (Decks 3-7) or later (Decks 8-10) stages of its work. During the earlier stage there was a sharp and well-sustained increase of support for economic liberalism (reflecting the presence on the Court then of Minton, Clark, and Brennan as well as of Warren, Black, and Douglas); but during the later stage equally strong support was given to civil liberties due to the appointments of Goldberg, Fortas, and Marshall to augment the minority support that previously had been provided by Warren, Brennan, Douglas, and—until the eighth period—Black. Indeed, the drop in period nine can be attributed directly and substantially to the loss of Black's support, while the rise in period ten can be identified with the appointment of Marshall, whose fifth vote in support of C made possible a solid majority not merely in the absence of Black's support but even notwithstanding Black's opposition.

Graphs for the subscales of C and E are reported in Figures 4.3 and 4.4, respectively. Figure 4.3 well illustrates, incidentally, how misleading it can be to direct attention to percentage differences of small

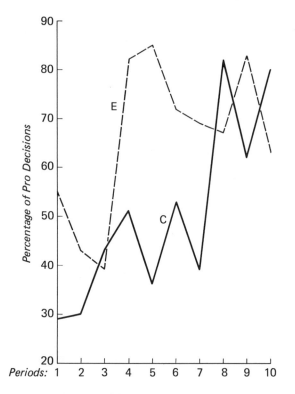

Figure 4.2 Major Scales, Degree of Support

samples: clearly we should not wish to make much of the violent swings
in the curve for PF, at a time (periods 3-5) when the maximal peak (for
period 4) represents 100 per cent of a sample of one and when the two
adjacent samples each consisted of three decisions. Substantially the
same is true of the equivalent peaking of the W curve, which represents
100 per cent of three decisions in period 5. What Figure 4.3 does show
is a steady and appreciable increase in support for all three of the
subvariables of political liberalism, initially of modest proportions
(from a range of 23-40% in the first period, to a range of 37-41 per cent
in the seventh), rising sharply thereafter to a range of 72-84 per cent
during the tenth—twice that of even the seventh period. In the case of
the subvariables of economic liberalism, the increase, from a range of
35-57 per cent in period one, to one of 60-92 per cent in period four,
came much sooner, and then tended to level off—with a corresponding
range of 61-92 per cent in the ninth period, for example. The sample

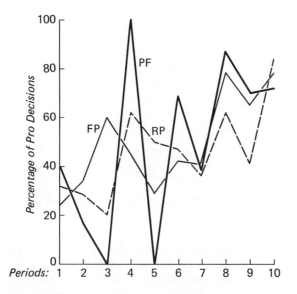

Figure 4.3 Selected Subscales of C, Degree of Support

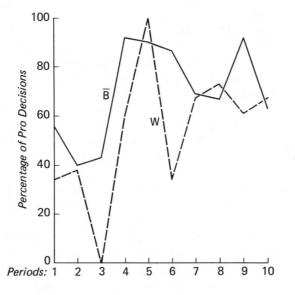

Figure 4.4 Subscales of E, Degree of Support

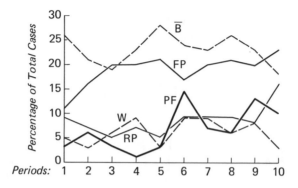

Figure 4.5 Subscales, Sample Sizes (as Percentage of Total Cases, by Periods)

sizes for the subscale variables are charted in Figure 4.5, which shows that the two major subscales ($\overline{\text{B}}$ for E and FP for C) both remained consistently larger than any of the other subscales throughout all ten periods. Figure 4.5 shows also that all three of the subscales of C tended to improve in sample size as time went on, although their relative weights (with FP>RP>PF) remained in the same order. Similarly, the curves for $\overline{\text{B}}$ and W are alike, although at quite different levels; and both terminate at points for the last period lower than those of their originating points in the first.

The sample sizes of the minor scales are charted (along with C and E) in Figure 4.1. The minor are (by definition) all consistently much smaller than the major, and although F begins with what appears to be a distinct size advantage over N and A, that differential disappears after period five, and during the last five periods none of the three minor scales have samples that include more than 12 per cent of the deck samples. Figure 4.6 shows the qualitative support given to these minor scale variables: only F tended to attract consistent support for most of the issues that it raised. Support for N and A tended to fluctuate much more sharply from period to period, no doubt reflecting the consistently small size of their samples (which never exceed a dozen decisions), although the Court did tend to give more support to N than to A.

What is clear in these figures is that the Supreme Court gave much more consistent support, both quantitatively and qualitatively, to the two major scales than to any of the minor scales. As between C and E, neither was given much favor during the Vinson Court and the beginning period of the Warren Court; support for economic liberalism was favored during the years of the middle and late fifties; and then at long last, with Felix Frankfurter and his long outmoded values gone from

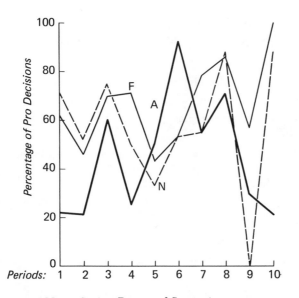

Figure 4.6 Selected Minor Scales, Degree of Support

the Court, the Warren Court of the sixties increased its quantitative support for political liberalism while at the same time supporting it qualitatively fully as much as it did economic liberalism.

Notes to Chapter 4

1. See Harold J. Spaeth, "Warren Court Attitudes toward Business: The 'B' Scale," chapter 4 in Glendon Schubert, ed., *Judicial Decision-Making* (New York: The Free Press, 1963), pp. 79-103.

2. Cf. my discussion of the lingering effects of the Warren Court's heritage, upon the policy output of the early Burger Court, in my *The Future of the Warren Court* (Honolulu: University of Hawaii Foundation, 1972), especially pp. 18-25 and 35-42.

3. Two-thirds of the total inconsistencies in the C scale for Deck 10 are attributable to its two most conservative respondents, Black and Harlan.

4. See my *Dispassionate Justice* (New York: Bobbs-Merrill, 1969), pp. 107-10.

5. See his *A Constitutional Faith* (New York: Knopf, 1968); and my *The Constitutional Polity* (Boston: Boston University Press, 1970), especially pp. 65-69 and 120.

6. 347 U.S. 497 (1954).

7. Beginning about three-fourths of the way through, but clearly during Deck 8, on June 22, 1964. See *The Constitutional Polity*, pp. 118-19.

8. *Ibid.*, p. 176.

9. 369 U.S. 186 (1962). See also my *Reapportionment* (New York: Scribners, 1965).

10. And—or so it might appear—the present author as well. See *Dispassionate Justice*, p. 140.

11. Cf. Louis L. McQuitty, "Elementary Linkage Analysis for Isolating Orthogonal and Oblique Types and Typal Relevancies," *Educational and Psychological Measurement*, Vol. 17 (1957), pp. 207-29.

12. The average value of the eight intransitivity ratios reported in Table 4.4 is .017, with a range of .000–.035.

13. *The Judicial Mind*, p. 119.

14. Marquis W. Childs, "The Man Who Has Always Been a New Dealer," *Forum* (March 1940), pp. 148-54.

15. *Dispassionate Justice*, pp. 16-17.

16. *The Judicial Mind*, p. 125.

17. *Ibid.*, p. 145.

18. In fact, as we shall observe in the next chapter, the average observed correlation between the C and E scales in four-dimensional, factorial (principal-component) space, is .516: a difference of .108, which is equivalent to an angular difference of only seven degrees. Moreover, the correlations by period between these two major scales are .636, .100, .430, .633, .738, .678, .783, .600, .661, and .276. The average for the first six of these decks is .536; for decks 7-10 it is .538; and overall it is .537, which equals an angle of $57°30'$.

5 Principal Components

The factor analysis was carried out by a standard principal-components program which uniformly extracted nine factors from the phi matrices reported in Appendix B; but for reasons that have been explained in Chapter 2, the analysis that follows is based upon the first four components only for each of the ten periods. The loadings of the respondents upon these dimensions are shown in Table 5.1. These loadings define a set of configurations each of which represents the ideal-points or ideological positions of the justices in a multidimensional space. Because these spaces are four-dimensional, it is not possible to model them with physical structures. On the other hand, as Table 5.2 demonstrates, of the twenty C' and E' scale vectors that can be observed in this set of ten four-dimensional spaces, only about one-third have any correlation with the fourth dimension, which suggests that by sacrificing a little in the way of goodness of fit, we might settle for a three-dimensional (Euclidean) principal-component space that could be physically modeled. That is certainly correct; and, as we shall see in Chapter 7, the average correlation of both scale vectors across all ten four-dimensional spaces is .96, which is only half-a-per cent higher than the equivalent correlation—which also rounds to .96—for *three*-dimensional smallest space. So I have considered the latter to be the clearly more parsimonious, and most satisficing, solution; and I have therefore preferred to construct the physical models of ideal-point configurations and their associated scale vectors in three-dimensional smallest space, and as a consequence the presentation of those models is deferred until Chapter 7.

TABLE 5.1
Principal-Component Factor
Loadings* (Four-Dimensional Space)

		Dimensions						Dimensions			
Deck	Vari-able	1	2	3	4	Deck	Vari-able	1	2	3	4
1	Vi	46	−38	−66	01	2	Vi	64	−28	−43	04
	Bl	−76	−05	−29	14		Bl	−57	−37	−30	−14
	Re	37	−64	21	57		Re	56	−05	33	48
	Fr	56	59	−13	01		Fr	−35	69	−15	−11
	Do	−65	−24	32	−30		Do	−54	−52	06	14
	Mu	−79	19	−31	17		Ja	03	80	−20	11
	Ja	64	40	02	28		Bu	23	−00	50	−77
	Ru	−77	02	−19	13		Cl	40	−14	−64	−32
	Bu	57	−36	−21	−45		Mi	62	−02	07	−05
3	Wa	07	64	49	−16	4	Wa	77	17	03	41
	Bl	83	09	−09	−09		Bl	85	06	−08	31
	Re	−72	21	−42	33		Re	−50	74	−11	−06
	Fr	−01	−58	59	03		Fr	−25	−68	19	51
	Do	78	17	−08	−12		Do	84	−03	−21	−11
	Ja	−31	−55	50	−09		Bu	−65	17	−33	40
	Bu	−70	24	06	−11		Cl	16	48	82	03
	Cl	−22	74	47	−11		Mi	−52	49	06	32
	Mi	−33	−17	−33	−85		Ha	−47	−72	22	−09
5	Wa	73	08	13	57	6	Wa	79	11	28	−07
	Bl	84	−10	03	15		Bl	86	11	25	05
	Re	−64	63	07	06		Fr	−53	68	−35	10
	Fr	−35	−63	37	−46		Do	83	14	03	−04
	Do	84	04	−19	−38		Bu	−66	−10	29	−47
	Bu	−56	−36	−07	36		Cl	−39	−77	−24	−20
	Cl	−31	76	45	−07		Ha	−67	57	04	−01
	Ha	−68	−43	−08	30		Br	49	34	−26	−72
	Br	30	−25	85	12		Wh	−62	14	64	−08
7	Wa	77	11	44	−18	8	Wa	59	50	−26	−21
	Bl	77	13	15	07		Bl	60	−17	−26	53
	Fr	−73	09	40	31		Do	67	−32	02	−07
	Do	82	−17	−21	06		Cl	−42	08	−60	−31
	Cl	−36	77	04	−45		Ha	−83	13	08	−11
	Ha	−72	03	40	34		Br	39	71	−24	−13
	Br	62	−08	61	−13		St	−51	39	33	24

TABLE 5.1 (continued)

Deck	Vari-able	1	2	3	4	Deck	Vari-able	1	2	3	4
	Wh	−68	−13	−05	−33		BW	−36	23	−41	69
	St	−45	−63	22	−43		Go	37	44	59	12
9	Wa	68	−53	−18	−12	10	Wa	30	−54	−52	−21
	Bl	−00	71	−43	14		Bl	−19	41	−62	12
	Do	75	33	01	15		Do	73	28	37	05
	Cl	−27	−43	−76	−07		Ha	−66	−28	31	−05
	Ha	−76	−36	26	−24		Br	25	−59	−37	29
	Br	62	−46	−08	12		St	−38	−41	47	16
	St	−64	−09	20	33		BW	−64	−14	−26	14
	BW	−33	−21	−15	83		Fo	35	−27	13	72
	Fo	59	−21	39	30		Ma	28	−53	12	−51

*Note: All matrix entries are two-place decimals.

The scale vectors denoted in Table 5.2, which were called "scale axes" in *The Judicial Mind*, are analogues of the two major scales discussed in the preceding chapter. Each such scale vector consists of a linear path through the origin of the space and extends to its spherical rim in such a position that the set of orthogonal projections onto the vector from the point configuration is maximally isomorphic with the rank order position of the same respondents on the corresponding linear cumulative scale (e.g., the sets of scales for C and E that are reported in Appendix C). The procedure for determining scale vector positions has been discussed in Chapter 3 and in greater detail in the original study.[1] It suffices for present purposes to note that no computer program to perform this task has to my knowledge yet been written; despite my sometime efforts to provoke a few persons, both skilled in computer technology (as I am not) and knowledgeable concerning the empirical data and problem, to undertake that task, none thus far has succeeded; but, the manual procedure that I have employed for, in effect, solving a set of nine simultaneous linear equations so as to satisfy an ordinal rather than an interval solution criterion guarantees neither that any acceptable solution will be found nor that if an acceptable solution is found, this will necessarily also be the best possible solution.

For purposes of this study, I posited the same ad hoc criterion of acceptability that was used in the earlier study: a rho correlation $\geqslant .90$

TABLE 5.2
Directional Cosines for, Correlations between, and Cumulative Scale Correlations with, Scale Vectors

A. *Directional Cosines for Scale Vectors*

Decks:	Factors:	C'	E'	Deck:	C'	E'
1	1	-.66	-.99	6	.81	.69
	2	.66	-.15		.57	-.69
	3	.33	.00		.00	-.21
	4	-.13	.00		.16	.00
2	1	-.89	.00	7	.86	.98
	2	-.45	-.93		-.51	.00
	3	.00	-.37		.00	-.10
	4	.00	.00		.00	.20
3	1	1.00	.56	8	.97	.73
	2	-.10	.56		.10	-.22
	3	.00	-.56		.24	-.65
	4	.00	-.22		.00	.00
4	1	.89	.88	9	.98	.69
	2	-.45	.44		.00	.24
	3	.00	.00		.20	-.69
	4	.00	-.18		.00	.00
5	1	.93	.88	10	.75	.67
	2	-.37	.13		-.53	.47
	3	.00	-.44		.37	-.54
	4	.00	.09		.07	.20

B. *Correlations between Vectors C', E'*

Deck:	Cosine	Angle
1	.5610	55°50'
2	.4185	65°20'
3	.5040	59°40'
4	.5852	54°10'
5	.7703	39°40'
6	.1656	80°30'
7	.8428	32°30'
8	.5301	58°00'
9	.5382	57°30'
10	.0676	86°10'
Avg.*	(.5160)	58°56'

C. *Correlations (rho)** between Scales and Scale Vectors*

Deck:	C/C'	E/E'
1	1.000	.970
2	.900	.867
3	.954	.966
4	1.000	.983
5	.881	.992
6	.996	.967
7	.996	1.000
8	.933	.983
9	1.000	.979
10	.967	.912
Avg.	.963	.962

*The average given is the mean angle size, for which the corresponding cosine is reported in parentheses; alternatively, the mean cosine is .4983, for which the corresponding angle (arc cosine) is 60°05'.

**With an N of 9, a rho $\geq$ .783 is significant (one-tailed) at the .01 level; evidently all rhos reported here are much more significant than that. Kendall's tau rank correlation coefficients also were calculated for both C' and E' in all ten factor spaces, with values $\geq$ .783 for C' and $\geq$ .778 for E', at significance levels $\leq$ .0019 (and averaging < .0005 for each scale). The rho correlations between the corresponding composite cumulative scales (Table 4.4) and scale vectors (Table 5.5) are .883 for C/C' and .894 for E/E'; with an N of 20, a rho of .534 is significant at the .01 level.

D. *Minor Scale Vectors*

Deck		1		2	3	4
Scale		F	N	N	A	F
Factors	1	−.39	−.38	.00	.07	.31
	2	−.16	−.64	−.99	.70	.92
	3	−.90	.21	.10	−.14	−.23
	4	.09	−.64	−.10	.70	.09
Correlation of Scale/Vector		.887	.886	.950	.903	.911
Scale Evaluation		P+	M	P+	M	P+

Deck		6			7		8	9
Scale		N		F	F	N	F	F
		a	b	c				
Factors	1	.09	.09	.10	.17	−.001	.21	.00	−.17
	2	.78	.78	.77	−.87	.999	.00	.64	.00
	3	.62	.61	.63	.17	.000	−.69	−.64	−.99
	4	.00	.00	.00	−.43	.000	−.69	−.42	.00
Correlation of Scale/Vector		.967			.852	.946	.847	.918	.936
Scale Evaluation		M			M	P+	P+	$\overline{A}$	F

Note: None, for Decks 5 or 10.

between the criterion cumulative scale and its analogue vector in a space (of whatever dimensionality) that was analytically derived from a phi correlation matrix of assent/dissent in decisional dispositions. Table 5.2 shows that eighteen of the twenty scale vectors are acceptable under this criterion: all except C' in the fifth period (for which the problem is strictly one of poor reliability for both the cumulative scale and the factorial configuration, because of very low sample size) and E' in the second period. Rho $\geqslant .966$ in six periods for C/C' and likewise in eight periods for E/E'. For four of the eighteen acceptable scales, the fit is perfect with correlations of unity. The averages for both scale vectors, at .963 and .962 respectively, clearly are very substantially above the minimal level of acceptability. What this signifies in operational terms for paired rankings of nine respondents is that on the average, the sequence of point projections upon either vector is identical with the ranking on the cumulative scale, except that a single respondent projects to a position two ranks above or below his rank position on the scale—and it should be noted that all nine points in a fixed configuration for each period project simultaneously upon two different vectors, for which the criterion rankings are also different. I should underscore the fact, however, that these measurements do *not* signify a better fit for the scales in the four-dimensional space of the present study than was achieved for the term scales in three-dimensional centroid space in the earlier study.[2] This finding contradicts my own anticipation: I had expected to find a better accommodation, for the scales, in the present study, partly because of the use here of better, in the sense of less contaminated by error variance, factorial dimensions and partly because of my use here of the fourth factorial dimension, one more than was invoked in the earlier study. One possible explanation for the failure of the present measurements to replicate in fact the consistency in analogue vectorization achieved in the earlier study is that the tau correlations reported therein are spuriously high; that is to say that even with the somewhat larger series of seventeen data sets, substantial error variance happened to favor an increase in correlation levels. A second possibility is that I was more successful in finding the best locations for scale vectors in the earlier study than in the present one. And a third possibility concerns the pooling of the data into larger sets. The ten sets for the present study average in duration some 2.4 times that of the earlier study, and even more than that in magnitude because of the consistent upward trend in the frequency curve for total decisions. These changes entail the inescapable empirical consequence of greater heterogeneity of issue content, with the probability of correspondingly greater inconsistency in response behavior. If this is true, then the present set of cumulative scales *should* scale less well than did the term scales of the earlier study.

Although I did not calculate or report the statistic for mean R and S scores for either C or E in *The Judicial Mind*, these index values are reported therein for all individual term scales,[3] and I have now calculated those means: they are .9488 and .7404 (for R and S, respectively, for C) and .9409 and .7455 (for E). Reference to Appendix C shows that the corresponding index values for the present study are .9314 and .7138 for C and .9210 and .7097 for E. The average extent to which the R scores for C and E combined of the earlier study exceed the corresponding datum for the present study is .0186; for S combined, the differential in the same direction is an even larger .0312. Consequently, the term scales reported in *The Judicial Mind* are more consistent, to the average extent of .02 to .03, than those reported in Appendix C herein; and a difference of that magnitude and consistency is not insubstantial when we are talking about scores that all are in excess of .90 for R and .70 for S. If the present scales have higher error variance than the older set, then we should expect to find it more difficult to analogize them in factorial or other multidimensional space, which implies that the explanation for the observed slightly poorer fit of these scale vectors lies in the slightly poorer quality of the criterion scales for which accommodation in the factorial spaces is sought. Indeed, the difference between the tau averages, with those for the earlier study being to this extent higher than the taus for the present study, are .0176 for C and .0390 for E; and the average difference for both scales is therefore .0283, which lies explicitly within the range of .02 to .03 poorer quality and greater inconsistency that we noted above to obtain for the present cumulative scales. Therefore, I personally favor this last as the most likely and most plausible explanation for the (to me) surprising finding that the scale/scale-vector correlations here are not quite as high as were those in the original study.

The factor loadings reported in Table 5.2 show three consistent relationships. Except for E' during the second and third periods, all vectors for both scales are strongly correlated at .66 or better with the first factor in all ten periods. Of course, the circumstance that these correlations are negative during the first two periods and positive otherwise has no importance because the directionality of factorial dimensions is, from a substantive point of view, an arbitrary consequence of statistical procedures. Again, with the exception of the second period (and this time for the second factor) and also the fourth factor in the tenth period, it is otherwise notable that when both scales load on the same one of any of the last three factors (II-IV), it is with opposite signs. In combination these two findings imply that both scale vectors are generally correlated in the same direction with the first factor, but they otherwise point in opposing directions on any of the remaining three factors with which both are correlated in a particular period. The third relationship pertains to the average size of loadings: it is of course inherent in the design of the principal-components program that first factor loadings will be, on the average, largest; next largest will then be second factor loadings, and so on. Accepting (as we must) that that is our model, it remains of some interest to note the empirical values that attach to this sequencing of relative factorial importance. Here the first factor is by far the most important—indeed, the average loading of .76 in absolute value on Factor I for both scales combined is substantially larger than the sum of the mean absolute loadings for the remaining three factors combined (.66). Similarly, the sum of the mean absolute correlations on the first two factors, on which we shall rely for most analyses in the next chapter, is about four times that of the third and fourth factors combined. As previously noted, very little weight is attached, by these vectors, to the fourth principal component.

Table 5.2 also reports the correlations between C' and E' in each period. Because the C' and E' vectors are of unit length identical to that of the principal component reference axes, the formula for their angular deviation reduces, by the law of cosines, to an identity relationship between their correlation and their cosine; and the correlation can be readily calculated by simply summing the cross-products of the two vector loadings on each of the four factors for any period. The angular equivalent for that correlation/cosine value can be looked up in any standard table of trigonometric functions. It is notable that in these spaces, the angle of deviation between the vectors ranges from a minimum of slightly over 30° (in the seventh period), to a maximum of over 86° (in the tenth period). Of course, an angle of 30° signifies a very close relationship between the two vectors, which means that in the seventh period virtually all of the judges responded very similarly to major questions of both economic policy and civil liberties. Contrariwise, the correlation of almost 90° signifies the opposite situation: that during the last (tenth) period most of the judges perceived civil liberties issues to be very different from economic issues, and they therefore responded in quite differing patterns of voting to the two types of issues. Or stated otherwise, during the seventh period, if one knew how any judge voted on questions of civil liberties, one could predict with considerable accuracy how that same judge would vote on questions of economic policy, and vice versa; while during the tenth period, knowledge of how one judge voted on either type of issue would in general be worthless in attempting to forecast how the same judge would vote on the other type of issue. The average deviation of almost 60°—and in most of the periods the angle is 59±06°—signifies a consistent, modest, but not unimportant degree of positive relationship between the two vectors and therefore also of consistency in the response patterns of at least a substantial minority of the justices, to the two major types of issues.

It is, of course, apparent that an alternative way of conceptualizing the relationships described in Table 5.2 would be to say that these data define, in an unconventional way, what amounts to oblique rotation of the first two reference axes, to oblique positions that are determined by an extrinsic (*viz.*, not a purely statistical) criterion. This is the way that educational psychologists, who got into factor analysis via attempts to investigate the common content of items on tests of mental traits, skills, and abilities, would naturally tend to think about any correlated vectors in relation to an orthogonal reference factor structure. That is their prerogative; but the fact that a particular mode of conceptualization is conventional makes it neither mandatory nor inherently useful when the method is employed, as we use it here, to investigate theoretical questions very different from those that were of concern to the pioneers of factor analysis. Hence I recognize the possibility of talking about my C' and E' vectors as "rotated oblique factors," and indeed I present the data of Table 5.2 in the paradigm of the transformation matrices that are employed in orthodox discussion to describe an oblique rotation. We shall, furthermore, explore the relationship between C' and E', and a set of oblique rotations of the very same principal component reference factors that are discussed here, in the very next chapter of this study. But for present purposes I prefer to use the alternative conceptual paradigm of criterion cumulative scales that are replicated by vectors, analogous in both content and meaning, whose positions can be determined in the factorial space generated by a matrix of (overall) agreement (and disagreement) scores.

We must consider in addition to the two major scales the possible relationships between the minor scales and the factorial space. Table 5.2D reports the results of the relevant investigation, for the purposes of which I accepted very lenient evidence of scalability under the presumption that poor scales would generally be harder to analogize and that one could always reject the analogues of poor scales after—and if—they could be located in the factorial four-space. The table does not by any means report the results of all of my tests but rather reports only the minor "scales" (with latitudinarian application of the criteria of acceptance) that could be analogized at a rho correlation level of .85 (or within rounding distance thereof) or better. This table reports the directional cosines and rhos for eleven analogizations, of which only six are for acceptable scales, as the evaluations in the table signify. Clearly F fits the best of the minor scales, thereby confirming, incidentally, one of the findings of the earlier study. Over half of the analogizations are for F, and four of the six scales rated as acceptable are F scales. Although its scores on all relevant indices of scalability are poor, the F non-scale in the eighth period also was tested, because its sample size is relative high (including twenty decisions).

As the note to Table 5.2 D concerning the fifth and tenth periods indicates, there were no minor scales available to be tested for these two periods, in the case of the fifth period because the deck N is so small. In the instance of N/N' in the sixth period, three isotypic solution sets are reported for the cosines to illustrate my statement earlier in this chapter that any scale analogue determined by my method will not be an unique solution; rather it is one of a set of solutions (which in geometric terms can be pictured as a cone of vectors) which produce the same rho correlation. I have not taken the trouble to calculate similar alternative solutions for the other analogizations in either part A or part D of this table, but I have no doubt that they can be found—and an iterated computer solution would necessarily calculate them (and could therefore be programmed to print them as output) as a stage in its search for the optimal solution.

The other two acceptable scales reported in Table 5.2D both are for N, in the second and seventh periods. There are, therefore, no analogues for acceptable scales for either A or J. And there are only a total of four minor scales which are both acceptable as scales and accommodated in factorial four-space at a correlation level of at least .90: N in the second period, and F in the fourth, seventh, and ninth. The average levels of correlation are .906 for the six F "scales," and .908 for the four N. But clearly the thrust of the table is to confirm _The Judicial Mind_ finding that none of these minor variables scales well or consistently enough to have a sufficiently large effect upon the configurations of the factorial structures to enable us to locate their analogue vectors in adequate depth to support a valid substantive interpretation concerning the role that they play in defining the ideologies of Supreme Court justices. Nothing in the present study can be said to negate the hypothesis that the minor variables do have a moderate impact upon Supreme Court ideology; but whatever that impact may be, we cannot measure it well enough using the methods that have been employed in the present study. Of course, we can and do include the F' and N' analogue vectors in the plots of the figures (6.2A-J) to be presented in the next chapter.

As I remarked above, the mathematical process for specifying the position of scale vectors involves an attempt to maximize rank-correlation coefficients, which are themselves based on the results of the solution of sets of simultaneous equations. The solutions to the equations are the (unknown) weights that, when normalized, are the factor loadings for C' and E', as reported in Table 5.2A. The constants that are substituted in those sets of equations are the respondent factor loadings reported in Table 5.1: those loadings function also as the Cartesian coordinates for locating the configuration of respondent points in relation to the reference axes that define the factorial space. When normalized, the results of these equations are the orthogonal projections of these respondent ideal points upon the scale vectors; and that set of projections is preferred that includes those of such a magnitude that the sequence they order, of the respondents, is maximally similar (and optimally is identical) to the ranking of these same respondents on the criterion cumulative scale. These projections are reported in Table 5.3, and one comment about them is necessary. In several instances (involving Black, Frankfurter, and Warren, on both scale vectors) a pair of average values (rather than a single one) is given. This is necessary because, in the cases of both Black and Frankfurter, their decisional behavior in regard to C' changes sharply, significantly, and negatively during their respective last two periods on the Court. In Warren's case, it is not quite the same: he was less favorable to both civil liberties and economic liberalism during his initial and final periods on the Court than he remained otherwise.

It is necessary now to consider the model described by Figure 5.1, before we proceed to a consideration of the data reported in Table 5.3. Figure 5.1 is a two-dimensional model of a circumplex.[4] Its external parameter is, by definition, a circle; and its internal structure is determined, also by definition, by the intersection of two cumulative scales. In this figure the two scales are shown as being correlated at an arbitrary (and strictly hypothetical) .707 (= 45°), and the area of the circumplex is partitioned symmetrically into nine segments which are color coded in a pattern that will be followed both in subsequent figures in this chapter and also in the photographic illustrations of Chapter 7. Each of the eight external segments is bounded either by one or both of the scale vectors or else by normals to them (*e.g.*, by vectors orthogonal to the scale vectors at the origin of the space [*i.e.*, the center of the circle]). The circular center segment has a radius of .333, and therefore it includes the middle third of each scale vector, which presumably corresponds to the most moderate attitudes toward the values represented by the scale. Each scale vector is thereby partitioned into two additional segments, one positive (from +.334 thru +1.000) and the other negative (from −.334 thru −1.000). Evidently there are nine (3 x 3) logically possible combinations of sectional positions on the two scale vectors, and these correspond to the nine segments that we observe in Figure 5.1: in the center oo (white), and then, proceeding counterclockwise from the segment bounded by the positive sections of both scale vectors, ++ (light blue), o+ (green), − + (chartreuse), −o (yellow), − − (orange), o− (red), + − (violet), and +o (dark blue).

Furthermore, we can designate these segments on the basis of the known substantive content of the scales, to which these scale vectors have been shown, statistically, to correspond. Thus, to be positive on both vectors is to be liberal by the ideological standards prevailing in the American culture at the time the underlying decisions, which constitute our data, were made. To favor civil liberties but to be a moderate on economic policy issues is to be a political liberal, and by

TABLE 5.3
Projections to Scale Vectors
(by Periods, in Two-Place Decimals)

Justice	Decks: 1	2	3	4	5	6	7	8	9	10	Average
Mu	53										53.0
Ru	44										44.0
Do	41	71	76	77	76	75	79	62	74	55	68.6
Bl	28	67	82	73	82	74	60	50	/−09	−59	64.5/−34.0
Fr	−02	00	05	08	−09	/−72	−67				00.4/−69.5
Ja	−19	−38	−25								−27.3
Bu	−62	−22	−72	−66	−38	−21					−46.8
Re	−68	−47	−74	−78	−82						−69.8
Vi	−77	−45									−61.0
Cl		−29	−29	−07	−57	−06	−70	−54	−41		−36.6
Mi		−54	−31	−69							−51.3
Wa			01	/ 61	65	71	60	56	63	/ 30	15.5/62.7
Ha				−10	−46	−51	−63	−77	−70	−23	−48.6
Br					37	59	57	38	59	45	49.2
Wh						−41	−51				−46.0
St							−06	−37	−59	13	−22.2
BW								−42	−35	−50	−42.3
Go								53			53.0
Fo									66	52	59.0
Ma										50	50.0

C' Vector

Decks:

Justice	1	2	3	4	5	6	7	8	9	10	Average
Ru	76	47	61	72	73	46	75	64	/ 47	42	76.0
Bl	76	-67	-79								64.2/44.5
Ja	-69										-71.7
Mu	75										75.0
Do	67	46	59	74	79	47	84	54	59	44	61.3
Re	-27	-08	-12	-11	-51						-21.8
Vi	-41	42									00.5
Fr	-63	-58	-67	-61	-60	/ -77	-69				-61.8/-73.0
Bu	-51	-19	-28	-55	-48	-45					-41.0
Cl		37	05	34	-38	32	-44	08	23		07.1
Mi		-01	10	-29							-06.7
Wa			15	/ 68	65	41	67	49	46	/ 19	17.0/56.0
Ha				-71	-59	-86	-68	-68	-79	-74	-72.1
Br					-14	16	52	28	37	14	22.2
Wh						-66	-73				-69.5
St							-54	-67	-60	-68	-62.2
BW								-05	-17	-33	-18.3
Go								-21			-21.0
Fo									09	18	13.5
Ma										11	11.0

E′ Vector

symmetry, we can also define the economic liberal, political conservative, economic conservative, and conservative segments. This leaves us with the −+ (top center) and +− (bottom center) sectors, which represent combinations of attitudes that are economically negative and politically positive on the one hand, and economically positive and politically negative on the other. As I have proposed elsewhere in discussing the same problem but in regard to the High Court of Australia, the ideological types that correspond best to these attitudinal combinations are those of classical liberalism and classical conservatism respectively[5]. So −+ is designated as classic liberalism and +−as classic conservatism. In regard to the ++ and −− combinations, it should be understood that these refer to "modern," contemporary twentieth-century American ideological concepts of liberalism and similarly to "modern" conservatism; but because the shorter designations "liberal" and "conservative," leaving the modifier "modern" unarticulated but nonetheless applicable, are quite unambiguous in the context of the present discussion and that which will follow, I prefer to follow the more parsimonious practice of using the shorter designations.

The central region is equivalent, therefore, to an ideological position of moderation toward both scales, and again proceeding in a counterclockwise manner, the sequence of other ideological types denoted in Figure 5.1 is from modern liberalism to political liberalism, classic liberalism, economic conservatism, modern conservatism, political conservatism, classic conservatism, economic liberalism, and thence back to (modern) liberalism. This is the model of the hypothetical ideological types, in terms of which we shall undertake to analyze the empirical data provided by the projections from principal-component ideal-point configurations onto the pairs of scale vectors in the factorial spaces that define those configurations.

There are two ways in which we can proceed empirically to examine the data of Table 5.3 in the light of the circumplex model suggested by Figure 5.1. One approach is to convert the data for each period into typal patterns and then to determine the composite typal assignments on the basis of the modal assignments for each respondent during the individual periods in which he appears. The composite types could then be shown in relation to each other in an empirical circumplex. Alternatively, mean scores could be calculated from the term scores reported in Table 5.3, and these mean scores could then be used as the plotting coordinates (e.g., as the structural correlation coefficients for oblique factors) for determining the projections onto the scale vectors from the traces of the projections onto the vector plane, which in turn emanate from the configuration of ideal-points in the factorial space from which the Table 5.3 scores were derived. Or we can do both, comparing the results, which we should predict to be equivalent except for measurement error.

The scale-vector types for each period are shown in Table 5.4. Clearly the most popular typal positions are LIB, POLIB, ECONS, CONS, and PCONS. Only two respondents appear in the ECOLIB category, and for neither of them is economic liberalism their modal assignment. Black's relatively modest support for civil liberties, during the first period when his colleagues included such politically liberal stalwarts as Murphy and Rutledge, was followed by seven consecutive periods of liberalism, after which he retreated in the face of rising racial and radical protest movements back through economic liberalism in the ninth period to classic conservatism during the final period of the Warren Court. Clark shows considerably more variation, with two assignments each to the politically conservative, conservative, and moderate types in addition to his two periods of economic liberalism. Classic liberalism is a completely null category, and there is only one assignment to classic conservatism—Vinson during the second period—in addition to that of Black mentioned above.

The moderate type appears to have functioned, like economic liberalism, as strictly a way station rather than a home—for Burton during the second period and Minton during the third, in addition to the two assignments there for Clark, and for Warren during his first (*i.e.*, the third) and his last (the tenth) period on the Court. Thus, Warren's change was similar to but less extreme than Black's: Black moved from a relatively more conservative position on civil liberties into a position of consistent support for both scales until he backslid during the last two periods; Warren moved from a position of moderation on both scales to a position of consistent support of both, only to return to a more moderate position during the final period. The last two columns of Table 5.4 cumulate for each period the frequencies of the four liberal types and the four conservative types respectively. These marginals show that conservative types predominated on the Court throughout the first five periods and again in the seventh period. There was a balance of power between the liberal and the conservative types during the sixth and tenth periods—the latter exclusively because of Black's defection on most civil liberties issues. Only for the short span of half a dozen years represented by the eighth and ninth periods during the early and mid-sixties was there a predominance of voting power and ideological support in behalf of liberalism on the Court. Thus conservative types predominated in six periods and liberals in only two; or stated in terms of individual assignments, 49 per cent are to conservative types, and 43 per cent to liberal types, with the remaining 8 per cent being assigned, of course, to the moderate type. We can also

TABLE 5.4
Scale Vector Types (by Periods)

Modal Types:

Period:	MODERN ECOLIB +o	MODERN LIB ++	CLASSICAL POLIB o+	CLASSICAL LIB -+	CLASSICAL ECONS -o	MODERN CONS --	PCONS o-	CLASSICAL CONS +-	CLASSICAL MODERATE oo	LIBS +o,++ o+,-+	CONS -o,-- o-,+-
1	Bl	Do,Mu,Ru			Fr,Ja	Bu,Vi	Re			4	5
2	Cl	Bl,Do			Fr	Ja	Mi,Re	Vi	Bu	3	5
3		Bl,Do			Fr, Ja		Bu,Re		Cl,Mi,Wa	2	4
4	Cl	Bl,Do,Wa			Fr,Ha	Bu	Mi,Re			4	5
5		Bl,Do,Wa	Br		Fr	Bu,Cl, Ha,Re				4	5
6		Bl,Do,Wa	Br		Bu	Fr,Ha,Wh			Cl	4	4
7		Bl,Br, Do,Wa			St	Cl,Fr Ha,Wh				4	5
8		Bl,Do,Wa	Br,Go			Ha,St	BW,Cl			5	4
9	Bl	Br,Do,Wa	Fo			Ha,St	BW,Cl			5	4
10		Do	Br,Fo,Ma		Ha,St		BW	Bl	Wa	4	4

		Bl,Do,Mu, Ru,Wa	Br,Fo, Go,Ma		Fr,Ja,St	Bu,Ha,Wh	BW,Cl,Mi, Re,Vi			9	11
Modal positions:											
Average (as %)	0.4 / 04	2.7 / 30	0.8 / 09	0.0 / 00	1.2 / 13	1.9 / 21	1.2 / 13	0.2 / 02	0.6 / 07	3.8	4.5
Projections (soft data) 11		Do	Br,Ma			Bl,BU, Ha,St	BW	BI		3	6
12		Do	Br,Ma		PO(?)	BU,RQ,St	BW,BL(?)			3	6

Legend: BL = Blackmun
BU = Burger
PO = Powell
RQ = Rehnquist

note that the stand-off in the sixth period, made possible by Clark's moderate posture then, was accompanied by Frankfurter's retreat during his last two periods on the Court to a position of straight conservatism in reaction to what he conceived to be the Court's excesses in behalf of political freedom as the nation began to back away from some of the more extreme repressions of the mood of McCarthyism that had characterized its decisions during the second and third periods. But in view of the fact that Frankfurter already had made his switch—one which he had, quite characteristically, signalled verbally in advance—by the sixth period, we must explain the swing back to conservative predominance during the seventh period not on the basis of Frankfurter changing, but rather on the basis that Clark moved from moderation during the sixth period to conservatism during the seventh.

The other stand-off, during the tenth period, finds both a necessary and a sufficient explanation in the movement of Black from economic liberalism during the ninth period to classic conservatism during the tenth, thereby supplying the fourth conservative vote in substitution for that of Clark (whose resignation marks the division between the ninth and tenth periods); plus the movement of Warren to a position of moderation, which made the stand-off possible. The question logically arises whether the stand-off in the tenth period is transitional to a return to conservative predominance on the Court; and we all know, in a general sort of way, that this is precisely what happened when Earl Warren retired and Nixon undertook the most whole-hearted campaign to pack the Supreme Court since Franklin Roosevelt had confronted the political problem of how to free himself of the Hughes Court. I regret that I have no equivalently hard data for the Burger Court that could be exploited for present purposes as a check upon our subjective impressions; but there must be closure at some point if research is to enter the public domain by becoming published, and I cut off systematic data collection with Earl Warren's retirement. There is, however, a kind of compromise alternative that we can consider: I do have available some partially ordered data, based upon selective rather than systematic analysis of the first three terms of the Burger Court, which I collected for an independent but by no means incompatible purpose. Therefore, I have added, below the totals rows of Table 5.4, two additional rows, based upon my qualitative analyses of the first period of the Burger Court and the initial year of the second period.[6] I am reasonably confident about most of the assignments to the periods that I have designated as eleventh and twelfth, but because of the relative inadequacy of the supporting data on which I have relied for the twelfth period, I have made explicit my uncertainty concerning the indicated assignments for Powell and Blackmun. But those doubts go to the choice of assignment *among* conservative types for PO and BL; I have no doubts in coming to the conclusion that both of these Nixon appointees belong in one or another of the four conservative types. Consequently, I am quite prepared to stand behind the marginal frequency totals for the eleventh and twelfth periods, just as much as I would feel bound to defend my judgment concerning the frequency totals for the first ten periods. And what the marginals for the eleventh and twelfth periods show is that the tenth period was indeed transitional and that the Supreme Court under Burger has been more extremely conservative in its ideological orientation than at any other time in the part quarter of a century, at least. All four of Nixon's appointees are assigned to one or another of the three principal conservative types, and with the continuing support of Stewart and White, plus that of Harlan and Black until their retirement before the opening of the 1971 term, the ideological balance of the Court has remained strongly conservative ever since Earl Warren's retirement in June 1969.

The typal assignments for the ten periods of this study proper are depicted, in the form of an empirical circumplex, in Figure 5.2. In this figure the two scale vectors are correlated at .5 (=60°), which approximates the observed correlations between the composite scales, the scale vectors that are defined by the mean projections from the ideal-point configurations as reported in Table 5.5, and the mean of the correlations between these vectors in all ten periods as reported in Table 5.2. This figure directs attention to the curvilinear relationship among the five principal types, which are the only ones populated on the basis of the modal assignments. None of the respondents was moderate sufficiently long and consistently enough to be modally assigned to that type. Modally, there are five liberals and four political liberals, followed by two economic conservatives; one respondent (Stewart) who could not be assigned other than arbitrarily because he was economically conservative in two periods and conservative in his other two periods of service; three conservatives; and five political conservatives. Thus, there are three empirical conservative types but only two such liberal types; and a majority of eleven of the respondents in this sample are assigned to one of the three conservative types, while the minority of nine liberals are assigned to one or the other of the two liberal types. These latter are divided by time of appointment—and therefore also (at least roughly) by age, generational culture, and related considerations. Earl Warren two full decades ago became the last consistent liberal to join the Court.

The five empirical types that are populated form a discontinuous U-shaped curve, so that from the perspective of Figure 5.2 the hypothesized circumplex appears to be a partially incomplete one. An alterna-

TABLE 5.5
Mean Scale Vector Projections
(in Two-Place Decimals)

VECTORS:

C'   E'

	Justice	Projection		Justice	Projection
	Do	69		Ru	76
	Fo	59		Mu	75
	Mu	53	+	Do	61
	Go	53		Bl	60
+	Wa	51		Wa	46
	Ma	50			
	Br	49		Br	22
	Bl	45		Fo	14
	Ru	44		Ma	11
				Cl	07
	Fr	−20	0	Vi	00
0	St	−22		Mi	−07
	Ja	−27		BW	−18
				Go	−21
	Cl	−37		Re	−22
	BW	−42			
	Wh	−46		Bu	−41
−	Bu	−47		St	−62
	Ha	−49	−	Fr	−65
	Mi	−51		Wh	−70
	Vi	−61		Ha	−72
	Re	−70		Ja	−72

tive empirical circumplex is depicted in Figure 5.3, which is constructed from the mean scale vector loadings of Table 5.5, treating them as structural correlations between the planar traces of the ideal points and the vectors which in this sense are treated as obliquely rotated factorial axes. Certainly there is no conceptual reason why we should not consider the scale vectors to be analogues not only of the cumulative scales but also of obliquely rotated factorial axes. The derivation of the data reported in Table 5.5 is straightforward enough: these data are the means of the projections, from the ideal-point configurations in the four-dimensional factorial space of each period, upon the scale vectors in those spaces. In the case of three of the justices, the means for two subgroupings of periods in lieu of the overall mean is reported in Table 5.3. This is because Warren's voting in his first and last periods on the Court and that of Frankfurter and Black in their respective last two periods of participation differed significantly, as previously noted, from their modal behavior: hence I report these average differences so that they can be taken into account in the structure of Figure 5.3. Table 5.5 arrays the vector sequences so as to distinguish among the three segments previously defined: + (.334 or higher), 0 (within the range ± .333), and − (−.334 or more extremely negative than that). In comparing the two vectors, it is evident upon visual inspection that the Court was more sharply divided over political liberalism than over economic liberalism: this is demonstrated by the larger size of both the + and the − segments on C', than on E'; or, stated otherwise, the much larger size of the 0 segment on the E' vector.

It is of course possible to correlate each of these vectors with its criterion, which is the composite scale that was constructed from the dominance matrix for the scale. We should not expect such correlations to be remarkably high because both the vector scores and the composite scale rankings are themselves the results of averaging processes, which differ considerably in the manner in which they weight the importance of differentials in the small number of periods that constitute the samples of observations. The rho correlation between C composite and C' is .883, while the rho between E composite and E' is .894. These levels are substantially less than the averages of the correlations by periods (.963 for C/C' and .962 for E/E') that are reported in Table 5.2, but I consider even correlations at about the level of .9 to be quite satisfactory for the purpose of substantiating the underlying identity between the cumulative scales as measurements of attitudinal differences, and the scale vectors as significants of ideological structures.

Figure 5.3 denotes in explicit form the structure of the ideological types that, in a more general way, we observed in Figure 5.2. Warren, Black, and Frankfurter each is shown in two different positions: one is his predominant place and the other is the position that he assumed (1) during his first and last periods, in the case of Warren, or (2) during the last two periods of his participation as covered by the present study, in the cases of Frankfurter and Black. None of the ideal points is located, in four-dimensional principal-component space, precisely in the positions in which we impute them in this figure. This must be the case for two reasons: there is no composite four-dimensional factorial space, as we already have noted above—instead we have averages of projections, upon scale vectors, from configurations in the four-dimensional spaces of particular periods; and in any event, such projections, even for particular periods, are orthogonals drawn from the ideal points to the scale vectors and will only rarely if ever, and then coincidentally, lie in the plane defined by a pair of scale vectors. Certainly when we deal with averages of projections, we may consider the projections themselves to fall on the vectors and therefore to lie within the scale-vectors plane, but that does not imply that the ideal points also lie in that plane. On the other hand, in the factorial space for any particular period, we could project orthogonals from each ideal point in the configuration to each scale vector and also to the plane that they define. A line drawn in that plane, from the trace of the ideal-point, defined as the point in the plane to which the ideal point projects orthogonally and from which it seems to project orthogonally (in the planar view) onto the scale vector, will constitute in four-dimensional space the leg of a right triangle, of which the projection from the ideal point to the scale vector will be the hypotenuse. So what we observe in Figure 5.3 are points that are *analytically* the analogues of ideal-point traces, which one might plot and observe empirically in the space for a particular period. But they are not, *empirically*, such traces in Figure 5.3 for the reason, already mentioned, that there is no composite four-dimensional ideal-point configuration of which they could be the traces of orthogonal projections to the plane. On the other hand, if it were possible to observe such projections to the plane, we should expect them to deviate from the means plotted here to such a relatively slight extent that it would not change in any important way the interpretation that we ought logically to make on the basis of the relationships depicted by Figure 5.3.

The most obvious finding from this figure is that assignment to ideological types is precisely the same as we observed in Figure 5.2, providing that we focus there on the modal positions of Warren, Black, and Frankfurter, and with the exception that Stewart, whose position was indeterminate as between conservatism and economic conservatism, appears to be clearly the latter in the present figure. In effect, Figure 5.2 directs attention to the differences between ideological types, whereas the present figure focuses attention on the more detailed differences within ideological types. Figure 5.3 also emphasizes the magnitude of the differences between the modal and idiosyncratic positions assumed by the three justices for each of whom we have denoted two points in this figure. Warren, for example, began his work on the Supreme Court in a posture of almost complete neutrality between the conflicting ideological positions that he found to divide his then more experienced colleagues on the Court; but after an initial year his position changed to one of pronounced and balanced liberalism as close to that of Douglas and the modal Black as either of the latter was to each other.[7] The second idiosyncratic change apparent in the figure is the move of Justice Frankfurter from what had been his modal and archetypal position of economic conservatism to an extreme posture of balanced conservatism. (I have provided elsewhere[8] an explanation for this phenomenon, which can be summarized as an endeavor on Frankfurter's part to apply the lessons taught by the Court-packing fight of 1937 to a new and inappropriate set of circumstances). The third such change is that of Black, from a position of core modern liberalism (adjacent to Douglas and the modal Warren) to a posture of classic conservatism as extreme as that of Frankfurter's final ideological repose. Indeed, as examination of Figure 5.3 makes evident, from one point of view there isn't such a great difference between the manifest relationships of these two superannuated judicial figures (*i.e.*, of Frankfurter and Black, in denouement) and the political liberalism vector; what these two former stalwarts still disagreed about was not civil liberties—which neither could continue to support—but rather it was the E' vector of economic liberalism; and here it was Black who continued to vote the populist position while the Harvard administrative law professor, who never could quite bring himself to affiliate with the Democratic Party, continued to oppose the liberties which bureaucrats took with the rights of property. Civil liberties had never been of much concern to Franklin Roosevelt's administrations, anyhow; and political liberalism began to emerge as an array of questions of national policy concern only during World War II when Roosevelt himself was ill and preoccupied with problems of military policy. So two of the leading gladiators of the New Deal era played out their Gotterdamerung on the Supreme Court, united in their opposition to civil liberties, but divided still by what had been the gut issue of the thirties: to what extent and how social justice can and should be furthered by greater equalization of economic goods.

I must also add an afterword concerning the fact that we have just considered three such changes in ideological position among the justices in the present sample. In the earlier study I had remarked about only one of these, that of Warren. But the Black switch began a full year after the end of the period of analysis included in *The Judicial Mind*, so I am left with Frankfurter to explain away. And I can't. As reference to the passage cited above in footnote eight will demonstrate, I was quite sufficiently sensitized to the drop in Frankfurter's support of civil liberties beginning in the 1958 term, and to the reasons therefor.[9] Furthermore, the very data for the earlier study that correspond best to those on which I rely in the present study for portraying Frankfurter in more conservative position during the sixth and seventh periods show exactly the same thing: Frankfurter's projections on C' are reported

there as ranging between +.201 and +.357 during the half-dozen terms
preceding 1955; as dropping to values of +.056, +.046, and −.008
during the next three terms; and then, beginning with the 1958 term, as
dropping sharply to values of −.693, −.673, −.610, and in his final term
on the Court, −.531.[10] Clearly there was support then for the same
finding that I make now, and clearly I should have made it then too.
One is reminded of the story of Samuel Johnson's reply, to the query
of a lady who wondered why his dictionary had defined "postern" as
"a part of the foot of a horse": "Ignorance, madame, ignorance" was
his retort; and I have none better.

A question might also be raised, I suppose, in regard to my classification of Clark—not as to his modal placement in the political conservative type, but rather whether he should be deemed a fourth case of
change in ideological position. I think not, and no doubt I should
explain why not. What we observe, as I pointed out above in discussing
Table 5.4, is that Clark is assigned for two periods each, to each of the
following types: ECOLIB, POLIB, CONS, and MODT. And there seems
to be a correlation with time: the sequence of assignments is ECOLIB,
MODT, ECOLIB, CONS, MODT, CONS, PCONS, and PCONS, which
suggests that Clark was weakly an economic liberal during his initial
three periods on the Court and that thereafter he overswung (see Figure
5.2) to straight conservatism, ultimately coming to rest (as it were) in
the PCONS type which mediates between ECOLIB and CONS in the
structure of the circumplex. The weakness of his economic liberalism is
demonstrated by the observation, from Table 5.3, that Clark's scores on
E' are confined to the range ±.38, so that he is never more than
marginally (by .05 or less) out of a moderate stance in regard to
questions of economic policy. But let us consider also some additional
perspectives of the matter. I have previously discussed at some length [11]
what I consider to be the most plausible explanation for Clark's early
perturbations—during, that is to say, periods two and three: that he was
as much influenced then by social influences, following the leadership
of whoever was Chief Justice, as he was by ideological convictions. But
those early differences, which show up better in the scales than in the
projections, are only superficially (and probably spuriously) relevant to
the present problem, because Clark's largest shifts in position (at least,
if these are to be measured in the space defined by Figure 5.3) occurred
subsequent to the third period as he alternated back and forth between
marginal economic liberalism and marginal conservatism during periods
four through seven. This observation suggests the possible utility of
plotting all eight of Clark's period trace points from Table 5.3, in the
space of Figure 5.3. I do not reproduce the result here because anyone

who wishes to do so can readily replicate the exercise, but what it shows is that six of the eight points are confined to a small area centered about his position in his final (the ninth) period; that these six points are either clearly political conservative, or moderate, or barely marginally economic liberal; and that even when the other two, marginally conservative points are considered, all eight trace points are spanned by approximately a quadrant of the circumplex centered in the politically conservative typal space. Moreover, his position in the ninth (his last) period is the closest to his position in the second (his initial) period, which again is negative as evidence that his ideological position underwent any fundamental change. And not least, his rank on the composite E scale is tenth (out of twenty), while his rank on the corresponding C scale is eighteenth; and such a combination (0−) of relative moderation on E combined with relatively extreme negative support for C is of course the prototype of the ideological position of political conservatism.

Notes to Chapter 5

1. *The Judicial Mind*, pp. 73-75.

2. The present averages are +.963 and +.962, true, but these are rhos; taus were used in the earlier study, thereby meeting a tougher standard of acceptability because a tau of .90 denotes greater consistency between two sequences than does a rho of the same numerical magnitude. The average taus for the present study are +.912 and +.884, as compared to .929 and .922 for the term-grouped data of *The Judicial Mind.*

3. *Ibid.*, pp. 104-12, 130-38.

4. See Louis Guttman, "A New Approach to Factor Analysis: the Radex," chapter 6 in Paul F. Lazarsfeld, ed., *Mathematical Thinking in the Social Sciences* (Glencoe: The Free Press, 1954), pp. 258-348.

5. See my "The Dimensions of Decisional Response" in Joel B. Grossman and Joseph Tanenhaus, eds., *Frontiers of Judicial Research* (New York: Wiley, 1969), p. 184; L. T. Hobhouse, *Liberalism* (New York: Henry Holt, 1911), especially chapter 2, "The Elements of Liberalism"; and cf. John Stuart Mill, *On Liberty* (London: Oxford University Press ed., 1933; The Worlds' Classics, Vol. 170), p. 116.

6. See my *The Future of the Nixon Court* (Honolulu: University of Hawaii Foundation, 1972), pp. 18-42.

7. Cf. *The Judicial Mind*, p. 119.

8. Cf. my *Constitutional Politics* (New York: Holt, Rinehart and Winston, 1960), pp. 636-38.

9. See also C. Herman Pritchett, *Congress versus the Supreme Court, 1957-1960* (Minneapolis: University of Minnesota Press, 1961).

10. *The Judicial Mind*, p. 218.

11. *Ibid.*, pp. 118-19.

6
Oblique Factors

Because of the manifestly positive correlation between the political and the economic liberalism scales, orthogonal rotation of the reference axes of principal-component factor analysis, whether to simple structure via varimax or to any other conventional criterion of orthogonal rotation, never has seemed appropriate to me as a basis for interpreting the data discussed in this book. Furthermore, no one else seems to have had much success in interpreting judicial decision-making data on the basis of orthogonally rotated factor analysis. It seems intuitively more plausible, however, to consider oblique rotation as a hypothesis that ought to be tested. This was not attempted in the earlier study for several reasons, of which a sufficient one is that computer programs, including the one that I used for the present study, were then in an experimental stage and not available to me; and manual operations were too tedious to be feasible. But the earlier study had indicated that, generally speaking, the variables tended to form three clusters in the configurations: one of the liberals, and in the other hemisphere, two of conservatives, economic and political. Oblique factors tend (again, generally speaking) to pick out the clusters in a configuration, in the sense that one could expect the two primary factors in a bi-factor oblique analysis to be directed near the respective centroids of one or another of the major clusters that might appear in a particular configuration. If that happened, then these primary factors might be hypothesized to project in vectors that would be co-aligned with, if not identical to, those of the two major scale vectors, C' and E'. The test for such isomorphism would be to determine the orthogonal projections, from the judicial ideal points of the configuration, onto the primary factors and then to compare their rank orders with those of the cumulative scales to ascertain whether either or both scales are highly correlated with either or both primary factors.

The "oblimin" program for oblique rotation used here permits a choice among three statistical criteria relating to the minimization of either the sum of the cross-products, or else the covariances of the squared factor pattern coefficients, or a mediating procedure which assigns equal emphasis to the two preceding alternatives. I chose the third or "biquartimin" alternative because it compensates for the opposite biases of the first two alternatives and is deemed most appropriate for moderately complex data[1] such as those with which we are here concerned. As I explained in Chapter 3, I carried out both two- and four-factor rotations, and after comparing them decided on grounds of marginal utility against making also a three-factor oblique analysis. We shall consider first the two-factor results, which I have preferred to use for purposes of exposition because of the not inconsiderable advantages in simplicity and economy that this choice entails; then I shall present a comparison of the results of the two- and the four-factor analyses. The chapter concludes with a discussion of a two-factor oblique analysis of the eight-scale matrix of rho correlations, which was introduced in Chapter 4, thereby permitting us to examine the appropriateness of a two-factor oblique solution to the question of the relationships among several liberalism scales and subscales, plus the F Scale. We shall re-examine this question in the next chapter, where it will be possible to compare the relative merits of one-, two-, and three-, and four-dimensional smallest-space solutions for the same matrix.

The structural correlations between the configuration points and the primary oblique factors (T_1 and T_2) are given in Table 6.1. These correlations denote the points of orthogonality between the primary factors and the configuration variables; thus, we know from Table 5.1 that Chief Justice Vinson's ideal-point is located, in the first period in two-dimensional principal-component space, at (+.46, −.38) and the shortest distance between that point and *any* point on the primary oblique factor T_1 is the line connecting the point (+.46, −.38) with the point (−.20, +.60). This is the point at which Vinson's point is orthogonal to T_1, because the orthogonal from the shorter to the longer vector is always the minimal distance between two vectors. We calculate the projection point (of orthogonality) by cross-multiplying the coordinates for Vinson's point, with the corresponding coordinates for the vector T_1 (which are given in Table 6.2A, as −.86, −.52); the algebraic sum of the pair of cross-products is −.3956 +.1976 = −.1980, or the

TABLE 6.1
Oblimin Oblique Structural Correlation Matrices
(Two-Place Decimals)

Deck	Variable	T_1	T_2	Deck	Variable	T_1	T_2	Deck	Variable	T_1	T_2
1	Vi	−20	60	2	Vi	67	−19	3	Wa	−07	64
	Bl	68	−52		Bl	−52	−44		Bl	−83	13
	Re	02	71		Re	56	02		Re	72	18
	Fr	−78	−01		Fr	−42	63		Fr	01	−58
	Do	68	−30		Do	−48	−59		Do	−78	21
	Mu	58	−70		Ja	−06	80		Ja	31	−56
	Ja	−75	18		Bu	23	03		Bu	70	20
	Ru	65	−57		Cl	42	−08		Cl	22	73
	Bu	−30	66		Mi	62	06		Mi	33	−18
4	Wa	−71	40	5	Wa	−67	40	6	Wa	76	−39
	Bl	−81	32		Bl	−68	60		Bl	83	−44
	Re	67	55		Re	23	−89		Fr	−21	86
	Fr	07	−73		Fr	62	27		Do	81	−39
	Do	−82	23		Do	−74	50		Bu	−64	32
	Bu	68	−03		Bu	66	−07		Cl	−67	−38
	Cl	−03	50		Cl	−11	−79		Ha	−37	86
	Mi	63	31		Ha	80	−08		Br	59	−03
	Ha	27	−83		Br	−13	38		Wh	−51	49
7	Wa	−77	10	8	Wa	−31	75	9	Wa	−18	86
	Bl	−78	11		Bl	−61	21		Bl	−46	−47
	Fr	73	11		Do	−75	13		Do	−78	35
	Do	−82	−19		Cl	41	−18		Cl	48	08
	Cl	35	78		Ha	80	−38		Ha	81	−34
	Ha	72	05		Br	−04	80		Br	−17	77
	Br	−62	−10		St	62	02		St	55	−42
	Wh	69	−12		BW	42	−02		BW	39	−11
	St	46	−62		Go	−14	57		Fo	−32	58
10	Wa	61	−04	10	Br	64	04	10	Ma	60	−03
	Bl	−45	−01		St	18	53				
	Do	11	−78		BW	−19	64				
	Ha	−07	71		Fo	41	−19				

−.20 indicated above. The same relationship is presented graphically in Figure 6.1, in which we can observe the two-dimensional principal-component configuration of judicial ideal-points, the pair of oblique factors T_1 and T_2, and also the pair of scale vectors C' and E', plus the minor scales in those periods in which they are acceptable. Only the positive half of each of the primary oblique factors and of the scale vectors is drawn in the figure in order to avoid obscuring, with unnecessary radials, the important relationships. One can visually confirm that Vinson's point position in Figure 6.1A is at least approximately located at (−.46, −.38), and that his loading on the first reference factor is negative rather than positive because that factor has been reflected (*i.e.*, reversed in direction), as the number one with a superscript asterisk (1^*) signifies. Similarly, one can estimate that a line drawn through Vinson's point and orthogonal to T_1 will intersect the latter in the second quadrant at a distance of approximately .20 (and, therefore, at −.20) from the origin on the first reference axis. All of the other relationships denoted in Figures 6.1A−6.1J are similarly determined by the information presented in Tables 5.1, 5.2A, 6.1, and 6.2.

Further inspection of Figure 6.1A shows that T_2 is almost perfectly though negatively correlated with $C'+$, while T_1 is highly and positively correlated with $E'+$; so at least during the first period the evidence seems to support the hypothesis. It is also notable that C' and E' are obliquely correlated, while T_1 and T_2 are more orthogonal than oblique with an angle of 105°. Also confirmatory of our expectation is the set of cluster relationships of the two primary factors: T_2 does pass through the middle of the larger conservative cluster (of Bu, Vi, and Re) while the negative segment of T_1 passes between the two points (those of Ja and Fr) that comprise the other conservative cluster. And the remaining four ideal-points, all of liberals, lie within the intersection of the T_2− and T_1+ axes. (No particular significance should be attached to the circumstance that T_2 is reversed in direction from the C scale and its vector; we can reflect the primary factor so that it then has projections of reversed polarity, and a correspondingly reversed rank order.) Similarly, we can observe that in Figure 6.1B, it would be necessary to reflect both primary factors in order for T_1 to become positively coaligned with C', and T_2 with E'. In Figure 6.1C, T_1 would need to be reflected; and I leave to the reader the judgment of which primary factor or factors would require reflection in the other subfigures in this sequence—both would in 6.1G, and one or the other factor would in the other periods. One's overall subjective impression is that when properly reflected, these oblique factors are generally well, but by no means perfectly, correlated with the scale vectors. But of

TABLE 6.2
Directional Cosines for and Correlations between
Primary Oblique Factors

A. *Directional Cosines for Primary Oblique Factors (T Matrix)*				B. *Correlations between Primary Oblique Factors (φ Matrix, T'T)*		
Deck:	Reference Factors	Primary Factors				
		T_1	T_2	Deck:	Cosine	Angle
1	1	−.86	.72	1	−.2593	105° 00′
	2	−.52	−.69			
2	1	.99	.14	2	.0234	88° 40′
	2	−.11	.99			
3	1	−1.00	.05	3	−.0493	92° 50′
	2	−.00	1.00			
4	1	−.97	.31	4	−.0554	93° 10′
	2	.25	.95			
5	1	−.86	.63	5	−.1464	98° 25′
	2	−.50	−.78			
6	1	.91	−.61	6	−.2285	103° 15′
	2	.41	.80			
7	1	−1.00	−.02	7	.0050	89° 40′
	2	−.02	1.00			
8	1	−.90	.58	8	−.1594	99° 10′
	2	.44	.82			
9	1	−.76	.76	9	−.1491	98° 35′
	2	−.65	−.66			
10	1	.48	−.90	10	−.0480	92° 45′
	2	−.88	−.43			
				Avg.	−.1067	96° 09′

course the criterion against which we must evaluate the question of goodness-of-fit is that provided by the cumulative scales rather than the scale vectors. We know the latter already contain an average of about four to five per cent error in their rank orderings of the judicial ideal-points, and we would not want to take advantage of the possibility of spuriously either overestimating or underestimating the goodness-of-fit of the oblique factors. One or the other such effect would

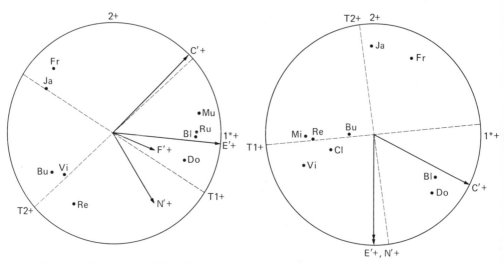

A. The Early Vinson Court (1946-1949)   B. The Later Vinson Court (1949-1953)

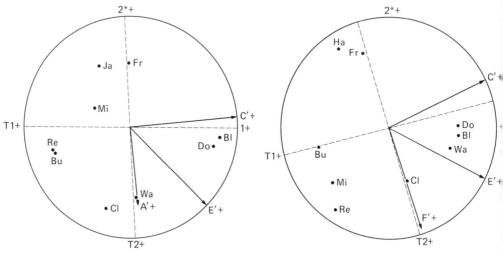

C. The Early Warren Court (1953-1954)   D. The Early Warren Court (1954-1956)

Figure 6.1 Oblique Factors and Scale Vectors in Two-Dimensional Principal Component Space (by Periods)

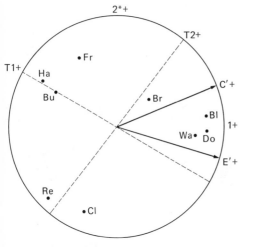

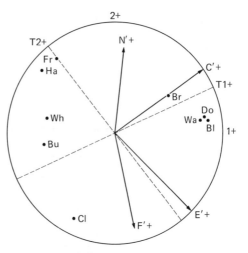

E. The Middle Warren Court (1956)

F. The Middle Warren Court (1956-1958)

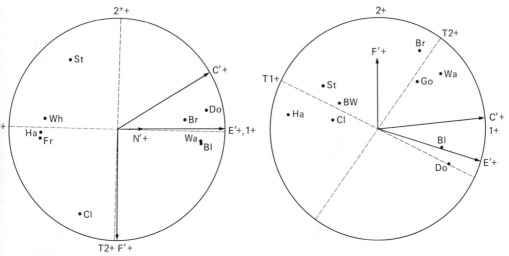

G. The Middle Warren Court (1958-1961)

H. The Later Warren Court (1961-1965)

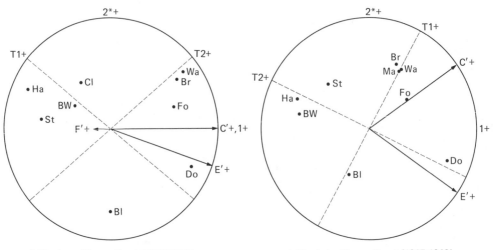

I. The Later Warren Court (1965-1967)   *J. The Later Warren Court (1967-1969)*

likely be the case if we used the scale vectors as criteria, depending upon which way the errors happened to lie in any particular paired comparison.

We can also observe the scale vectors, and when we do so we note that all liberals are within the sector of the space demarked by C'E' during the first six periods, with the exceptions of Douglas in the first period, Warren in the third, and Brennan in the fifth. Only half of the four liberals are so contained in the seventh period, and thereafter only two out of a total of eleven are between the vectors during the last three periods. Stated otherwise, the proportion of those persons who were classified in the preceding chapter as among one of the liberal types, and who appear in these figures as consistent liberals, drops from 89 per cent during the first six periods to 18 per cent during the last three periods. Such an extreme difference can be accounted for only by both of two conditions: (1) that persons who strongly supported both economic and political liberalism—an ideological posture that we might identify with the liberalism of the late New Deal era, which still predominated during the initial period of the present analysis—no longer continued to be appointed to the Court during the latter portion of the Warren Court era; and (2) that most of the persons remaining on the Court during the latter portion of the Warren era, who had been themselves balanced liberals during the earlier part of that era, no longer adhered to that position.

The models depicted by Figures 5.1 and 5.2 can readily be applied in the interpretation of the non-liberal configurational (trace) points of Figure 6.1. Of course, this necessarily is true; Figures 6.1A-J are a mode of representation alternative to that of the scale vector types presented in Table 5.4, but they are based in part, and to the extent that is relevant here, on the same information. What seems apparent in these figures is that cohesiveness seems to be strictly a function of size: during the first five periods, except for the transitional third when the change in Chief Justices occurred, a cohesive minority group of liberals confronts a majority of conservatives who are clearly divided into subgroupings of political conservatives and economic conservatives; then these two subgroups of conservatives, while by no means uniting, do appear to be back in closer rapport because of the emergence of a more balanced conservative center during the sixth and seventh periods when Whittaker was on the Court; and then, once the liberals comprise a majority, as they do during the last three periods, a conservative minority that seems to be just as cohesive as the liberals of the first five periods faces a liberal majority that is divided between political and balanced liberals—with Douglas alone left in the latter type during the ninth and tenth periods because of Black's descent into classic conservatism.

The inclusion of both the major scale analogues and the oblique factors in these figures directs attention to an anomalous finding: that the pair of major scale vectors (C' and E') are conspicuously correlated in an acute oblique relationship except in the sixth period, while the pair of supposedly oblique factors (T_1 and T_2) are consistently shown in a quasi-orthogonal relationship to each other. The range of differences in degree in the angle of $T_1 T_2$ is only $16°20'$, and their average of $96°09'$ shows that what the biquartimin program employed here for the oblique factor analysis produced was in fact virtually an orthogonal solution. Moreover, as we shall see presently when we consider Table 6.4D, a second oblimin factor analysis (this time, of the matrix of correlations among the C and E scales and subscales and the F Scale) confirms the fundamental orthogonality of the biquartimin solution: the angle reported there between T_1 and T_2 is $99°10'$, only three degrees different from the estimate provided by Figure 6.1. It should be kept in mind that the oblique factors observed in Figure 6.1A-J are derived from the rotation of principal components produced by the factor analysis of phi correlation matrices of decisions classified strictly according to paired agreement and disagreement in assenting and dissenting voting on the disposition of cases and without regard to their policy or issue parameters. The oblique scales observable in Figure 6.2, quite to the contrary, were derived from factor analysis of a matrix of rho correlations between pairs of composite cumulative scales, themselves products of dominance matrices based upon the individual cumulative scales for each period, which were constructed from subsets of decisional data classified by support or non-support of policy issues.

Figure 6.1 also shows those minor scales that are correlated with their scale vector analogues at rhos of approximately .85 or better. Even with this lower criterion of acceptability for analogization, only eleven minor scales are listed in Table 5.2D, and their apportionment is strictly proportional to the numbers of minor scales evaluated as acceptable (or as marginal or quasi—and in one instance, that of the F scale in the eighth period, as non-scalable); the table includes six out of nine F scales, four out of six N scales, one of three A scales, and none of the three possible J scales. Two of the F scale vectors, in Figures 6.1A and J, show F as very highly correlated with one of the oblique axes, but two others in periods eight and nine are congruent with reference factors instead; and generally no consistent relationship between either F or the other minor scales, and the oblique axes, . apparent in these figures.

It is possible, of course, to examine in a more systematic and precise manner the relationships between the scales and the oblique axes. Furthermore, we can do this so as to compare the relative goodness-of-fit provided by two- and by four-dimensional oblique space, for the scales; and that is something that we cannot do by planar perspectives such as the graphs of Figure 6.1. (It would of course be possible to correlate with the oblique factors the scale *analogues* [which, necessarily, appear in Figure 6.1, rather than the scales themselves], but that would involve the problem of fortuity in the apportionment of the error variance, mentioned above, and so I have preferred to compare the cumulative scales themselves directly with the oblique axes.)

Table 6.3 lists the scales and their respective correlations with the factors of both oblique two-space and also oblique four-space. (Those minor scales that were not evaluated as acceptable in their scalability, but which are nevertheless included in this table, are tagged with the ascriptive designation symbols introduced in Table 4.1). The descriptive information of Table 6.3A is summarized in Table 6.3B, and together these show the following. Both major scales are relatively highly correlated with one or the other of the oblique factors in all periods for both two-space and four-space. In two spaces, in most of the periods both C and E are most highly correlated with the same oblique factor, which generally (five times out of six) was T_1. The same phenomenon is evident in four-space, although less strongly so there (in three out of four times, on T_1). In two-space there is a tendency for both major

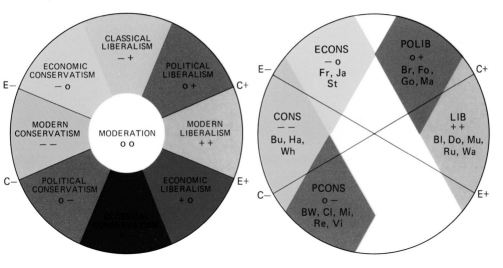

Figure 5.1 Circumplex Model of Scale Types (Hypothetical)

Figure 5.2 Empirical Circumplex of Scale Types (Modal Positions)

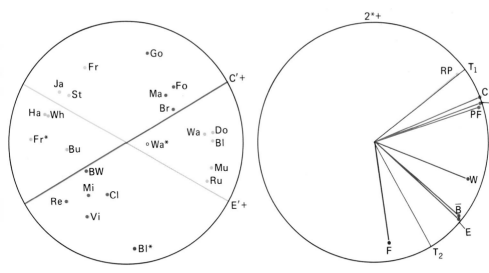

Figure 5.3 Empirical Circumplex of Mean Orthogonal Projections to Scale Vectors, from Average Ideal-Point Loci (as Projected on Scale-Vector Planes from Configurations in Four-Dimensional Principal-Component Space)

Figure 6.2 Oblique Factors and Vectors for Eight Scales and Subscales

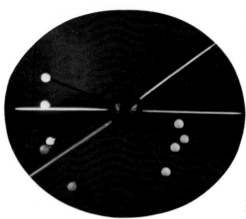

Figure 7.1 Three-Dimensional Smallest-Space Configurations with Scale Vector Analogues (by Periods)

A. The Early Vinson Court (1946-1949)

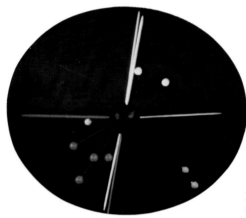

B. The Later Vinson Court (1949-1953)

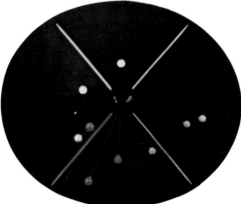

C. The Early Warren Court (1953-1954)

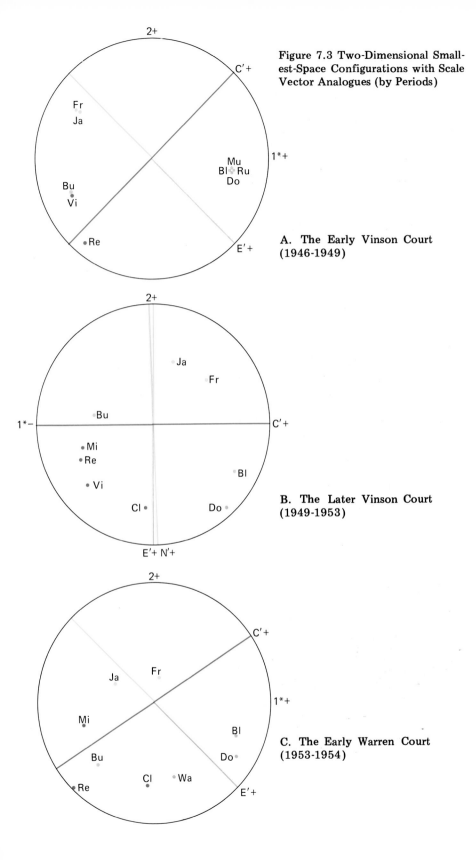

Figure 7.3 Two-Dimensional Smallest-Space Configurations with Scale Vector Analogues (by Periods)

A. The Early Vinson Court (1946-1949)

B. The Later Vinson Court (1949-1953)

C. The Early Warren Court (1953-1954)

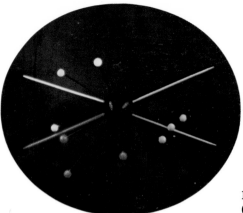

D. The Early Warren Court
(1954-1956)

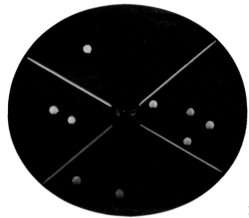

E. The Middle Warren Court (1956)

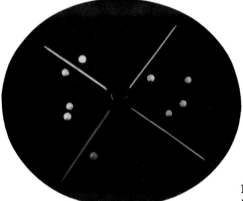

F. The Middle Warren Court
(1956-1958)

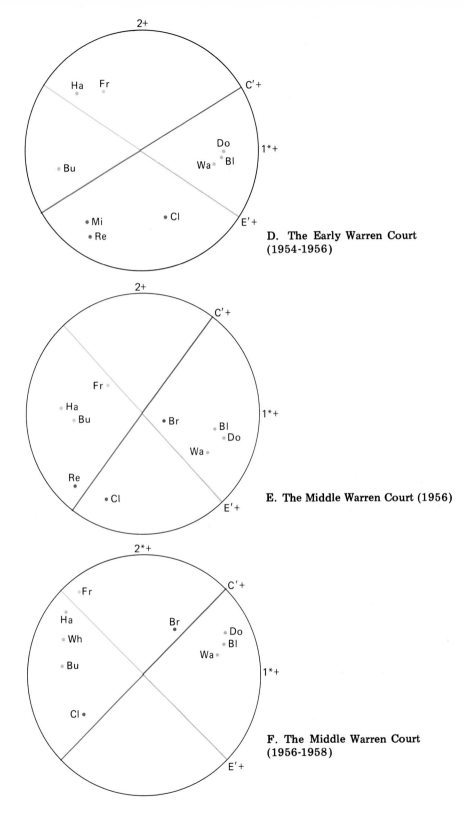

D. The Early Warren Court
(1954-1956)

E. The Middle Warren Court (1956)

F. The Middle Warren Court
(1956-1958)

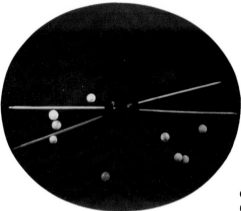

G. The Middle Warren Court
(1958-1961)

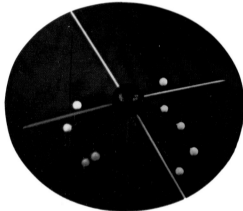

H. The Later Warren Court
(1961-1965)

I. The Later Warren Court
(1965-1967)

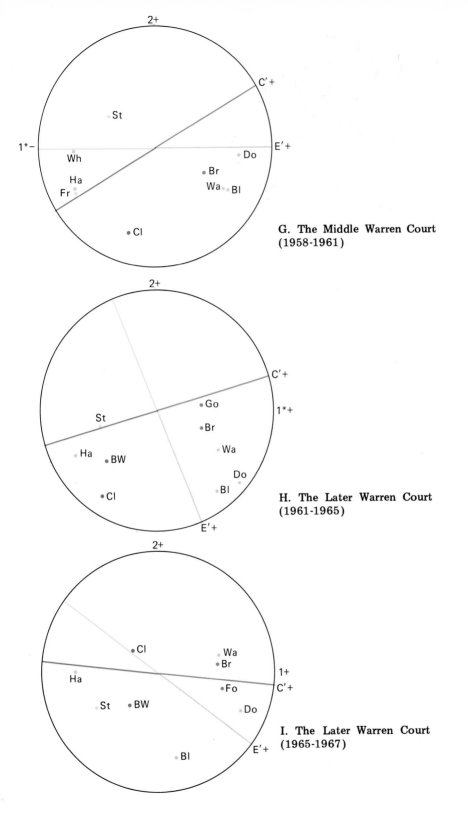

G. The Middle Warren Court
(1958-1961)

H. The Later Warren Court
(1961-1965)

I. The Later Warren Court
(1965-1967)

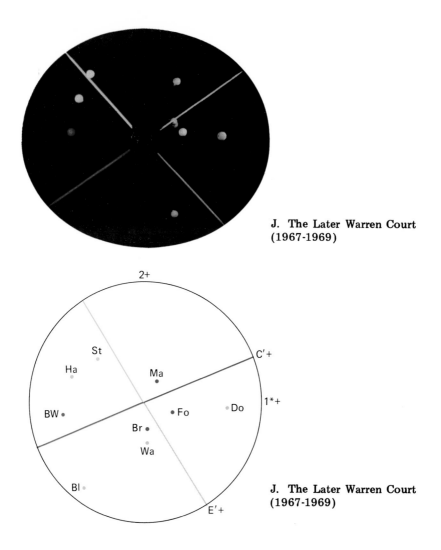

**J. The Later Warren Court
(1967-1969)**

**J. The Later Warren Court
(1967-1969)**

scales to be correlated with equal frequency with T_1; in four-space, however, the modal relationships clearly are between C and T_1, and E and T_2. The average correlations between C and E, and whichever of the oblique factors can be optimally analogized to either of them, are approximately .805±.048 for two-space; and the two scales are virtually identical at .876±.002 for four-space. Clearly C fits better than E in two-space, and both scales fit better in four-space, although it should be noted that the only substantial gain is for E rather than for C. In only three instances out of twenty is either C or E most highly correlated with either T_3 or T_4 in the four-space.

The minor scales, on the other hand, tend to fit better in two-space. Looking first at the more important minor scales F and N, we see that just as many (3 + 3) are accommodated in two-space as are (4 + 2) in four-space, and that the levels of correlation are substantially higher for the two-space fits. However, only one marginal A scale shows up in two-space; whereas five, of which all except one are either marginal or quasi, do appear in four-space. The four-space A scales are correlated at an average level less than that of the single one in two-space, but the level for that single scale in the third period is higher in four-space than in two. And the single J scale is apparent only in four-space.

The evidence clearly goes both ways, but generally the major scales fit better in four-space and the minor scales in two-space. This conclusion is exactly the opposite of what I had expected to find. My presumption was that the two major scales would be better delineated in oblique two-space but that the more complex oblique four-space would be necessary to accommodate the additional variance provided by the minor scales in addition to the major scales. Table 6.3 certainly contradicts that assumption. Two-space provides a much more parsimonious frame of reference for the interpretation of interscale relationships than does four-space, and on this evidence it is hard to conclude that the four-space frame is in any relevant sense "better" than that of the two-space. It is for these reasons that I decided to forgo the luxury of undertaking a comparison with oblique three-space as well. But there is one additional way in which we can examine the proposition that the two-space oblique solution is satisficing, at least among this set of oblimin oblique solutions.

It will be recalled that the direct (rho) correlations between pairs of the C and E composite scales and subscales and also between them and the F Scale, which was selected as the best of the minor scales, were reported in Table 4.5. That matrix was factor-analyzed with a biquartimin oblique program with the results shown in Table 6.4 and Figure 6.2. That figure shows one of the best empirical circumplex arrays that

TABLE 6.3
Cumulative Scale Structural Correlations* with Oblimin Oblique Factors,
Comparing Two- with Four-Dimensional Solutions (in Three-Place Decimals)

A. *Listing*

Period:	Two-Dimensional		Four-Dimensional			
	1	2	1	2	3	4
1	E 870 N 730(M)	C −933	E 870		C −912	
2	C −867	E −745 N −900	C −879	E −904	A −862(M)	N −536
3	C −887 E −731	A 658(M)	C −828 E −781	A −763(M) N 528(Q)		
4	C −950 E −739	F 860	C −783 E −850			F 521
5	E −927	C 882		C −877 F 588(Q)	E 920	
6	C 983	E −958 F 749(M) N 491(M)	C 946	E −933 F −852(M)		
7	E −942 C −824	F 931		E −946 J −878(Q) A −793		C −933
8	C −854 E −854		E −879 C −854 A −667(Q)			
9	C −895 E −794		A −623(Q)	E 887 C 833	F 654	
10		C −817 E −649	C −895	E −812		

TABLE 6.3 (continued)

B. *Totals*

Scale:	Two-Dimensional		Totals	Average	Four-Dimensional				Totals (Accept/ Dubious)	Average
	1	2			1	2	3	4		
C	7	3	10	853	6	2	1	1	10/0	874
E	7	3	10	757	4	5	1	0	10/0	878
F	0	3	3	847	0	2(M)(Q)	1	1	2/2	654
N	1	2	3	707	0	1(Q)	0	1	1/1	532
A	0	1(M)	1(M)	658	2(Q)(Q)	2(M)	1(M)	0	1/4	542
J	0	0	0	—	0	1(Q)	0	0	0/1	878
Totals	14	9	27		12	13	4	3	24/8	

*Except for the N scale in the 6th Period (= .491), all scale/analogue pairs listed are correlated at the criterion level of ≥ .500.
Legend: (M) = Marginal; (Q) = Quasi.

I have ever encountered. It has been a dozen years since I first read Louis Guttman's theoretical discussion of simplex and circumplex matrices,[2] and I have been aware throughout the intervening time that my phi matrices of United States Supreme Court voting behavior are quasi-simplex/circumplexes,[3] which explains, of course, my earlier efforts to provide a general interpretation of Supreme Court ideology, in *The Judicial Mind*, based on Guttman's theory.[4] I now think that my intuitions about the matter were entirely correct, but that my earlier data were inadequate for the use that I attempted to make of them. For reasons that I explained in the earlier study,[5] I had available to me at the time of its publication only partial data on the subscales of C and E, and even those data were grouped in subsample sizes too small to be very helpful. One advantage of the present re-analysis is that I have of course been able to learn from my earlier mistakes so that I now do have available complete and more rationally organized data on the subscales, although it should be noted that the earlier study does include a matrix strictly analogous to that of Table 4.5.[6]

TABLE 6.4

Reference Factor Loadings, Oblimin Oblique Structural Correlations, and Directional Cosines for and Correlations between Primary Oblique Factors for Eight Cumulative Scales and Subscales*

A. *Reference Factors*   B. *Structural Correlations*

(*Primary Factors*)

Variable:	1	2	Variable:	T_1	T_2
RP	.702	−.544	RP	.899	−.153
C	.909	−.368	C	.959	.102
FP	.910	−.330	FP	.938	.137
PF	.898	−.306	PF	.913	.152
W	.806	.314	W	.462	.663
E	.731	.639	E	.203	.918
$\overline{B}$	.730	.634	$\overline{B}$	.206	.913
F	.131	.833	F	−.401	.807

C. *Directional Cosines*   D. *Correlation*
   for Primary Oblique   *between Primary*
   Factors (T̄ Matrix)   *Oblique Factors*
                                     (*φ Matrix, T'T*)

Reference Factors:	Primary Factors		Cosine	Angle
	T_1	T_2		
1	.810	.474	−.1595	99° 10'
2	−.608	.894		

*See Table 4.5 for the rho correlation matrix for these scale variables.

Figure 6.2 arrays the variables of Table 4.5 in a semi-circumplex ("semi" because it spans only slightly more than a single quadrant, and at that the same one that is designated in Figure 5.1 as the liberalism sector) in precisely the same sequence except for the trivial (because minute) transposition in order of E and $\overline{B}$. The table shows that E is slightly more highly correlated with W than is $\overline{B}$, whereas $\overline{B}$ is even more slightly highly correlated with PF than is E, and because *both* PF *and* W precede both E and $\overline{B}$ in the sequence, there is at least a linear intransitivity explicit in these relationships, and it shows up as such in Figure 6.2. But the points for E and $\overline{\text{B}}$ are virtually indistinguishable, and I do not wish to overemphasize what is clearly the only exception to the rule of an extraordinarily symmetrical structure of ideological patterning.

Three closely aligned values constitute the core of civil liberty: the C scale and its fair procedure and political freedom subscales. Above and to the left of the C cluster (and therefore, of the C scale in this figure) lies the right to privacy, clearly in the segment of the circumplex attributed to political liberalism in Figure 5.1 and the region of the space that I previously have interpreted as being that of pragmatic, individualistic libertarianism.[7] This finding also confirms my long-standing belief[8] that the right to privacy raises issues that are fairly closely correlated with the core values of civil liberties, but that it also loads strongly on another dimension. This second dimension causes many individuals to view privacy as an issue somewhat different from other questions of civil liberty, and to act (and for the justices among them to vote) accordingly.[9] Supreme Court justices who have responded differently to privacy than to civil liberties issues generally include Robert Jackson, Felix Frankfurter, and Hugo Black, and they are only the most conspicuous examples.

The pro-union variable shows about the same degree of distinction from the E cluster as does RP from C, except that W lies within the liberalism quadrant and on the civil liberties side of the E scale. This placement is consistent with the point of view of many students of politics, who have tended to argue that the collective organization of workingmen into union associations raises important questions of political as well as of economic liberalism. We already have noted the virtual identity of the anti-business subscale with its parent E scale; and much lower than that cluster lies the F point, located beyond the economic liberalism sector and within the sector of classic conservatism. This locus for F is confirmatory of most of the limited observations on F that it was possible to make in the earlier study.[10]

The C and E scales are correlated at an angle of $63°$, which is of course the same, apart from error variance, as the $65°55'$ that is equivalent to the rho of .408 between C and E that is reported in Table 4.5. That relationship was input; what we could not have known in advance of the biquartimin analysis is precisely how the oblique factors would interpret the simplex matrix. Figure 6.2 shows that the basic function provided by T_1 and T_2 is to provide a frame for the six core values of liberalism: C, FP, PF, W, B, and E. On the other hand, RP is clearly a marginal value from this point of view, and indeed it falls precisely on the T_1 vector which demarks one boundary of the sector to which I refer; while F is sharply distinguished from all of the other seven values. The two oblique factors themselves are, as previously remarked, virtually orthogonal rather than oblique, with a correlation of less than $-.16$ and an angle of $99°10'$ (Table 6.4D). Table 6.4A provides, of course, the plotting coordinates for the variables; but Table 6.4B gives their correlations with the oblique factors, and what this table shows is that the six values that I referred to above as "the core values of liberalism" all correlate positively with both oblique vectors, but neither of the other two variables does so. RP is strongly loaded on T_1 but is negative with T_2, while F is strongly loaded with T_2 but negative with T_1. This finding, together with our observation of the corresponding Figure 6.2, obviously suggests the interpretation that oblique primary factor T_1 represents the combination of liberalism and privacy while T_2 represents a very different combination, that of liberalism and governmental fiscal authority. T_1 denotes the political emphasis of liberalism-plus, just as T_2 denotes the economic emphasis of liberalism-plus, and it is of course the presence of these two "pluses" that accounts for the deviations, of T_1 from C and of T_2 from E: if neither RP nor F had been included in the underlying matrix of interscale correlations, then we can be entirely confident that T_1 would appear as congruent with C, and T_2 as congruent with E. And this, of course, helps to explain the seeming anomaly, on which our analysis in this chapter has focused attention: that our criterion major scales are quite obliquely correlated, while our putatively "obliquely" rotated factors come out virtually orthogonal to each other. In Figure 6.2 we know that the presence of F and RP is what keeps T_1 and T_2 in a position of apparent independence, and the same explanation holds for the ten two-dimensional period perspectives that we observe in Figure 6.1: it is the presence in the phi matrices underlying those spaces of values, other than those of liberalism, and together averaging a third or more of the total content,[11] that accounts for the only fairly close relationship, between the primary oblique vectors and the cumulative scales, that has been brought out by our analysis in this chapter.

Alternatively, we can note that because oblique rotation tends to pick out the major clusters, T_1 projects into the most populous cluster and T_2 into the next most populous. But the principal (typal) clusters during most of the periods of the present analysis typically were *not* coaligned on any pair of axes, and this is another reason why, contrary to the major hypothesis stated at the beginning of this chapter, oblimin rotation did only a fair job of locating the C and E scales. If the aggregation of conservative type justices had been somewhat consistently larger and sufficiently more homogeneous to have partitioned consistently into two clusters—say, ECONS and PCONS—rather than

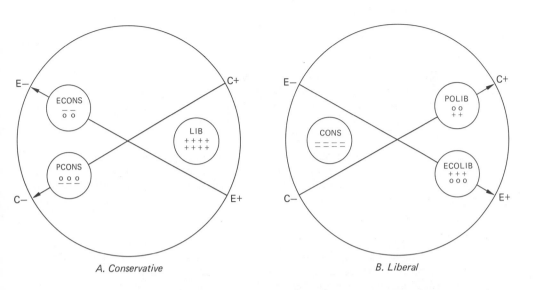

A. Conservative   B. Liberal

Figure 6.3 Two Paradigms of Predominance Clusters

into the three that in fact it was divided, then the diagram indicated in Figure 6.3A would have supplied a better-fitting model and then oblique rotation would have provided a more satisfactory solution. On the other hand, if the situation that was foreshadowed by Figure 6.1J—but that was not in the event experienced because of the election of Nixon rather than of Humphrey as President in 1968—had come to pass, with a large and consequently[12] splintering majority of liberals confronting a small but closely clustered coterie of conservatives, then the model of Figure 6.3B would have applied, and evidently, the fit of oblimin factors would have been just as good in that speculative case as was in fact that for Figure 6.3A during, say, the first, fourth, and fifth periods.

Notes to Chapter 6

1. See Rudolph J. Rummel, *Applied Factor Analysis* (Evanston: Northwestern University Press, 1970), Table 17-11, p. 422.

2. Louis Guttman, "A New Approach to Factor Analysis: The Radex," chapter 6 in Paul F. Lazarsfeld, ed., *Mathematical Thinking in the Social Sciences* (New York: The Free Press, 1954).

3. Edgar F. Borgatta, "On Analyzing Correlation Matrices: Some New Emphases," *Public Opinion Quarterly*, Vol. 22 (Winter 1958-59), pp. 516-28.

4. *The Judicial Mind,* chapter 8.

5. *Ibid.,* chapter 6, pp. 158ff.

6. *Idem,* Table 27, p. 173.

7. *Ibid.,* pp. 224, 271, shows a rank correlation matrix (but tau rather than rho) of ten scales and subscales—the same ones included in our present Table 4.5 except that two of those included earlier are deleted here, PE because of inadequate sample sizes and FC because of its amalgamation with $\bar{B}$, with which it is very highly correlated.

8. As evidenced, for example, by the chapter on physiological and psychological privacy, in my *Constitutional Politics* (New York: Holt, Rinehart and Winston, 1960), Part IV of which organizes the discussion of civil liberty into three chapters, dealing respectively with "First-Amendment Freedoms" (PF), "Procedural Due Process" (FP), and "The Implications of Ordered Liberty" (RP). Indeed, the book closes with the quotation of Justice Brandeis's well-known postulation of "the right to be let alone—the most comprehensive of rights and the right most valued by civilized men" and, in the citational footnote appurtenant thereto, his less well-known claim that the Founding Fathers of the Constitution of the United States "sought to protect Americans in their beliefs, their thoughts, their emotions and their sensations." Dissenting in *Olmstead* v. *United States,* 277 U.S. 438, 478 (1928).

9. After an intensive and extensive review of the evidence, a study that focuses upon the FP and RP subscales during the later Warren Court arrives quite independently at a similar conclusion, suggesting "the presence in search and seizure cases of a unique attitudinal factor." G. Gregory Fahlund, *Feedback in the Judicial Process: The Warren Court and Criminal Procedure* (in press; ms. p. 182).

10. See the first two reference-axis (I/II) perspectives of the centroid factorial spaces for 1957, 1959, and 1960, in *The Judicial Mind,* pp. 214-16.

11. Almost precisely two-thirds (67.02 per cent) of the total sample consists of C and E scales content, although this basis for categorization includes RP while excluding F; if RP (which includes 8.8 per cent of the total sample) is also excluded, the percentage of "other than core liberalism" content rises to over 40 per cent of the total.

12. The larger the majority (whether conservative or liberal) subuniverse, the more heterogeneous the *non*-liberalism/conservatism correlates of the dominant ideological position, as well as the greater the complexity of the social relations among the humans in whom the individual ideological phenotypes are embodied. It is much easier to remain united in opposition than in victory. For a more technical discussion of some of the relevant considerations, see the statement, discussion, and development of "the size principle" in William H. Riker, *The Theory of Political Coalitions* (New Haven: Yale University Press, 1962).

7
Smallest Space

In this chapter we shall consider a second alternative to the principal component factorial analysis that was presented in Chapter 5. The general approach of non-metric, multidimensional scaling, of which smallest-space analysis is a particular type, is, as Chapter 2 discussed, more appropriate to employ for the investigation of the empirical data for the samples here from the point of view of psychometric measurement theory, because it presumes ordinal rather than interval observations of the data and otherwise makes less demanding and therefore less unrealistic assumptions about the statistical properties of the data than does factor analysis. In addition, smallest-space computer programs are based upon an algorithm that readily makes possible sequential analysis at levels of increasing spatial complexity, thereby facilitating selection of that level of complexity that is in some relevant sense optimal.

Our discussion in this chapter will proceed as follows. First I shall present the data to support an analysis in three-dimensional smallest space, a level that I accepted as satisficing for reasons that I shall explicate below. Then we can consider in some detail the substantive findings about Supreme Court ideology that follow from our time-series examination of the (Euclidean) three-dimensional spaces. After that we shall compare the relative adequacy of the corresponding solutions at other levels (one, two, and four) of spatial complexity.

The matrices to be interpreted by smallest-space analysis may be composed of correlation coefficients, and in the present instance they are. But one advantage of smallest-space over factor analysis is that it can be used with many other measures of association besides correlation coefficients. Output takes the form of "coordinates" for "dimensions," rather than of correlations with (loadings upon) factors. These coordinates are normalized (in the program that I used) to range between values of ± 100; but it should be noted that, unlike orthogonal factor analysis—which apportions the variance allocated to *each* factor approximately equally between the positive and negative vector segments—smallest space makes such an equal apportionment consistently only for the first dimension. The reported coordinates for the second and higher order dimensions range mostly between −100 and zero with only a few, and these mostly on the second dimension, having positive coordinate values. This reflects the circumstance that factor analysis proceeds in relation to a fixed centroid point of origin, while the center or origin of a smallest-space structure is determined, in a sense arbitrarily, by rank-order rather than by least-squares considerations. What is relevant here is that the first dimension places liberals and conservatives in different, vertically defined hemispheres; but generally speaking, all points tend to be positions within the negative segments of the second, third, and fourth dimensions. This means that the center of a two-dimensional smallest space will typically be closer to the point (00, −30) rather than to the point (00, 00)—which is where it *would* be in a two-dimensional factorial plot. Stated alternatively, a two-dimensional,

TABLE 7.1

Smallest-Space Coordinates

A. *Three-Dimensional Space*

Deck	Variable	Dimensions			Deck	Variable	Dimensions		
		1	2	3			1	2	3
1	Vi	75	−48	−100	2	Vi	88	−87	−67
	Bl	−99	−25	−86		Bl	−100	−74	−26
	Re	52	−100	−62		Re	89	−43	−100
	Fr	85	47	−59		Fr	−53	63	−53
	Do	−93	−56	−58		Do	−91	−100	−75
	Mu	−98	10	−65		Ja	10	74	−80
	Ja	100	09	−68		Bu	49	−10	27
	Ru	−100	−18	−45		Cl	43	−57	−38
	Bu	92	−53	−35		Mi	100	−36	−30
3	Wa	−22	−77	−55	4	Wa	−73	−42	−78
	Bl	−95	−32	−84		Bl	−95	−02	−71

TABLE 7.1A (continued)

Deck	Variable	Dimensions			Deck	Variable	Dimensions		
		1	2	3			1	2	3
	Re	100	−100	−64		Re	72	−100	−44
	Fr	00	51	−31		Fr	24	59	−79
	Do	−100	−52	−23		Do	−100	−06	−13
	Ja	73	31	−29		Bu	100	−21	−31
	Bu	91	−48	−16		Cl	−11	−75	−35
	Cl	22	−88	−06		Mi	73	−47	−100
	Mi	82	−18	−100		Ha	85	61	−32
5	Wa	−79	−44	−40	6	Wa	−74	−28	−46
	Bl	−89	−05	−37		Bl	−94	−23	−52
	Re	89	−73	−75		Fr	61	44	−84
	Fr	47	39	−95		Do	−100	−00	−76
	Do	−100	−17	−100		Bu	100	−34	−83
	Bu	75	01	−16		Cl	61	−100	−83
	Cl	31	−100	−76		Ha	87	31	−58
	Ha	100	16	−67		Br	−39	02	−100
	Br	−30	10	−74		Wh	82	−15	−23
7	Wa	−70	−66	−65	8	Wa	−74	−35	−42
	Bl	−82	−71	−65		Bl	−74	−100	−73
	Fr	100	−52	−89		Do	−100	−74	−100
	Do	−100	−20	−65		Cl	63	−89	−22
	Cl	37	−100	−62		Ha	100	−35	−66
	Ha	99	−46	−100		Br	−49	−09	−15
	Br	−49	−30	−82		St	70	−08	−95
	Wh	96	−47	−19		BW	53	−81	−96
	St	48	05	−58		Go	−51	19	−90
9	Wa	76	16	−71	10	Wa	35	−16	39
	Bl	08	−100	−83		Bl	−45	96	−21
	Do	100	−54	−56		Do	100	−15	−100
	Cl	−31	03	−100		Ha	−93	−52	−49
	Ha	−100	02	−63		Br	35	−17	34
	Br	65	15	−58		St	−69	−100	−35
	St	−73	−55	−29		BW	−100	−05	−23
	BW	−32	−08	03		Fo	53	−19	−41
	Fo	68	−25	−03		Ma	37	−84	09

TABLE 7.1 (continued)

B. *One-, Two-, and Four-Dimensional Space.*

Dimensions:		I	II		IV			
Deck	Variable	1	1	2	1	2	3	4
1	Vi	−99	99	−41	76	−73	−20	−01
	Bl	100	−100	−14	−95	−29	−36	−35
	Re	−99	82	−100	56	−100	−100	−61
	Fr	−100	89	56	87	44	−86	−52
	Do	100	−100	−15	−85	−62	−89	−43
	Mu	100	−100	−13	−99	02	−28	−58
	Ja	−100	90	55	100	26	−49	−47
	Ru	100	−100	−14	−100	−23	−53	−74
	Bu	−100	100	−41	91	−70	−13	−100
2	Vi	100	80	−75	90	58	−92	−29
	Bl	−91	−100	−58	−100	73	−51	−29
	Re	100	88	−44	92	34	−100	−100
	Fr	−36	−63	51	−60	−87	−60	−39
	Do	−100	−85	−100	−92	87	−67	−99
	Ja	52	−12	69	−02	−100	−94	−70
	Bu	37	74	10	40	−09	38	−86
	Cl	25	47	−37	56	28	−39	−03
	Mi	90	100	−23	100	19	−38	−61
3	Wa	31	−22	−90	−33	45	−71	−100
	Bl	97	−100	−42	−100	−21	−10	−82
	Re	−100	100	−99	99	67	−12	−83
	Fr	−16	−04	30	23	−100	−85	−100
	Do	100	−100	−68	−93	12	−46	−11
	Ja	−49	49	22	73	−81	−72	−32
	Bu	−66	71	−73	100	22	−74	−51
	Cl	15	09	−100	27	69	−100	−51
	Mi	−75	87	−28	81	−28	25	−52
4	Wa	67	−88	−16	−73	−43	−92	−50
	Bl	89	−97	−08	−98	−05	−82	−43
	Re	−52	63	−100	73	−100	−64	−77
	Fr	−11	46	70	29	70	−100	−57
	Do	100	−100	00	−100	11	−43	−92
	Bu	−74	100	−20	100	−17	−85	−100
	Cl	24	−30	−78	−12	−50	−09	−46

TABLE 7.1B (continued)

		I	II		IV			
		1	1	2	1	2	3	4
	Mi	−43	65	−83	79	−42	−79	−13
	Ha	−100	78	68	84	74	−25	−49
5	Wa	−81	−80	−45	−67	−22	−100	−80
	Bl	−87	−88	−18	−84	−02	−76	−30
	Re	94	83	−85	90	−75	−51	−56
	Fr	52	44	34	44	40	02	−21
	Do	−100	−100	−28	−100	−25	−22	−32
	Bu	78	85	−07	75	11	−97	−06
	Cl	25	44	−100	38	−100	−31	−46
	Ha	100	100	06	100	31	−64	−90
	Br	−28	−25	−09	−25	11	−18	−100
6	Wa	81	−90	−22	−74	−31	−57	−31
	Bl	98	−98	−35	−95	−27	−66	−45
	Fr	−42	79	−100	65	52	−15	−38
	Do	100	−100	−50	−100	−02	−46	−61
	Bu	−100	100	−11	100	−43	−64	−100
	Cl	−74	72	46	62	−100	00	−33
	Ha	−80	95	−75	94	24	−44	−39
	Br	43	−39	−53	−38	−02	−16	−93
	Wh	−88	99	−42	87	−23	−100	−40
7	Wa	100	−81	−49	−70	−51	−66	−58
	Bl	100	−86	−50	−82	−38	−53	−44
	Fr	−100	98	−51	100	−46	−43	−85
	Do	100	−100	−10	−100	−03	−82	−90
	Cl	−99	33	−100	43	−100	−92	−100
	Ha	−100	98	−48	98	−23	−23	−64
	Br	99	−58	−16	−54	−16	−37	−99
	Wh	−100	100	−04	97	−08	−100	−40
	St	−99	58	18	58	27	−82	−100
8	Wa	−69	−73	−48	−85	−45	−23	−60
	Bl	−82	−72	−96	−84	−96	−98	−79
	Do	−100	−100	−86	−100	−72	−89	−12
	Cl	77	68	−100	55	−100	−18	−22
	Ha	100	100	−52	100	−42	−60	−54
	Br	−44	−52	−21	−57	−35	−04	−99
	St	80	71	−19	71	−03	−79	−52
	BW	66	62	−60	47	−87	−100	−100
	Go	−53	−54	06	−56	28	−84	−51

TABLE 7.1 (continued)

		1	1	2	1	2	3	4
9	Wa	84	75	21	63	28	−21	−75
	Bl	11	21	−100	00	−100	−06	−81
	Do	100	100	−44	100	−47	−41	−69
	Cl	−28	−31	26	−41	04	31	−62
	Ha	−100	−100	01	−100	25	−47	−100
	Br	72	72	11	61	28	−24	−59
	St	−77	−77	−40	−81	−41	−71	−78
	BW	−45	−34	−37	−46	−17	−61	−03
	Fo	80	79	−19	55	−06	−100	−82
10	Wa	−22	−04	−47	35	13	46	−74
	Bl	100	73	−100	−43	−100	−05	−21
	Do	−100	−100	−06	100	17	−100	−62
	Ha	54	90	31	−100	46	−34	−42
	Br	−22	−04	−31	35	19	40	−82
	St	32	58	52	−79	97	−22	−44
	BW	68	100	−13	−98	−02	−33	−100
	Fo	−38	−33	−11	54	19	−34	−52
	Ma	−32	−15	25	40	72	25	−22

TABLE 7.2

Directional Cosines for, Correlations between, and Cumulative
Scale Correlations with Scale Vectors in Two- to Four-
Dimensional Smallest Space

A. *Directional Cosines*

Dimension-
ality: Decks:

		1		2			3	
		C'	E'	C'	E'	N'	C'	E'
2	1	−.71	−.71	−1.00	.00	.71	−.84	−.52
	2	.71	−.71	.00	−1.00	−.18	.54	−.85
3	1	−.62	−1.00	−.99	.00	.00	−.70	−.46
	2	.62	.00	.00	−.94	−.90	.70	−.76
	3	.49	.00	−.15	.33	.43	−.17	−.46
4	1	−.70	−1.00	−.99	.00	.00	−.67	−.84
	2	.70	.00	.00	.94	−.89	−.47	.17
	3	.00	.00	−.15	.00	.45	−.33	.51
	4	−.14	.00	.00	−.35	.00	−.47	.08

TABLE 7.2A (continued)

Dimen-
sionality: Decks:

		4		5		6		7	
2	1	−.86	−.82	−.60	−.69	−.71	−.71	−.86	−1.00
	2	.52	−.57	.80	−.73	−.71	.71	.52	.00
3	1	−.89	−.89	−.80	−.79	−.71	−.78	−.89	−.99
	2	.36	−.45	.52	−.61	.71	−.62	.45	.00
	3	.27	.00	−.31	.00	.00	.00	.00	−.10
4	1	−.93	−.75	−.89	−.92	−.71	−.69	−.63	−.99
	2	.33	−.45	.36	−.28	.71	−.69	.63	.00
	3	.00	.45	.00	−.28	.00	−.07	−.44	−.10
	4	−.14	−.30	−.27	.00	.00	−.21	.00	.00

		8		9		10	
2	1	−.96	−.37	.99	.80	−.93	−.54
	2	.29	−.93	−.10	−.60	.37	−.84
3	1	−.75	−.57	.97	.82	.85	.66
	2	.18	−.82	−.24	−.41	−.51	.73
	3	.11	.08	.00	−.41	.09	.15
4	1	−.94	−.49	.96	.88	.89	.65
	2	.28	−.71	−.29	−.44	.36	−.65
	3	.09	.11	.00	.18	.00	.03
	4	−.19	.49	.00	.00	−.27	−.39

B. *Correlations between Vectors C'/E'*

Dimensionality: 2   3   4

Deck	Cosine	Angle	Cosine	Angle	Cosine	Angle		
1	.0000	90°00′	.6155	52°00′	.7001	45°35′		
2	.0000	90°00′	−.0491	92°50′	.0000	90°00′		
3	−.0286	91°40′	−.1327	97°40′	.2763	74°00′		
4	.4092	65°50′	.6350	50°35′	.5986	53°55′		
5	−.1668	99°35′	.3157	71°40′	.7141	44°25′		
6	.0000	90°00′	.1105	83°40′	.0000	90°00′		
7	.8576	31°00′	.8900	27°10′	.6747	47°35′		
8	.0869	85°00′	.2889	73°10′	.1820	79°30′		
9	.9245	22°20′	.8910	27°00′	.9693	14°15′		
10	.1876	79°10′	.2022	78°20′	.4531	63°00′	*Avg.*	
Avg. *Cos.*	.2270	(76°47′)	.3767	(67°52′)	.4568	(62°49′)	.3535	(69°18′)
Avg. *Ang.*	(.2692)	74°27.5′	(.4161)	65°24.5′	(.4972)	60°13.5′	(.3956)	66°42′

TABLE 7.2 (continued)

C. Correlations between Scales/Scale Vectors (Three-Place Decimals)

Dimensionality

Deck	C/C'				E/E'				N/N'			
	1	2	3	4	1	2	3	4	1	2	3	4
1	857	915	983*	983	861	953	987*	962#	—	—	—	—
2	828	917	967*	967	225	800	800	933*	067	833	900	950
3	879	983	996*	996	622	810	925	992*	—	—	—	—
4	833	1000*	1000	1000	900	967	967	983*	—	—	—	—
5	831	936	966*	966	920	945	936#	987*	—	—	—	—
6	895	996*	996	996	766	929	967	983*	—	—	—	—
7	857	900	900	1000*	857	996	1000*	1000	—	—	—	—
8	867	967	996*	979#	833	967	983*	967#	—	—	—	—
9	967	1000*	1000	1000	753	711#	921	937*	—	—	—	—
10	979	967#	967	983*	214	941*	929#	929#	—	—	—	—
Avg.	879.3	958.1	977.1	987.0*	695.1	901.9	941.5	967.3*	—	—	—	—

Note: * signifies the highest correlation between each pair of vectors, for each set of dimensionalities, for each deck; if more than one dimensionality is equally high, only the lower dimensionality is asterisked.
signifies a higher dimensionality with a lower correlation than that of a corresponding lower dimensionality, for the same pair in the same deck.

smallest-space configuration will characteristically appear to be clustered in the lower half of the space; and typically the ideal-point vectors of a three-dimensional configuration will appear as directed primarily *forward* (*i.e.*, toward the viewer) and *downward.* Such an aspect is a result of the format of the analytical technique rather than a result of any substantive implications of the data.

Table 7.1A reports the coordinates for three-dimensional space (3D); part B of the same table reports the corresponding coordinates for one-, two-, and four-space (1D, 2D, and 4D), to which we shall turn later in this chapter. The scale vector analogues are located in two- to four-dimensional space by the same method employed for the factor analysis, and therefore equivalent information concerning directional cosines for the scale vectors, for their intercorrelations, and for their correlations with the criterion scales, is presented in Table 7.2.[1] This table includes, in addition to complete data for the two major scales, corresponding information (in parts A and C) for the N scale in the second period, which was the only instance in which any of the minor scales could be accommodated at a satisfactory level of rank correlation in any of the three-spaces.

The data of Tables 7.1A and 7.2A provide all the empirical information needed for the construction of physical (*i.e.*, 3D Euclidean) models of Supreme Court ideology during the ten periods of our analysis. These physical models were constructed primarily as a guide to the substantive interpretation that will be presented in the next section of this chapter, but they proffer also the most helpful basis for reader apprehension of the relationships involved. To the latter end these physical models were coated with fluorescent paints and then photographed in color under ultraviolet light, so as to direct attention to the patterning of the configuration of ideal-points (rather than upon the indispensable—from a mechanical point of view—supporting apparatus of base, pedestal, and vectors which direct the ideal-points themselves); all of the supporting structures have therefore been blacked out in the photographs that are presented in Figure 7.1. To carry out this scheme it has been necessary to make certain minor compromises in order to keep within the bounds of feasibility. Fluorescent paints are available, for example, in only half a dozen colors, of which chartreuse *is* one such but plain yellow is not: this result is a consequence of the laws of optical physics rather than of those laws imputed (depending upon one's ideology) to the marketplace. Consequently I have used chartreuse as the color for the ECONS type and orange for the negative vector segment of the E$'$ scale analogue (rather than the yellow specified by Figure 5.1) in Figure 7.1 (but not in Figure 7.3, below, where it was of course possible to follow Figure 5.1, and I have therefore done so.) For similar reasons, I have used light blue rather than dark blue as the color for the positive vector segment of the E' scale analogue in Figure 7.1; again, the colloidal restrictions are such that dark blue is neither an available fluorescent color nor visible, in any case, under ultraviolet light. But the two-dimensional patterning of the colors in the photographs follows, like Figure 5.1 that of the color wheel, including the use of complementary colors (green/red and blue/orange) for the C' and E' scale analogues respectively.[2]

The models of Figure 7.1 have been constructed in the conventional format, so that the first dimension is abscissal and its positive direction is to the right-hand side of each figure. The second dimension is vertical, and its positive direction is toward the top of the figure. The third dimension is orthogonal to the other two at their point of intersection, so that its positive direction points away from the viewer, and the ideal points with negative coordinates with the third dimension are the ones that are closest from the viewer's perspective. Generally speaking, therefore, we should expect to find (using a clock metric for specifying locations) that *all* types will tend to project forward, with liberals in the three-o'clock region; political liberals (POLIBS) will be above them and closer to 1:30; economic conservatives (ECONS) will be around 10:30; conservatives at 9:00; and political conservatives (PCONS) at 7:30. Similarly, the $C'+$ vector should generally appear in the region of 1:00 to 2:00, with $E'+$ tending to fall near the region of 4:00 to 5:00 o'clock.

Certain dimensions must be reflected for certain periods in order for the configurations to be equivalently positioned in the structures. Only the first dimension needed to be reflected in the first five periods, and also in the seventh and eighth; both the first and second dimensions were reflected in the sixth period; and only the second dimension was reflected in the tenth period. No dimensions needed to be reflected, but the positions of the second and third are *reversed* (i.e., the third is the vertical dimension) in the structure of model 7.1I for period 9. This is tantamount, of course, to viewing the structure in conventional format, but from the perspective of the top (instead of the front) and with the second dimension reflected. Otherwise the perspective from which the figures are viewed is generally very similar, although I have shifted it slightly from period to period in order to present views that would delineate the significant relationships in the configuration better than a dead head-on view sometimes would have done (as when, for example, one ideal-point would have appeared eclipsed, by another with a more negative loading on the third dimension). Clearly no two-dimensional object, including a photograph, can be more than suggestive of depth perception and therefore of the shifting aspects of any three-dimensional object. But it is not possible to distribute a set of three-dimensional models along with this book, so we must settle for the second-best alternative provided by the photographs. Of course, there is nothing to preclude any reader from constructing the models himself on the basis of the information presented here. Apart from some elementary knowledge of analytical geometry and, preferably, access to a desk calculator, all of the information that I used is in Table 7.1A and 7.2A, as I stated above.

The color coding is designed, as we noted in Chapter 5, to facilitate the identification, in the discrete setting afforded by particular periods, of characteristic ideological positions, and also to facilitate tracking them through time—because although the structures are static, I am acutely aware that their significance is in their dynamic import. Individuals can be most readily identified by comparing any of the photographs of Figure 7.1 with the corresponding plot, for the same period, of Figure 7.3, in which points are identified by name. The correspondence between the two-dimensional plots of the latter figure and the views presented in Figure 7.1 is sufficiently close so that in most instances identification will be instantaneous and effortless. In the few cases in which it is not, reference to Table 7.1 should resolve the question without too much difficulty. The structure for each period is designated as A, B, C . . . J, corresponding to the periods 1, 2, 3 . . .10; and for convenience of reference I shall refer to these elements of Figure 7.1 by their subdesignation letters (as A, B, etc.) in the discussion that follows. I shall take full advantage of the fact that I do have before me the three-dimensional physical structures to observe and that I am not confined to their perception from any particular standpoint.

From the Euclidean Point of View

The first period was that of the waning heyday of what had been the Roosevelt Court, and seven of its nine members were his selections, including several, such as Black, Reed, Frankfurter, and Douglas, whose appointments stemmed from the immediate aftermath of the Court-packing episode of 1937 although they constituted almost as mixed an ideological bag as had the New Deal itself. View (A) shows that this court was bifurcated into two clusters, one consisting of the four liberals (Murphy, Rutledge, Black, and Douglas) and the other a somewhat broader-ranging array composed of the remaining five justices. But even at that and even though they include individuals representing all three of the conservative ideological types, various subsets of four of these five non-liberals—for instance, all except Frankfurter or all except

Reed—are as tightly clustered as are the same number (four) of liberals. The liberalism plane—and it is an empirical manifestation of the same phenomenon about which I had hypothesized in *The Judicial Mind*[3]—is clearly evident, transecting the space from the seventh to the first octant. The seventh octant is where the two political conservatives, Reed and Vinson, and the conservative Burton all project, and Jackson is almost with them (in the light of his marginal placement within the sixth octant): these four all are arrayed around the $C'-$ vector. But there are no liberals clustered around the $C'+$ vector; instead, all four of them are much more closely related to $E'+$ than to $C'+$, and the position in which we observe them in this initial period is definitely that of the economic liberal (ECOLIB) type, with which none of the justices in our sample is characteristically associated. But when seen from above, Frankfurter and Jackson, as well as Burton, are placed midway between the $C'-$ and $E'-$ vectors. As Table 7.2C shows, both scales are exceptionally highly correlated with the scale vectors in Figure 7.1 (A), at .98 and .99; and in general, there is nothing apparent about the structure that contradicts either the theoretical implications of Chapter 2 or the substantive findings of the factor analysis for this same period.

The structure for the second period as shown in (B) is markedly different from not only the initial period but also all of the remaining periods that follow. The reason for this sharp change in structure is also evident: there was a double change in personnel (instead of the single change that usually occurred) between the first and second periods, due to the replacement of both Murphy and Rutledge—probably the two most consistently liberal justices ever to serve together on the Supreme Court—by the very much more conservative Minton and Clark. From a typal point of view, what occurred was the transfer of two LIB positions to the PCONS category; and with only half as many liberals but twice as many political conservatives, a major change in structure was unavoidable. For one thing, the first smallest space dimension does, as previously pointed out, apportion the variance between a major and minor subset; and given the rule of equality in voting weight, there is no way in which a minority of two individuals could carry enough weight to determine the cutting point for the first dimensional division. Conceivably Black and Douglas could have joined with the two new political conservatives or with others of that type to define what the structure might have interpreted as an economically oriented plurality, but that did not happen. Instead, Frankfurter appears in octant five and Jackson is at the margin between the fifth and sixth octants, with Black and Douglas still in octant eight, as they were in (A), so that these are the four who constitute the most positively oriented plurality subset on the first dimension in (B). And the explanation is obvious when we examine the scales: C is both larger and more consistent than E, and therefore it follows that the relationship of Black and Douglas with Frankfurter and Jackson on the C scale carries greater weight, that is, assumes more statistical importance, than does the alternative relationship of Black and Douglas with Minton and Reed on the E scale. The next most obvious aspect of the second period structure is that C' and E' are almost perfectly correlated with the first and second dimensions respectively and that the two scale vector analogues are therefore virtually orthogonal to each other, as Table 7.2B indicates. Somewhat less obvious is the appearance of a third scale vector, that for N', which is the only minor scale to fit these structures, and then only in this second period. For reasons explained in the second footnote of this chapter, the $N'+$ vector is very highly and positively correlated with $E'+$ in (B), and therefore it is behind it (*i.e.*, slightly more positively correlated with the third dimension) in the lower half of the structure; but the $N'-$ vector is plainly evident in front of $E'-$ in the center of the upper half of the structure shown in (B). The substantive inference demanded by this finding is that, at least during the second period, attitudes of the Vinson Court toward policy issues of federalism were indistinguishable from the attitudes of the same group of judges toward economic liberalism. Burton is the only representative of the modern conservative type in (B), and he is the only one to coordinate positively with the third dimension—and therefore to project into the third octant in the posterior hemisphere of the structure. The (B) structure otherwise manifests an almost perfectly balanced division of the Court into three clusters, separated by angles of about $120°$ in each instance with Black and Douglas at four to five o'clock, Jackson and Frankfurter at 12:00 and 1:00, and with the four political conservatives, Clark, Vinson, Reed, and Minton, at 7:00 to 8:00 o'clock. As we observed to be true in the case of the first period, this structure in no way disconfirms the predictions of our theoretical model or the findings from the factor analysis for this period.

The third dimension of the structures for these first two periods denotes a number of relationships that would necessarily be obscured in a two-dimensional space. For example Burton, who is the only representative of the conservative type in either period, is separated from the ECONS and the PCONS types in both periods by appearing, as required by the Figure 5.1 paradigm, medially between them, but he is also separated from both types by being more positive on the third dimension. And in the second period, Burton the conservative is in a position that would be—except for the second dimension—directly opposite to that of liberals Black and Douglas.

The structure for third period (C) shows a partial reversion to that of the initial period, reflecting Vinson's replacement by Warren, and the consequent augmentation of the weight of the liberal point of view— although it should be noted that in this, Warren's first, term on the Court, his position is closer to that of Clark and just as close to that of the other two political conservatives, Reed and Minton, as it is to that of Black and Douglas. The scale analogues remain orthogonal to each other, but rotated back counterclockwise about $45°$; and $E'-$ is rotated slightly positively on the third dimension. Accompanying and partially causing the rotation of the scale vectors is a similar counterclockwise rotation in the positions of Frankfurter and Jackson: Frankfurter in (C) appears in the same position occupied by Jackson in (B), while Jackson in (C) has moved to a much more conservative position near the other boundary of the fifth octant. Burton's position has also moved counter-clockwise with the rotation of the scale vectors, but he is no longer positively coordinated with the third dimension, and he is, indeed, slightly more negative than Clark, although otherwise his position as the only representative of the modern conservative type remains relatively very much the same in relation to the economic conservatives and the political conservatives—below the former and behind the latter. In this third period both Clark and Warren appear in the sector assigned by Figure 5.1 to the classic conservative type, which is not the correct modal type for either of them. As I had remarked in *The Judicial Mind* and as figures (B) and (C) show clearly, during the second period, which was Clark's first period, he assumed an ideological position that was closest to, but slightly more liberal than that of Chief Justice Vinson. The third period was Warren's first, and what (C) shows is that Clark had moved—partly in strict accord with the rotation, of course, but beyond that into a much less negative relation to the third dimension— so that he is right on the liberalism plane and almost precisely equidis-tant from the $C'-$ and the $E'+$ vectors. This left him now closer to the new Chief Justice Warren than to anyone else. Whether the apparent switch in affinity from the old Chief Justice to the new was coinciden-tal could not be determined, of course, on the basis of (B) and (C) alone; but certainly we can pick up this thread again when we turn, as we shall presently, to (D). The other general aspect of (C) worth remarking is that although appropriately and transitively sequenced, the typal clusters are less sharply demarked from each other, which is due primarily to the failure of either Clark or Warren to adhere more closely to others of their respective modal types. But the change in the Chief Justiceship clearly had as much effect upon the Court's structure as did the substitution of two persons at the end of the first period; and the direction of the change accompanying Warren's appointment was away from the strong political conservatism symbolized by the structure of (B) and toward a more balanced consideration and disposition of questions of both civil liberties and economic policy.

In the fourth period the scale vectors are much more obliquely correlated, reflecting Warren's movement into the liberalism cluster with Black and Douglas. This was a position that for Warren remained unchanged during his remaining six periods on the Court, with a consequent sharpening of the division between the liberal and the conservative weights on both major scales. Indeed, we can now see the second and third periods as transitional between two isotopic expressions of the normal structure of the Court, the attainment of which requires a critical mass of sufficiently committed liberals: Warren was not yet sufficiently committed during his first period on the Court, but he was so in (D). Otherwise, the structure of the configuration of (D) is remarkably similar to that of (C), with two exceptions. Clark is *positive* on the first dimension in (D) for the only time during his eight periods of service on the Court, and he has therefore moved further in the same direction as Warren, but not nearly so far. The other change was in personnel rather than in position: Harlan replaced Jackson in (D), and he moved directly into what we would have to predict, on the basis of figures (A) through (C), would have been Jackson's position had the latter remained on the Court during the fourth period. Such placement as an ECONS was not, of course, what became modal for Harlan, who is identified instead as a modern or balanced conservative during the next five periods. Evidently, his initial experience in the role of Supreme Court justice was, as we have observed to be true also of Warren, a time of learning during which he was working to define the ideological posture that he would be prepared to stand by and defend. My opinion is that Warren's affiliation with the LIB cluster—and Clark's continuing to tag along—was the principal both signifier and significant of change in the fourth period, whereas in this particular instance the personnel change of Harlan for Jackson was *de minimus* in its effect on the ideological structure.

In the fifth period Harlan did move into a CONS position, very similar, except for Harlan's greater intensity, to that of Burton. Clark, however, had retreated; and while Warren moved even more strongly into the center of the liberal cluster, Clark moved negatively backward on the first dimension into a normal PCONS position closer to Reed. One possible explanation for Clark's backsliding may be found in the personnel change: Minton, who had remained firmly ensconced in the seventh octant throughout his three periods on the Court, as seen in figures (B), (C), and (D), had been replaced by Brennan, who appears in the fifth octant of (E) in a position of moderately positive orientation toward both scale vectors, which remained his characteristic standpoint during the next five periods also. In effect as well as in appearance, as figure (E) suggests, Brennan had interposed himself between Clark and Warren, proffering a point of view that was more generally congenial than Clark's could be to Warren: Clark continued to vote in support of Warren on economic issues, but experience served to underscore his fundamental differences with the Chief on many aspects of civil liberties policy; whereas Brennan could and did continue to go virtually all the way—of Warren's limited way, at least—on both major issues. And in figure (E), Brennan appears to be almost as much a part of the LIB cluster as any of the other three, who are modern liberals, although technically he does project into the fifth octant while the three LIBS all project into the eighth octant. The critical consideration that accounts for his identification with the POLIB type is, it will be recalled, the consideration that his scale vector projections in four-dimensional principal-component space are C+/Eo in a majority (four out of six) of instances—including this fifth period, in which his projections in the factor space are +.37 on C' and −.14 on E'. Evidently, Brennan projects moderately positively on both C' and E' in the smallest *three*-dimensional space of figure (E); in fact, it is +.52 on C' and +.18 on E'. From the perspective of (E), the ideal-points for Brennan as well as the three LIBS all fall within the angle formed by the $C'+$ and the $E'+$ vectors, while the ideal-points for both of the CONS (Burton and Harlan) fall on the opposite side within the angle defined by $C'-$ and $E'-$. Furthermore, Frankfurter, the only ECONS in this period, projects above and slightly forward of $E'-$ in the sixth octant, while the two PCONS Reed and Clark project into the sixth octant, below and in front of $C'-$. Thus, the structure of this fifth period conforms precisely to the paradigm of Figure 5.1, subject to the sole exception created by Brennan's placement, which would have to have been more closely aligned to and slightly above $C'+$ in order for figure (E) to have conformed perfectly with the paradigm.

The structure of the sixth period is remarkably similar to that of the fifth, with Whittaker's replacement of Reed the only personnel change. This left Clark as the only PCONS, and he continued to move further to the left (negatively) on the first dimension, to about the position that Reed had occupied in the previous period. Frankfurter, the only ECONS, also continued his parallel shift toward a more negative position on the first dimension, which began in the third period with Warren's appointment and persisted through the seventh, his own final period on the Court, when Frankfurter was completely negative on the first dimension and, as we shall observe presently, he projected as a balanced conservative. In this fifth period, the consequence of Frankfurter's incremental movement toward conservatism on C' as well as on E' was to put him in the CONS cluster even as early as this period; and since there is no change in the position of the three LIBS and Brennan between the fifth and sixth periods, the overall result was to restore the sort of balance that characterized the first period, with five conservatives of one type or another arrayed in opposition to a smaller and therefore tighter cluster of four liberals (of both types). The two scale vectors are orthogonal to each other, but oblique with regard to the first and second reference dimensions, and both are independent of the third dimension, which is, therefore, itself orthogonal to the plane defined, alternatively, by the C' and E' vectors and the first and second dimensions. Consequently, we can say with some confidence that in our perspective of (F), what we observe *are* the projections of the ideal-points onto the liberalism plane; and conversely, to the extent that our sense of depth perception permits us to infer the varying degrees of negativism on the third dimension, ranging from Clark's foremost projection, to the scale vectors themselves, we can sense the effect of non-liberal/conservative influence upon the ideal-point vectors—and these seem to be equivalently apportioned, in their effects, among LIB and CONS types alike.

In the seventh period the relevant space is almost entirely compressed into the quadrant defined by the seventh and eighth octants. This was Frankfurter's last period, and he spent it in a posture of almost perfectly balanced conservatism, in a position hardly distinguishable from that of Harlan. Stewart, an ECONS who replaced Burton in this period, appears only marginally in the fifth octant; but Clark and Whittaker are in appropriate modal positions as a PCONS and a CONS, respectively. $C'+$ and $E'+$ are highly correlated and therefore quite oblique in their relationship, and the liberal plane is tilted forward as it had been during the first period. And as happened in the change from the first to the second periods, so again in the change from the seventh to the eighth periods, a double substitution of personnel occurred with Frankfurter and Whittaker being replaced by Goldberg and White.

This time, however, the effects of the double replacement of personnel were very slight. As figure (H) shows, White moved into a position appropriate for his type (PCONS), and although Stewart and Harlan appear in the predicted sequence of typal relationships, together with Clark and White they form one cluster which projects into the seventh octant in the characteristic PCONS mode. On the liberal side, Goldberg projects into the fifth octant in the POLIB mode, but Brennan is marginally in the eighth octant closer to the LIB cluster. The scale vectors are in a more normal posture, except that E' is more highly correlated with the second dimension and C' with the first than characteristically occurs, so the liberalism plane is rotated clockwise some 25-30° from its usual position. But there is one more difference between figures (G) and (H) that is most remarkable: as in all of the preceding periods, so also in (G) a majority of the justices were conservatives of one type or another. In the eighth period consequently, for what was probably the first time in the entire history of the United States Supreme Court, a majority of the justices represented, at least modally, one or the other of the two liberal points of view. But this did not entail any apparent major change in the ideological structure of the Court, the most predominant feature of which was the delineation of two clusters that divided primarily on the first dimension—a statement which applies equally to the first and sixth periods, when the majority cluster was composed of conservatives rather than liberals. It should also be noted that this eighth period was the one in which Black began to withdraw his support for most issues of civil liberty, as discussed in Chapter 4 and as Appendix C shows. Black's shift toward the conservative direction of the C scale is reflected in figure (H) in the increasing distance between his ideal-point and that of Warren, as Black moved into closer alignment with the negative segment of the second dimension.

By the ninth period, Black's continued movement toward classic conservatism had put him into such a position that, as viewed in figure (I), he appears to be projecting directly toward the middle of the bottom of the space, and therefore in coalignment with what would ordinarily be 2−, but in this particular period is 3− (as explained above). But Black remained within, although at the border of the eighth octant; while Clark, who projects even more negatively on this third dimension, is actually quite a distance from Black on the second dimension. Clark in fact projects marginally into the third octant, which does not leave him too far from what had become his customary placement as an ECONS; but none of the other three conservatives appears close to where we should expect them to be according to their modal classifications. White is, indeed, positive on the third (here, the vertical) dimension, so that his ideal-point appears within the sector defined by the angle of $C'-/E'-$, which is the characteristic position of a balanced conservative; and Harlan, who is classified modally as a CONS, appears instead in the PCONS mode, and so also does Stewart, whose own classification is as an ECONS. On the liberal side, the two POLIBs,

Fortas, who had replaced Goldberg, and Brennan, are in proper sequence, ranking above the two LIBs Douglas and Warren; but Brennan and Warren are contiguous, and in order for the liberal subconfiguration to better fit the paradigm it would be necessary for the two POLIBs to appear above the $C'+$ vector and for the two LIBs to appear within the sector defined by the angle of $C'+/E'+$. The angle between the scale vectors is quite oblique, and one's general impression is that the smallest-space configuration provides in this particular period only a so-so fit to the factor analysis paradigm. The reason why this is true is also obvious: it is because of the tendency of the smallest-space algorithm to keep folding the remaining variance into smaller and smaller corners of the space (*e.g.*, by attributing negative coordinates to most ideal-points on the second dimension and to virtually all ideal-points on the third and higher-order dimensions), instead of partitioning them equivalently along positive as well as negative reference dimension segments.[5] Rank orders may be preserved, but the distance facet of the paradigm gets distorted when everything is squeezed into about a fourth of the available reference space.

In the tenth period, there are five liberals without counting Black, and figure (J) shows that the resulting structure appears once again to be back closer in accord with the factor paradigm. Clark had been replaced by Marshall, so there are now three POLIBs (for the first time) in this final period, and all of them are in close alignment with or else projecting above the $C'+$ vector. Two of them, however, are very closely paired with LIBs: Brennan with Warren (projecting like Marshall into the first octant and positively on 3D), and Fortas with Douglas (projecting into the fifth octant, negatively on the third dimension). Both Douglas and Warren but also Brennan and Fortas appear within the sector defined by the angle $C'+/E'+$, which is the expected position for LIBs. On the conservative side, Stewart projects above the $E'-$ vector in the customary ECONS mode, and Harlan and White appear, in that order from Stewart, in the sector defined by the angle $E'-/C'-$, which is where we should expect to find Harlan, but not White, whose projection, to be consistent with the factorial paradigm, should have been below $C'-$ and into the lower portion of the seventh octant (instead of marginally into the sixth). The two scale analogues are orthogonal and in the expected rotation from the first two reference dimensions, and the liberalism plane is tilted only very slightly (as Table 7.2A shows) toward 3D+ (reflecting, no doubt, the positive projections of Warren and Brennan and Marshall on that dimension).

When all ten structures are viewed from the criterion of their exemplification of the factorial paradigm of Figure 5.1, it is readily possible to rank them in the order of their goodness-of-fit, which I shall denote by using the subfigure symbols for Figure 7.1: (E), (F), (J), (D); (C), (H), (A); (G), (I); (B). The first four of these are clearly best; the next three are generally good; for (G) and (I) (ranking eighth and ninth) it is fair; and for (B) (ranking tenth) it is least satisfactory. Only in the case of B are the $C'+$ and $E'+$ vectors rotated substantially away from their customarily high positive correlation with 1D; in I, ranking ninth, the second and third dimensions appear transposed; while in (A) and (G), ranking seventh and eighth, and $C'+$ and $E'+$ vectors are highly correlated and the liberalism plane is tilted obliquely downward and forward in relation to 3D.

Alternative Solutions of Other Dimensionality

We shall now compare the adequacy of the three-dimensional solutions, which we have been considering, with the alternative provided by both simpler (one- and two-dimensional) and more complex (four-dimensional) smallest-space interpretations of the same set of matrices. There are two ways in which we can do this: subjectively, by contrasting what is apparent in Figure 7.1 with similar reactions to Figures 7.2 and 7.3; and objectively, by considering the data presented in Table 7.2B and C. We shall do both. In the concluding chapter, we shall consider in greater detail the question of the relative adequacy of any of the smallest-space solutions in comparison with those provided by principal component and by oblimin oblique factor analysis.

Figure 7.2 presents the set of one-dimensional spaces for our ten periods. A comparison of these sequences with the corresponding projections to the first dimensions of Figure 7.3(A)-(J), indicates that with a few exceptions (such as Black in period ten concerning which one should compare Figure 7.3J and 7.1J) these are identical. Consequently, we can infer that the 1D solution provides the best linear ordering of the configuration, although what it typically suggests is neither the C scale nor the E scale, but rather a compromise between them. Hence, the 1D solution constitutes the best index to general liberalism except in those periods, such as one and seven, when the program reports only the two clusters rather than discriminating within each of them.[6]

Figure 7.3 includes the two-dimensional spaces, which seem to conform to the factorial paradigm even better than do the three-dimensional spaces that we have just finished discussing. Moreover, the sequence in which I judge (subjectively) the goodness-of-fit of these two-dimensional spaces is significantly different (with rho = .08) from the three-dimensional sequence suggested above. In my opinion

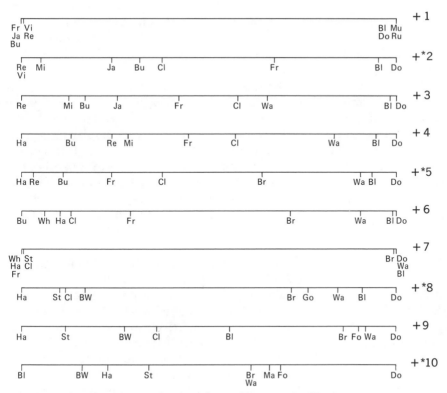

Figure 7.2 One-Dimensional Smallest Space Solutions (by Periods)

the best-conforming are (D), (B), (F), (E), (H), and (A) (all of which are perfectly transitive circumplexes), followed by (C), (G), and (J) (each of which involves a single intransitivity), with (I) least satisfactory because of its triple intransitivity. I think that from a completely subjective point of view, one might well conclude that these two-dimensional spaces provide as good or better solutions than do the three-dimensional spaces, and certainly they are vastly easier both to construct and appraise. Obviously we cannot discuss the four-dimensional spaces subjectively, so we turn now to the evidence provided by Table 7.2B and C concerning all four levels of dimensionality.

One measure of goodness-of-fit is the statistical criterion that is reported with the output of each smallest-space analysis solution. This "coefficient of alienation" indicates the extent to which the reported structure deviates from the matrix that it purports to model. The average coefficient values for 1D, 2D, 3D, and 4D solutions respectively are .212, .076, .032, and .013. These measures show that, generally speaking, the 1D solutions are only fair replications, the 2D ones are much better, and both the 3D and 4D solutions are quite good, with the 4D better—although whether enough so to justify the much higher costs and other disadvantages entailed by working with space of that complexity is certainly a serious question.

Table 7.2B indicates that the average correlation between $C'+/E'+$ is, in angular terms, about $74°$ for the 2D spaces, about $65°$ for 3D, and about $60°$ for 4D. The angle in 4D principal-component space is slightly less than $60°$, so the two 4D solutions provide very similar interpretations of the relationship between the two scale vectors. But the rho correlation between the two composite scales is equivalent (when treated as a cosine) to an angle of $65°55'$—which is, of course, indistinguishable from the average angle of $65°25'$ that separates the vectors in the 3D smallest space; so we must conclude that, on the basis of this criterion, the 3D smallest spaces are to be preferred.

The most important criterion, however, is probably that of how well the criterion scales can be accommodated to the different levels of space complexity; and Table 7.2C shows that, focusing on the mean values, each vector fits increasingly better as the space increases in level of complexity, and C' fits better than E' at all levels of complexity. On the other hand, the big improvement in fit comes with the move from one-space to two-space; and the difference between the average of the means for both scale vectors (.959 in 3D, and .963 in 4D—with both rounding to .96) is so small that we must deem the 3D solutions to be completely satisficing. This part of the table also denotes the highest level of correlation for each scale in each period; and by observing the asterisks by columns, we can see that there are no instances in which either scale fits best in one-space; there are three such for C, and one for E in two-space; but there are five occasions in which C fits best in 3D, and also three in which it fits as well as those that were maximal in 2D, plus three in which E fits best in 3D. For 4D, there remain two best-fits for C and six for E, but that total of eight is no better than the total of best-fits for the three-dimensional space. Certainly on this evidence we must conclude that the 3D spaces provide an entirely satisfactory accommodation for the C scale, and one that is adequate for E even though it is not quite so satisfactory as the 4D.

Table 7.2C shows also the instances of recession, when the space of higher order provides a less adequate accommodation for either scale than does any space of lower order. There is one instance of such recession for each scale in 2D; there are none for C but two for E in 3D; and there is one for C and three for E in 4D. It should be noted that from a probability point of view, the opportunities, for such recessions to occur, increase as the level of space complexity becomes higher; so it is not remarkable that there are twice as many recessions for 4D as for

2D—but by the same reasoning, it perhaps *is* remarkable that there are no more recessions for 3D than for 2D. This evidence, although hardly compelling, nevertheless is again supportive of the choice of three-dimensional space as the level of complexity that minimaxes between the benefits of goodness-of-fit, and the detriments that accompany multidimensional complexity.

On the whole the objective indices tend to support, and they certainly do not contradict, my decision to construct the 3D physical models, and to rely upon them as the primary basis for providing a smallest-space interpretation of our data.

Notes to Chapter 7

1. In the one-dimensional case, the question of directional cosines like that of intervector correlation is trivial: one compares the sequences for the dimension and each scale serially, and directionality is signified by the sign of the correlation coefficient.

2. For the N scale in Figure 7.1B I have used the fluorescent chartreuse color for both segments of the scale, which is highly positively correlated with $E'+$ at $+.908$ so that $N'+$ points (in the absence of any rotation) downward and away from the viewer, as its directional cosines of zero on 1D, $-.90$ on 2D, and $+.43$ on 3D require.

3. See p. 271, Figure 16, which should be compared with Figure 7.1 here.

4. In order for the same observation to be made for the first period, it would have been necessary for Burton not only to have been least negative (as he is) on 3D; it would also have been necessary for him to have been—as he is *not*—positively correlated with that dimension.

5. The degree of this increasingly negative bias in the smallest-space configuration becomes evident when we note that for Table 7.1A the algebraic mean of all first-dimension coordinates is $+06.2$; for 2D it is -28.5; for 3D it is -54.6; and for 4D all ninety coordinates reported in Table 7.1B are negative with an average value of -58.7.

6. Cf. the figure (No. 1: "Deviations Expressed in Percentages") suggested by C. Herman Pritchett, in his pioneering article on Supreme Court ideology, published over three decades ago: see his "Divisions of Opinion Among Justices of the U.S. Supreme Court, 1939-1941," *American Political Science Review*, Vol. 35 (1941), pp. 890-98. Pritchett's scale is not without a certain minor conceptual dissonance (Reed's schizophrenic placement on both sides of the zero-point); but what Pritchett sought to infer from his matrix of interagreement scores is precisely what smallest-space analysis reports as the first dimension (and that irrespective of whether the program is instructed to calculate one, two, three, four, or more dimensions).

8
Reappraisal

In this concluding chapter we shall reconsider what now appear to to be the most important results of our investigation. Let us proceed by turning first to the question of methodology, so as to compare the relative advantages and disadvantages of the three different approaches to multidimensional scaling that we have utilized. Next we shall review the major substantive findings concerning ideological changes resulting from this study. After that we can consider the question to what extent it is necessary to reject or modify, in the light of the present findings, those that were reported by the earlier study. Finally, we can consider to what extent if any the present study constitutes an improvement on the earlier one.

Principal Component, Oblique, and Smallest Space Compared

One empirical finding of this study that seems well established is that the plane of liberalism/conservatism, defined by vectors that represent the two major cumulative scales, determines the first two dimensions that are produced by any conventional computer method of multi-dimensional analysis, and these first two reference dimensions will be the same irrespective of which method is used. After reflection where appropriate, the first and second dimensions of principal-component factor analysis are the same as the first and second dimensions of four-dimensional smallest-space analysis, as a comparison of Tables 5.1 and 7.1B readily demonstrates. Furthermore, if we compare both of these sets of paired dimensions with the first two centroid factorial dimensions reported in *The Judicial Mind*,[1] then again we find that, after allowing for the necessary grouping of the latter data so that they will better correspond to the time periods of the present study, and recognizing that the earlier study terminates part way through the eighth period of the present study, the first principal component equals the first smallest-space dimension equals the first centroid factor; and the second principal-component equals the second smallest-space dimension equals the second centroid factor. This equivalence extends throughout both studies without exception. But there the equivalence ends, at least for the centroid factors. The third centroid factor during the earlier study corresponds to *none* of the third or fourth smallest-space dimensions of the present study; and if we employ the weak criterion of rank correlation of at least .75, then there are only two instances in which the third centroid factor can be identified with a higher principal component: with the fourth principal component in *⸍* e fourth period and with the third principal component in the ⸍⸍⸍⸍ h period. The observation of a moderate correlation between ⸍⸍⸍red rankings in two out of sixteen trials is hardly a sufficient ⸍⸍⸍rovement upon chance to warrant any further consideration of these relationships. The situation is rather different, however, if we compare the third and fourth smallest-space dimensions with the third and fourth principal components: the third smallest-space dimension matches (at rho $\geqslant$ .75) one or the other principal component in nine of the ten periods (the third component in periods 1, 3, 6, 7, and 9 and the fourth component in periods 2, 4, 5, and 8). Moreover, the fourth smallest-space dimension is the equivalent of the third principal component in the second period; so in this single period—the only one in which the strength of liberal ideology is so weak that there is no first-dimensional general factor of liberalism/conservatism—all four smallest-space dimensions match (although not in precisely the same sequence) all four principal components. Otherwise, however, the fourth smallest-space dimension cannot be identified with the remaining principal component in any of the other nine periods. And in the tenth and most liberally oriented period, neither the third nor the fourth smallest-space dimension matches either the third or the fourth principal component.

I believe that these findings imply the following conclusions. First of all, my hypothesis that principal-component factor analysis might clarify the attempt in the earlier study to provide a valid and consistent interpretation of the third centroid factor must be considered without support in the present study. If the third centroid factor cannot be significantly related to any of the higher-order dimensions of the present study, then whatever meaning the latter may have cannot be construed as supportive of the interpretation ventured for the third centroid factor in *The Judicial Mind*. But the fact that the third smallest-space dimension is replicated by a higher-order principal component in nine of the ten periods indicates that three-dimensional smallest space is measuring very much the same configuration as three- or four-dimensional principal-component factorial space.

Let us now recapitulate the evidence previously presented in Tables 5.2, 6.2, and 7.2 concerning the ability of the various types and levels of space complexity to accommodate the two major criterion scales. The best fit is provided by 4D smallest space, for which the average correlation for both scales for all ten periods is .977. Next comes 4D principal-component space at .962; but within rounding distance of that is 3D smallest space at .959—and I have previously stated the argument that a 3D space is clearly to be preferred on grounds of parsimony to a 4D space that improves upon it by the margin of only .003, just as it is also to be preferred, although in this case on grounds of simplicity, to the 4D smallest space which improves upon it by the relatively larger but still small margin of .018. Fourth best is the set of the 2D smallest-space solutions at an average of .930, followed by the oblique spaces at correlation levels of .876 (4D), .84 (3D, estimated), and .805 (2D), while the poorest fit is provided by one-dimensional smallest space at .787. In the light of these data, one might well question my decision to accept 3D smallest space as satisficing, arguing that *two*-dimensional smallest space at a correlation average of .93 is good enough and is much simpler to work with than the 3D space. I think the answer to this argument is best stated in two parts. In the first place, we know from the cumulative scaling measurements that only two-thirds of the total decisional content is measured by the two major scales, and hence we know also that if the first two dimensions of a multidimensional scaling analysis of a matrix encompassing the total decisional content are defined by those two major scales, then it necessarily follows that a third of the content and variance remains unaccounted for by such a two-dimensional analysis. From this point of view, three-space is the level of complexity that corresponds best to the known complexity of the matrices and underlying data.

The other answer to the two-space argument relies upon the 3D physical models which we considered in the previous chapter. There we discovered that although the plane of liberalism/conservatism *typically* appears as virtually orthogonal to (or independent of) the third reference dimension, there were three periods (1, 3 and 9) in which the plane defined by C'/E' is correlated with (*i.e.*, oblique to) the third dimension, and one period (the ninth) in which the second and third dimensions are transposed. Furthermore, there is sufficient variation on the third reference dimension that the perception and apprehension of the configurational relationships for the physical structures are substantially different and considerably more refined than for their enfoldment into the 2D representations of Figure 7.3. So one's understanding of either the relationship between the scales or that between the scales and the ideal-points is not the same for 2D space as it is for the plane of liberalism/conservatism embedded in 3D space; and in my opinion, the gains derivable from the latter justify the additional time and difficulty that are involved in their construction.

My overall conclusion is that all three methods will lead to the same basic substantive findings and conclusions, but if only one is to be employed, then smallest space appears to be the most parsimonious choice. Oblique factor analysis seemed to be the least helpful of these three methods, except in regard to the oblimin analysis of the interscale correlation matrix (Table 4.5) that we considered in Chapter 6. We can also examine the results of smallest-space analysis of these data. The one-dimensional solution arrays the eight scales and subscales in the following sequence: RP; then a triplet of C and its subscales FP and PF; next W; then E and its principal subscale $\overline{B}$; and last in rank, F. This is a perfectly satisfactory solution which denotes the two major scales and their subscales as a segment-bounded by the right to privacy on the civil liberties end and by governmental fiscal authority on the economic liberalism end, and this is the same as the curvilinear sequence of the vectors in the oblique solution of Figure 6.2. The 2D smallest-space solution is similar, except that the oblique configuration occupies a sector of only $120°$, while the 2D smallest space requires twice as large a sector as that. But the sequence in 2D smallest space is the same, except that RP (at one end of the sequence) is virtually zero and F (at the other end) is completely negative on the second dimension; while the first dimension distinguishes between RP, C, FP, and PF (all personal rights), and W, B, E, and F (all property rights). Thus the 2D smallest-space solution suggests the following interpretation: (1) that personal rights are different from property rights and (2) that F is different from the liberalism/conservatism scales and subscales. The 3D smallest-space solution continues to attribute the second dimension to the discrimination of F, while the third dimension discriminates RP from the remaining variables. The 4D solution is degenerate, providing an obfuscated interpretation of relations that had been clear and apparent in all of the solutions of lower dimensionality. Either the simplex (1D) or the circumplex (2D) is quite adequate for present purposes. The indication of the 3D solution, that the right to privacy defines a dimension separate from both liberalism/conservatism and F, does support the hypothesis that I stated in the preceding chapter, but this hardly constitutes evidence that can be considered to be more than suggestive.

An Overview of Ideological Change

Our analysis of changes in the ideological structure of the group showed that with so small a population any change in personnel was a major change, in its effect upon within-group interrelationships, and was directly reflected in changes in the configurational structure. Because each individual is a living and therefore changing organism, acting in a dynamic ideological environment subject to continuous stresses and realignments, it is inconceivable that we could find invariable constancy in the ideological position of any individual justice throughout the quarter of a century spanned by this study; but I think it is surprising that the amount and degree of such change was so relatively small as it appears. Virtually every individual position can be defined by a cone (in 3D space, for example) which delimits a relatively minute region of the total sphere, and the same argument applies by symmetry to 4D space or to less complex spaces than 3D. We found, for example, that this analogy even applies in the case of Clark, whose location, tracked through eight periods, remains confined to a region of the seventh octant that for him was characteristic. This finding suggests that a person's ideology is better conceptualized not as a point, not as a line, not even as a field, but rather as a multidimensional spatial region within an even more complex ideological space which has a potentially specifiable set of parameters. We sample that personal ideological space when we observe, for example, a justice's vote in a particular decision; or his rank on an empirical cumulative scale; or his ideal-point in a configurational structure derived from multidimensional analysis of all non-unanimous decisions during a particular period; or when we observe even more exotic and abstract, because further removed from the underlying empirical events, structures based on means of ranks on cumulative scales, and projections upon scale analogue vectors in sets of 4D spaces. The most that we can reasonably expect is that such samples will lie, subject to the effects of error (including measurement) variance, of course, within the region of personal ideological space whose bounds we demark by means of our samples. The better (including the larger in volume) our samples, the more confidence we should feel entitled to repose in our having staked out with acceptable validity the ideological parameters of the individuals in whom we are interested. Of course we ought also to anticipate, in studying a population of judges, for whom constancy and stability in value affirmation are at least nominally both public and professional virtues, that change in individual ideological stances will be relatively small in comparison with what we could expect to find among groups of the same size but consisting of persons who are not trained as lawyers and not cast in the official role of judges. We must keep in mind, also, that the relatively advanced age of the persons in our present sample probably had the effect of reinforcing stability in their ideological standpoints, at least until an individual among them sustained physiological deterioration to such an advanced degree, as with senescence, that the internal neurological structures that provide the information retrieval and association functions that make possible a stable ideological stance, themselves break down and his mind is changed because of stresses that arise within himself, rather than within the environment in which he acts. Unfortunately, the data of the present study give us no control over exogenous variables such as health or cultural change, and therefore we are confined to a descriptive rather than a causal interpretation.

There were three instances in which differences in observations of an individual's ideological region were sufficiently large and consistently in a particular direction that it seems necessary to characterize these sampling differences as changes in the individual's ideological position. In confirmation of a similar finding (concerning Warren's initial period) reported in *The Judicial Mind*, the first of these was for Warren who projected the viewpoint of a moderate during his initial and final periods on the Court, and that of a modern (or balanced) liberal otherwise. The fact that Warren did appear as a moderate in the context of the exceptionally liberal majority that dominated the Court in his final period is an important finding, and one that seems to have escaped notice prior to the present study. The second instance involved Frankfurter, who appeared consistently as an economic conservative throughout the first five periods of our analysis, but who was a balanced—and extreme—conservative during his final two periods on the Court.[2] The third instance is that of Black, who changed from an economically liberal position during the first period, and otherwise a position of balanced liberalism throughout the next seven periods, to a position of increasing political conservatism during the last two periods, and therefore to typal positions of first economic liberalism and then classical conservatism. I have offered interpretations for each of these changes, but these explanations are, of course, beyond the scope of the data analyzed in the present study, and they must all therefore be deemed strictly speculative. I offer them only in that spirit and with the thought that they may be of some value as hypotheses for future work. I have suggested, for example, that Warren's change may have been a function of his socialization into his role as Chief Justice,[3] but such an observation leaves wide open, of course, the query: why Earl Warren, but not Warren Burger or Fred Vinson? Or, if we assume that it was socialization into the role of Supreme Court justice rather than the more particular role of the Chief Justice that was relevant, then why Warren but not Stewart, Harlan, or Whittaker? And continuing to confine ourselves to Eisenhower appointees, why not Brennan, who moved immediately into the POLIB position that became characteristic for him?[4]

The Frankfurter denouement was due, I continue to believe, to a combination of prudence[5] and cultural dissonance,[6] but we know also that Frankfurter was suffering from hardening of the arteries during his final period on the Court, which resulted in the heart attack that killed him during the summer of 1962; and we know enough now about the side effects of hardening of the arteries that it would have been surprising if his physiological condition also had *not* contributed to his change in ideological stance. Similarly, I believe—but can hardly prove—that Black's more gradual movement in the same direction and with the same ultimate effects in terms of C scale position as Frankfurter's, but beginning about two years after Frankfurter's had terminated, reflected cultural dissonance that was perceived as such because of the inexorable physiological changes that accompanied relatively advanced old age. So we are left with three instances of change out of a possible total of twenty-eight,[7] if we presume that each individual had two particularly sensitive chances, at the beginning and again at the end of his affiliation with the Court group. This is supportive of a theory of group ideological stability but hardly adequate to support a theory of ideological change for this group. For the latter purpose, we would require a larger sample of instances of change and systematic data bearing on one or more hypotheses concerning its causation.

Apart from the three denoted examples of change, however, the configurational positions are remarkably stable, and they are well described by the typology suggested in Figure 5.1. POLIBs typically appear in the fifth octant (defined as ++−, with the first octant defined as +++) of the smallest-space structures (Figure 7.1), although often in a lower position than that forecast for them by the factorial model. But we know that this deflection in the LIB vectors is strictly a consequence of the smallest-space negative bias on the second dimension and that it has no substantive importance. The POLIBs appear in proper *rank* sequence in the smallest-space structures, invariably appearing (1) above the LIBs; (2) between the LIBs and the ECONS; and (3) within the liberal rather than the conservative hemisphere. Crossing into the conservative hemisphere, we observe the ECONS invariably projecting into or at the borders of the sixth octant, with the modern conservatives below and often behind them, followed by the PCONS who characteristically project into the seventh octant below both the CONS and, necessarily, the ECONS. Furthermore, these typal loci are directly and consistently correlated with the best-fitting positions for the scale analogue vectors. We can consider, therefore, the physical structures presented in Figure 7.1 to be a direct test and confirmation of the theory of ideological structure presented in the fifth chapter.

The Judicial Mind Revised

Let us turn now to an examination of the extent to which *The Judicial Mind* must be considered revised in light of the findings of the present study. Most obviously, the earlier study has been revised in the sense of updating. *The Judicial Mind* pointed out that on the basis of the 1962 term with which it ended, the Court had a libertarian majority bias for what was probably the first time in history; and the logical prediction that one would have to make would be, therefore, that a quite liberal policy output could be expected from the Court during the sixties, which is what happened. But the empirical study of the symbiosis between the ideological structure of the Supreme Court and the liberal thrust of policy-making by the later Warren Court came too late to be included in the earlier study. It constitutes instead a part of the revision made herein.

The identification of major scales and their general patterning and interrelationship as reported by the earlier study are strongly confirmed by the present study. The same comment applies to the subscales in so far as sample sizes were empirically adequate to permit their being tested, and none of the present evidence is directly contrary to that presented in *The Judicial Mind* concerning either subscales or minor scales. But the subscale findings of *The Judicial Mind* were based on very limited samples, equivalent in volume to little more than that of one or two of the present ten periods; and the earlier study expressly assumed that given a systematic examination of data grouped in larger subsets over a longer period of time, it should prove possible to observe and measure relationships along most, if not all of the hypothesized subscales. That expectation has been only partially realized in the present study: the same subscales that turned up strongly in the earlier study ($\overline{B}$ and W, and FP, PF, and RP) are also the ones that scale best under the more systematic and extended scrutiny provided by the present study.

The other subscale that showed up in the samples analyzed by *The Judicial Mind* was political equality, which we have dealt with here as three different subscales. Of these, one (racial equality) scaled well but in only three periods, while the other two (voting equality and civic equality) each scale in only a single period. The other hypothesized civil liberties subscale, religious freedom, may well constitute a distinctive attitudinal dimension for Supreme Court justices, but no empirical sample adequate for measurement and the testing of that hypothesis showed up in either *The Judicial Mind* or the present study. So the present study generally confirms but does not carry very much further, except in regard to the oblique and smallest-space analyses of the matrix of scale variables (Table 4.5), the subscale analysis of the earlier study. Similarly, the results of more adequate data samples must be deemed disappointing as concerns the testing of the minor scales. Four term F scales and a single term N scale are reported in *The Judicial Mind*, whereas Table 4.1 here lists F as scalable in a majority of the periods, N in three, J in two, and A in only a single one. The problem with the minor scales is that their sample sizes tend to be considerably smaller on the average than those of the better subscales of the major scales. Consequently, our failure to observe more minor scales more frequently is a comment upon the relative infrequency with which the Vinson—and more particularly, the Warren—Courts chose to deal with them rather than upon their validity as distinctive attitudinal issues. Whether they are distinctive and valid or not, one cannot resolve the question on the basis of the methods employed in the present study.

I had expected, in *The Judicial Mind*, that re-examination of the data concerning the minor scales might shed further light upon the substantive meaning of the third centroid dimension. That has not happened. I now think after rereading and after having reconsidered the earlier study that it remains a question mark, notwithstanding whatever was said and done there concerning it. A few of the F scales and a few of the N scales can be analogized in one or another of the different types of multidimensional space that we have examined, but only one minor scale could be accommodated in any of the 3D smallest-space physical models, and that one turned out to be best interpreted (at least, in that context) to be a subscale of E! The most relevant evidence concerning F is that provided by the 2D smallest-space analysis of the interscale correlation matrix of Table 4.5, which indicated that F is maximally loaded on the second dimension in the direction opposite to that of all of the liberalism/conservatism scales and subscales. But the data here are simply inadequate to permit anything to be said about how the minor scales relate generally to either the major scales or the reference structures, except that (1) F is clearly much closer to E than to C; and (2) the minor scales tend to be uncorrelated with the first reference dimension of general liberalism, but they do load upon the second and higher-order dimensions (*e.g.*, cf. Table 6.3).

Beyond that, I am now convinced as the result of the present re-examination that empirical proof is lacking concerning whatever, if any, substantive meaning should be attributed to the third dimension, to say nothing of the fourth. What the present study does, I think without any doubt, is to establish a strong, valid, and reliable substantive identification for both the first and second dimensions. But the proof of the ideological pudding (and, therefore, of the configurations produced by such multidimensional methods of analysis as principal component and smallest space) has been supplied by the two major cumulative scales; and it is their consistent interrelationship that has made possible a consistent interpretation of the factorial and smallest-space configurations. And that interpretation has gone no further than the discrimination of the relationship between those configurations and the plane defined by the major scale vectors, irrespective of whether the dimensionality of the criterion space was two, three, or four. If F or any of the other minor scales—or if any other additional variable—had been discovered to correlate consistently with the higher-order dimensions, then we would have an empirical basis for determining the substantive meaning of the third and fourth dimensions. In the absence of such information, we are in about the same position—in regard to these higher-order dimensions, but not in regard to the first and second dimensions—as was Thurstone himself when he reported the first factor analysis of Supreme Court ideology, which he denoted as a set of structural relationships which he could and did describe but which he could not interpret without a validated substantive theory and relevant substantive empirical data.[8] Of course this does not necessarily mean that the third (and possibly fourth) dimensions may not be identified through other and future work; but in the meantime, confirmation of the identification of the first two dimensions doubtless constitutes some advancement.

Contrary to the position that I took in *The Judicial Mind,* I now think that it is better to let the present interpretation rest with what can be clearly supported at the manifest level with empirical evidence. This does not necessarily mean that the rather elaborate discussion in *The Judicial Mind* (concerning the substantive ideological meaning to be attributed to the third reference dimension, the psychological components of intensity and closure, and the psychological dimension of dogmatism/pragmatism) is necessarily incorrect. But it does mean that in my present opinion, nothing discovered in this re-examination lends any additional support to the original argument, which must continue to rest on whatever persuasion it may command in the context of its initial statement.

There is also one particular finding of the earlier study which evidently must be modified in the light of the findings announced here. *The Judicial Mind* is emphatic in rejecting the hypothesis that Frankfurter actually had changed to a more conservative position, either behaviorally or ideologically, during his last few years on the Court.[9] This argument is made, it is true, in a context of an attempt to explain the highly relative nature of the scaling content and rank differences and of the importance of appraising ranks in relation to the ideological structure of the decisional group. Although I do not now wish to retract in any respect from *that* aspect of the earlier discussions that I have cited here in footnote 9, I am convinced that the claim that Frankfurter did not change from an ECONS position in the sixth period to a CONS position in the seventh is inconsistent with the evidence that we have examined in the present study.

Conclusion

We can consider also the respects in which the present study constitutes an improvement over the earlier one. Clearly the longer periods of analysis provided by the socially, rather than legally, defined subsample periods provide better data for the purposes of both linear scaling and multidimensional analysis. The data themselves, in the sense of the archived decisions described by Appendix A, are cleaner, that is, more free of errors of observation and recordation, and more complete as well as more extensive than those of the earlier study. Most of this improvement must be attributed, however, to the time and effort, incidental to the present project, that necessarily were expended in order to make the data suitable for archiving. The scales, at least in part because they are now based on initial computer analyses (instead of completely manual operations, as in the earlier study) are both more valid and more reliable instruments than those reported in *The Judicial Mind*, although I suppose that my failure to include herein the details of all of the scales as was done in the earlier study may be considered a deficiency by some. Indubitably, the multidimensional scaling upon which the present work rests is technically superior to the centroid factorial output on which the original study was based. The three different types of programs employed here—principal-component, oblimin oblique, and smallest-space—are more diverse, thereby making possible a comparative analytical approach. Moreover, each of them is in many respects superior to the centroid program, which did not even iterate. My present use of unities for communalities is a detail, but one which makes the results both in statistical theory and from an empirical point of view—putting all other differences aside—better than those produced by the use of the centroid program. Generally, I believe, the decade of intervening experience during which the political science profession grew substantially in its sophistication vis-à-vis the use of multivariate techniques of data analysis must have had a favorable effect in making me more skilled in my use of the techniques and more sophisticated in my understanding of the associated theory in related fields of behavioral science, now as compared to a dozen years ago. At least I have this time avoided premature commitment of my data and findings, to presentation in any particular format.

The present analysis relies heavily upon a typology, of which five subdivisions are used extensively throughout much of the analysis. These five include, but are no longer limited to, the three types that were the basis of the original analysis. The development of the present more complex typology depended in part, no doubt, on the availability of the more recent data that are included here but not earlier; but whatever the reason, the present typology is supported by a more general theory of ideological structure, and thus transcends the somewhat ad hoc character that tended to distinguish the tri-part typology of *The Judicial Mind*. In its more general present form, the theory applies equally well, as the earlier theory could not do, to a liberally dominated ideological structure, as it does to a conservatively dominated structure;[10] and it can now be related to more general theories of political coalition-building[11] instead of remaining, as I fear the earlier study tended to be viewed, at a level that was (however unfortunately) widely understood to be uniquely applicable to a unique political institution, the United States Supreme Court.

The present study limits its interpretation to the manifest, empirical level. Its method of interpretation is strictly inductive rather than deductive; and as a consequence, for example, the plane of liberalism/conservatism that was discussed hypothetically in the earlier study has become both empirical and manifest in the photographs of the physical structures of the present study. I believe that this represents, on the whole, an improvement over the more ambitious endeavors of *The Judicial Mind* to explain all relevant dimensions and to deal with psychological as well as substantive causal factors. Work in bio-political behavior in recent years makes me more convinced than ever of the importance of both physiological and psychological components of ideological stances; but for that very reason, I now think it is preferable to wait until such variables can be observed and measured rather than merely to speculate about their possible effects.

I think that the construction of the ten physical models of the 3D smallest-space configurations was a worthwhile activity which has improved the present analysis as compared to the earlier one. A dozen years ago I spent a considerable amount of time staring at two-dimensional perspectives of three-dimensional ideological structures, trying to imagine what the 3D relationships really looked like. There is no use asking why I didn't go ahead and build them then; let's just say that I was then brainwashed by natural science chauvinism to such a degree that I passively accepted the notion that physical models were something that chemists and other natural scientists built and used, whereas social scientists studied people, who are more complicated than natural phenomena, and so forth around the academic maypole. But this time I dared to make them and found them helpful in developing my own insight into and comprehension of the relevant multidimensional interrelationships. Hopefully, this may also have had some positive impact upon my attempts to elucidate this subject.

Notes to Chapter 8

1. *The Judicial Mind*, pp. 204-5.

2. Frankfurter, ranking 5th, supported a majority (45 of 86) of the civil liberties claims in the sixth period, but in the seventh period he ranked eighth and supported only 15 per cent (18 of 125).

3. Cf. Eloise C. Snyder, "The Supreme Court as a Small Group," *Social Forces*, Vol. 36 (1958), pp. 232-38.

4. Warren was the only one of the Eisenhower appointees who had had absolutely no previous judicial experience. That of Brennan, Whittaker, and Stewart was quite extensive.

5. See my *Constitutional Politics*, pp. 168-69, 636-38.

6. See J. C. Grant, "Felix Frankfurter—A Dissenting Opinion," *UCLA Law Review*, Vol. 12 (1965), pp. 1013-42.

7. Adjusting for experience before and after the limits of the present study.

8. Louis L. Thurstone and J. W. Degan, "A Factorial Study of the Supreme Court," *Proceedings of the National Academy of Sciences*, Vol. 37 (1951), pp. 628-35. Thurstone and Pritchett were faculty colleagues at the University of Chicago when that study was done, and they were indeed in close communication in regard to the project. If further evidence were needed of the pernicious effect of academic disciplinary boundaries, it is perhaps supplied by the observation that the marriage of the extraordinary insight of Pritchett's initial (1941) article on the subject (cited here in note 6, p. 137, *supra*)—which was right on target and superior to any of his increasingly diluted formulations that followed—with the technical competence in methodology of Thurstone's study, certainly would have produced the same basic interpretation as I proposed in *The Judicial Mind*—but a full dozen years earlier, in the early fifties rather than the mid sixties. But political scientists of Pritchett's genera-

tion were not trained in factor analysis; nor did psychometricians then (any more than now) read the *American Political Science Review*.

9. *The Judicial Mind*, pp. 121, 284.

10. A graphic demonstration of this point is supplied by Figures 6.1G and H, which show a scattered conservative majority confronting a tightly clustered liberal minority during the seventh period, followed by a tightly clustered conservative minority confronting a scattering liberal majority during the eighth period. Frankfurter's retirement at the end of the seventh period had converted the former conservative majority of five into a minority of four, just as Goldberg's appointment at the beginning of the eighth period converted the former liberal minority of four into a majority of five. And observation of Figures 6.1I and J, for the ninth and tenth periods, shows that the conservatives stayed tightly clustered while their minority shrank to three while the liberal majority, now grown to six, is spread over slightly more than half of the circumplex of the final period of the Warren Court.

11. For a useful statement of the general theory, see William H. Riker, *The Theory of Political Coalitions* (New Haven: Yale University Press, 1962).

Appendix A

Coding Manual for Combined
Schubert Data on Non-Unanimous and Unanimous Formal Decisions
of the United States Supreme Court, 1946-1968 Terms*

1. IDENTIFICATION CODES

Summary

Columns	Category
1–19	Case Identification Codes
21–40	Individual Voting Codes
78–80	Scale Variable Codes

Case Identification

Codes	Variable
1–2	Deck number (01 = 1946-48 terms, . . . 10 = 1967-1968 terms; se part 2, *infra*, for terms and card frequencies).
3–4	Tenths and units digit of term year (1946-1968)
5–6	Tenths and units digit of volume number of *United States Reports* (329-395)
7–10	Page number in *United States Reports*
11–14	Docket number of case [0000 = no docket # assigned in preliminary reports or published bound volume (N=5)]

*See footnote 1, p. 41, *supra*.

15	Docket Type of Case

    0. Appellate
    1. Miscellaneous Docket, as assigned for Term coded in cols. 3 & 4
    2. Original
    3. Appellate
    4. Miscellaneous Docket, as assigned for Term prior to that coded in cols. 3 & 4
    5. Original
    9. No Information Available on Docket Type of Case (N=5)

16   Type of Decision[a]
    1. Non-Unanimous
    2. Unanimous

17   Decisional Type of Case
    7. Formal (with individually assigned majority opinion and oral argument)
    8. Per Curiam

18   Total of Majority Votes (1 or 4 punches in cols. 21-40)

19   Total of Dissenting Votes (2 or 4 punches in cols. 21-40)

20   Blank

Individual Voting Codes

21–40   Individual Votes[b] (Chief Justices [cols. 21-22] and other respondents [cols. 23-40] are listed in the order of their appointment to the Court. See part 3, *infra*).

Blank. Not a member of the Court when the decision was announced
1. Assented (voted in the majority)[c]
2. Dissented (voted in the minority)
3. Did not participate in the decision
4. Non-ascertainable votes in 3-3 or 4-4 voting divisions (e.g., the partitioning of individual votes between the two subsets, as assents or dissents, cannot be objectively made). (Note that although the two subsets are equal in numbers of votes, one subset is the majority and the other subset is the minority, and case outcome *can* be specified in col. 80.)
5. Jurisdictional dissent (a vote limited to protesting the grant of jurisdiction in a case decided non-unanimously on the substantive merits.)

Scale Variable Codes

78	*Subscale[d] variables*

Blank. Non-scale
1. F (national government fiscal claims)
2. FP (fair procedure)
3. VE (voting equality)
4. PF (political freedom)
5. RF (religious freedom)
6. RE (racial equality)
7. RP (right to privacy)
8. W (pro-union)
9. $\overline{\text{B}}$/FC (anti-business or pro economic-underdog fiscal claims)
0. CE (civic equality)

79	*Scale variables[e]*

1. A (judicial activism)
2. C (political liberalism)[f]
3. E (economic liberalism)
4. F (national government fiscal claims)
5. J (judicial centralization)
6. N (nationalization)
9. Unknown
0. Non-scale

80	*Outcome direction*

1. pro
2. con[g]
9. unknown
0. non-scale

[a,b,c]For further discussion of the concepts of "decision," "vote," and "majority," see Glendon Schubert, *The Judicial Mind: Attitudes and Ideologies of Supreme Court Justices,* 1946-1963 (Evanston: Northwestern University Press, 1965), pp. 44-47.

[d]See *The Judicial Mind,* ch. 6, for further discussion of the definition of these subscale variables. (Note: PE [political equality], as used in the chapter, equals VE + RE + CE here.)

[e]See *The Judicial Mind,* ch. 5, especially pp. 146-58, for further discussion of the definition of these scale variables.

[f]Column 78 collates with column 79 as follows:

	78		79
	(1	=	4
Row punches	(2–7, 0	=	2
	(8, 9	=	3

gNote that because the Individual Votes (cols. 21-40) are coded as assent/dissent, the 1 and 2 punches in these columns (21-40) must be reversed for all decisions coded as row 2 punches (con) in col. 80 in order to align consistently all individual votes as pro (or con) the scale or subscale variables. To accomplish this result, a transgeneration of the data step must be written into standard Guttman (cumulative linear) scaling computer programs.

2. DATA DECK FREQUENCIES

Deck	Volumes	Term	Non-unanimous Data Cards By Deck	Unanimous Data Cards By Deck
1	329-338	1946		
		47		
		48	342	240
2	338-346	1949		
		50		
		51		
		52	384	241
3	346-348	1953		
		54	098	107
4	348-351	1954		
		55		
		56	110	132
5	352	1956	039	038
6	353-358	1956		
		57		
		58	206	166
7	358-369	1958		
		59		
		60		
		61	324	261
8	369-381	1961		
		62		
		63		
		64	364	455
9	382-388	1965		
		66	215	248
10	389-395	1967		
		68	277	331
	Total: all ten decks		2359	2219

Total N: 4578

3. COMPOSITION OF NATURAL COURTS

Column	Individual	Deck:	1	2	3	4	5	6	7	8	9	10
	Chief Justices:											
21	Vinson		X	X	—	—	—	—	—	—	—	—
22	Warren				X	X	X	X	X	X	X	X
	Associate Justices:											
23	Black		X	X	X	X	X	X	X	X	X	X
24	Reed		X	X	X	X	X	—	—	—	—	—
25	Frankfurter		X	X	X	X	X	X	X	—	—	—
26	Douglas		X	X	X	X	X	X	X	X	X	X
27	Murphy		X	—	—	—	—	—	—	—	—	—
28	Jackson		X	X	X	—	—	—	—	—	—	—
29	Rutledge		X	—	—	—	—	—	—	—	—	—
30	Burton		X	X	X	X	X	X	—	—	—	—
31	Clark			X	X	X	X	X	X	X	X	—
32	Minton			X	X	X	—	—	—	—	—	—
33	Harlan					X	X	X	X	X	X	X
34	Brennan						X	X	X	X	X	X
35	Whittaker							X	X	—	—	—
36	Stewart								X	X	X	X
37	White									X	X	X
38	Goldberg									X	—	—
39	Fortas										X	X
40	Marshall											X

Key: Blank = Not yet appointed
     — = Deceased, retired, or resigned
     X = Member of the Court during the
         period (deck) specified

Appendix B

PHI Correlation Matrices

Deck 1

	2	3	4	5	6	7	8	9	
	-219	240	143	-244	-273	146	-301	313	1
b	-141	-230	-418	360	609	-399	518	-346	2
c	205	-319	-066	-153	-333	094	-214	213	3
d	-264	010	-197	-416	-293	414	-334	124	4
e	-180	268	-133	-098	353	-444	358	-298	5
f	-093	-209	-021	353	-300	-347	632	-429	6
g	-013	-144	038	-057	-111	-082	-450	194	7
h	338	-069	048	-088	-091	-004	050	-346	8
i	268	-193	185	-160	-312	-053	087	087	9
	a	b	c	d	e	f	g	h	

Deck 2 (lower-left triangle of the matrix above)

Deck 3

	2	3	4	5	6	7	8	9	
	111	-046	-082	002	-108	-046	509	-100	1
b	685	-519	-095	488	-320	-471	-168	-183	2
c	-276	-369	-300	-549	-100	349	055	119	3
d	-170	-127	-313	-168	323	-027	-164	-072	4
e	544	613	-432	-258	-309	-369	-015	-199	5
f	-327	-413	395	098	-469	042	-075	064	6
g	201	099	160	-212	-005	-146	372	176	7
h	-208	-328	487	-091	-393	368	115	-116	8
i	-417	-470	-326	468	-363	118	-242	-030	9
	a	b	c	d	e	f	g	h	

Deck 4 (lower-left triangle of the matrix above)

Note: All self-correlations are unity, and the matrix entries are three-place decimals. The variables (respondents) are identified by the numbers 1-9 (upper matrices, for odd-numbered decks) or by the letters a-i (lower matrices, for even-numbered decks) in the same sequence in which they are listed in Appendix A.3.

Deck 6

		2	3	4	5	6	7	8	9		
		650	−327	−426	386	−294	−158	−335	321	1	
b	761		−548	−190	554	−317	−270	−520	223	2	
c	−374	−405		−120	−498	048	596	257	−259	3	Deck
d	512	666	−386		−239	247	−131	311	211	4	
e	−422	−473	179	−486		−561	−316	−639	095	5	
f	−340	−411	−209	−445	280		−022	358	−142	6	
g	−388	−454	640	−464	364	−090		−250	016	7	
h	374	328	−040	436	−203	−244	−149		−078	8	
i	−345	−415	197	−442	436	040	456	−274			
	a	b	c	d	e	f	g	h			

Deck 8

		2	3	4	5	6	7	8	9		
		663	−419	486	−144	−430	625	−438	−261	1	
b	224		−454	514	−229	−450	396	−478	−356	2	
c	242	247		−613	219	638	−283	381	247	3	Deck
d	−051	−197	−229		−381	−605	407	−549	−304	4	
e	−359	−530	−572	234		185	−204	172	−043	5	
f	448	095	052	−048	−221		−286	355	272	6	
g	−198	−281	−302	086	321	−068		−365	−137	7	
h	−114	017	−217	163	229	002	194		324	9	
i	217	084	104	−284	−216	178	058	−140			
	a	b	c	d	e	f	g	h			

Deck 10

		2	3	4	5	6	7	8	9		
		−184	243	137	−328	579	−350	−209	447	1	
b	−039		124	−024	−276	−177	038	−070	−126	2	
c	−080	−256		−254	−651	323	−354	−229	347	3	Deck
d	−122	−123	−374		184	−028	106	167	−231	4	
e	322	−082	−034	−130		−286	506	078	−302	5	
f	−129	−183	−224	265	042		−238	−038	286	6	
g	−048	053	−403	258	028	070		257	−146	7	
h	078	−067	167	−048	155	025	−119		−063	8	
i	220	−173	040	−001	117	055	−148	084			
	a	b	c	d	e	f	g	h			

Appendix C

Scale and Subscale Descriptions
(including ranks, indices, and interscale correlations)

C Scale (Political Liberalism)

1. *Scale ranks*

Respondent rank	Deck 1	2	3	4	5	6	7	8	9	10
1	Mu	Do	Do	Do		Do	Do	Do	Do	Do
2	Ru	Bl	Bl	Bl	Do,Bl,Wa	Bl	Bl	Wa	Fo	Fo
3	Do	Fr	Fr	Wa		Wa	Wa	Br	Wa	Ma
4	Bl	Ja	Ja	Fr	Br	Br	Br	Go	Br	Wa
5	Fr	Bu	Wa,Cl	Cl	Fr	Fr	St	Bl	Bl	Br
6	Ja	Vi	Wa,Cl	Ha	Ha	Ha	Wh	BW	BW	St
7	Bu	Cl	Mi	Bu	Cl	Wh,Bu	Ha	St	Cl	BW
8	Re	Mi	Bu	Mi	Re	Wh,Bu	Fr	Cl	St	Ha
9	Vi	Re	Re	Re	Bu	Cl	Cl	Ha	Ha	Bl

2. *Scale indices**

	1	2	3	4	5	6	7	8	9	10	Avg.
S	578	697	690	650	867	833	728	707	708	680	714
R	912	933	928	928	973	956	953	929	908	893	931
R'	913	924	933	917	—	943	942	934	906	901	923
M	791	774	789	801	830	777	829	796	742	735	786
M'	728	681	689	765	—	725	781	747	721	696	726
R−M	121	159	139	127	143	179	124	133	166	158	145
N	89	120	33	34	10	88	126	195	117	161	97
Characterization**	P	G	F	F	G	E	G	G	F	P+	F+ (3.9)

*Three-place decimals
**See the legend to Table 4.1 for definitions of these symbols

3. *Interscale rho correlations** (upper matrix)
   and sample size of rankings (lower matrix)

Decks	1	2	3	4	5	6	7	8	9	10	
1		967									
2	7		929								
3	6	8		934							
4		7	8		927						
5				8		951					C Scale avg.
6		5		7	8		905				921
7			5			8		867			
8							7		976		
9								8		833	
10							5	7	8		

*Three-place decimals

FP Subscale (Fair Procedure)

1. *Scale ranks*

Respondent rank	Deck 1	2	3	4	5	6	7	8	9	10
1	Mu	Bl	Do	Do,Bl	Do,Bl	Do	Do	Do,Bl	Do	Do
2	Ru	F	Bl			Bl	Bl		Fo	Ma
3	Do	Do	F	F	Fr	Br	Wa	Go	Wa	Wa
4	Bl	J	J	Wa	Wa	Wa	Br	Wa	Be	Fo
5	F	Bu	Mi	Cl	F,Ha	F,Ha	St	Br	Bl	Br
6	J	Vi	Wa	Ha			Wh	BW	Cl	St
7	Re	Cl	Cl	Mi	Cl,Re	Bu	F	St	BW	Bl
8	Vi	Re	Bu	Bu,Re		Wh	Ha	Ha,Cl	St	BW
9	Bu	Mi	Re		Bu	Cl	Cl		Ha	Ha

2. *Scale indices*

	1	2	3	4	5	6	7	8	9	10	Avg.
S	667	655	657	568	800	733	709	829	809	689	712
R	940	899	919	914	963	943	951	973	944	933	938
R'	940	910	894	899	—	923	953	965	922	923	925
M	824	756	778	800	839	798	841	819	754	785	799
M'	801	643	683	747	—	731	768	778	744	745	738
R–M	116	143	141	114	124	145	110	154	190	148	138
N	38	57	19	21	07	34	61	76	43	64	42
Characterization	F	F	F	P	Q	G	F	G+	G+	F+	F (3.4)

3. *Interscale correlations*: see **PF**

PF Subscale (Political Freedom)

1. *Scale ranks*

Deck

Respondent rank	1	2	3	4	5	6	7	8	9	10
1		Do	—	—	—	Do,Bl	Do,Bl	Do	Do	Do
2	Do,Mu,Ru	Bl	—	—	—	Do,Bl	Do,Bl		Bl	Bl
3		Fr	—	—	—	Wa	Wa,Br	Wa,Br,Go	St	Br,Ma
4	Bl	Ja	—	—	—	Br	Wa,Br		Fo	
5	Re		—	—	—	Fr	St	Bl	BW	Wa
6	Bu	Bu,Mi,	—	—	—	Ha	Wh,Cl	St	Br	St
7			—	—	—	Wh	Wh,Cl	BW	Wa	Fo
8	Vi,Fr,Ja	Vi,Re,Cl	—	—	—	Bu	Fr	Cl	Cl	BW
9			—	—	—	Cl	Ha	Ha	Ha	Ha

2. *Scale indices*

	1	2	3	4	5	6	7	8	9	10	Avg.
S	750	828	—	—	—	932	750	727	644	797	775
R	971	974	—	—	—	980	975	957	897	939	956
R'	—	—	—	—	—	—	—	—	898	905	902
M	884	831	—	—	—	810	903	822	752	745	821
M'	—	—	—	—	—	—	—	—	704	685	694
R−M	087	143	—	—	—	170	072	135	145	194	135
N	8	24	3	1	1	28	23	22	27	29	17
Characterization	Q	F+	I	I	I	E	F+	G	P	G+	F (2.7)

3. *Interscale correlations* (FP and PF)

Decks	1	2	3	4	5	6	7	8	9	10	
1		750	(943)								
2	505		763								
3				916							FP avg.
4					890						874*
5						970					
6		974					898				
7						793		982		(700)	
8							844		795	(649)	
9								635		905	
10									643		

PF avg. 732

*The average does not include correlations in parentheses, either in this matrix for FP or in those for E, B̄, or W.

RP Subscale (Pro Privacy)

1. *Scale ranks*

| | Deck | | | | | | | | | |
Respondent rank	1	2	3	4	5	6	7	8	9	10
1	Mu	Do	—	Do,Bl	—	Do	Do	Do	Do	Do
2	Ja	Bl	—	Do,Bl	—	Bl	Wa	Wa	Wa	Fo
3	Bl	Fr	—	Fr	—	Wa	Bl	Br	Fo	Br
4	Do	Bu	—	Wa,Cl	—	Br	Br	Go	Br	Wa,Ma
5	Ru		—	Wa,Cl	—	Fr,Ha	St	Bl	Bl	
6	Fr	Ja,Cl,Mi	—	Bu	—	Fr,Ha	Fr	BW	Cl,BW	Ha
7	Bu,Re		—	Ha,Mi	—	Wh		St	Cl,BW	St
8	Bu,Re	Vi	—	Ha,Mi	—	Cl	Wh,Ha	Ha	St	BW
9	Vi	Re	—	Re	—	Bu	Cl	Cl	Ha	Bl

2. *Scale indices*

	1	2	3	4	5	6	7	8	9	10	Avg
S	661	842	—	100	—	848	800	698	862	759	809
R	921	965	—	100	—	969	962	932	954	946	956
R'	—	—	—	—	—	—	952	933	926	856	917
M	769	821	—	817	—	803	784	775	782	846	800
M'	—	—	—	—	—	—	741	731	676	758	726
R–M	152	144	—	183	—	166	178	157	172	100	156
N	27	25	5	8	2	19	29	32	17	45	21
Characterization	F	G	I	Q	I	E	E	G	E	G+	F+ (4.0

3. *Interscale Correlations* (RP, RE, and VE)

Decks	1	2	3	4	5	6	7	8	9	10
1		522								
2				927						
3										
4						734				
5										
6							952			
VE:7/8 — 7								964		
RE:8/9 — 8							942		898	
9/10 — 9								807		691
8/10 — 10								(761)	801	

RP avg. 813

Respondent rank:	VE Subscales (Pro Voting Equality) 1. Scale ranks: Decks:			RE Subscales (Pro Racial Equality) 1. Scale ranks: Decks:				CE Subscale (Pro Civic Equality) 1. Scale ranks: Deck:
	8	9	10	2	8	9	10	9
1	Do							
2		Do,Fo		Do	Do	Do	Do	Do
3	[Wa,Br,Bl,BW]*		[Do,Wa,Br,Ma]*	Bl,Fr	Go	Br,Fo	Ma	Fo,Br
4		Wa,Br			Wa			
5			Bl	Ja,Bu,Cl	Br	Wa	Wa,Br,Fo	Wa
6	Go	Bl,BW	Fo		Cl	BW		Bl
7	Cl	Cl	BW	Vi,Re	St	Cl	Ha	Cl
8	St				Bl,BW	Bl	BW,St	BW / St
9	Ha	St,Ha	St,Ha	Mi	Ha	St,Ha	Bl	Ha

	VE Subscales (Pro Voting Equality)				RE Subscales (Pro Racial Equality)					CE Subscale (Pro Civic Equality)
	2. Scale indices				*2. Scale indices*					*2. Scale indices*
	8	9	10	*Avg.*	2	8	9	10	*Avg.*	9
S	960	1000	375	778	889	881	933	909	903	609
R	992	1000	935	976	**	965	1000	979	981	909
R'	—	1000	800	900	—	—	989	974	982	—
M	906	873	896	892	739	813	848	653	763	768
M'	—	775	778	776	—	—	830	675	752	141
R–M	086	127	039	084	**	152	152	326	210	—
N	30	8	9	15	8	25	11	11	6	11***
Characteri-zation	F+	Q	I	Ā (0.4)	I	E	G+	F+	P+ (1.7)	P

3. Interscale correlations: See RP

*Quadruple tie
**Only four computable decisions.
***The average number of cases of CE is 4, and all other scales rated are I, so the average characterization is 0.1 or Ā. For N's of other decks see Table 1.

E Scale (Economic Liberalism)

1. *Scale ranks*

Respondent rank	Deck 1	2	3	4	5	6	7	8	9	10
1	Ru,Bl	Bl	Bl	Do	Do,Bl	Do	Do	Bl	Do	Do
2		Do	Do	Bl		Bl	Bl	Do	Bl	Bl,Wa
3	Mu	Mi	Wa	Wa	Wa	Wa	Wa	Wa	Wa	
4	Do	Re	Mi	Cl	Cl,Br	Br	Br	Cl	Br,Cl	Br
5	Re	Vi	Re,Cl	Mi		Cl	Cl	Br		BW
6	Vi	Cl		Re	Bu	Bu	St	BW	BW	Fo
7	Fr	Bu	Fr	Bu	Re	Wh	Ha	Go	Fo	Ma
8	Bu	Fr	Bu,Ja	Fr	Fr,Ha	Ha	Fr	St	St	St
9	Ja	Ja		Ha		Fr	Wh	Ha	Ha	Ha

2. *Scale indices*

	1	2	3	4	5	6	7	8	9	10	Avg.
S	758	700	706	717	619	780	724	726	624	743	710
R	955	891	918	924	920	958	933	915	907	889	921
R'	942	891	—	936	—	950	926	906	903	896	919
M	818	681	742	763	790	797	786	727	779	667	755
M'	746	631	—	733	—	746	739	677	724	589	698
R−M	137	210	176	161	130	161	147	188	128	222	166
N	114	107	31	45	12	68	114	117	70	61	74
Characterization	G+	P+	F+	G	P	E	G	F+	P	F+	F+ (3.9)

3. *Interscale correlations (E and $\bar{B}$)*

Decks	1	2	3	4	5	6	7	8	9	10
1		967								
2	750		951							
3	(943)	786		910						
4			759		964					
5				919		984				
6					975		929			
7						902		929		
8							917		970	
9							(971)	951		994
10							(943)		958	

E avg. 955

$\bar{B}$ avg. 880

B̄ Subscale (Anti-Business)

1. Scale ranks

Respondent rank	1	2	3	4	5	6	7	8	9	10
1	Ru	Bl	Bl	Bl,Wa,Do,Cl	Bl,Do	Bl,Do,Wa	Do	Bl	Do	Do
2	Bl	Do	Wa				Bl	Do	Bl	Wa
3	Mu	Mi	Do	Wa	Wa	Br	Wa	Wa	Wa,Br,Cl	Bl
4	Do	Vi	Mi	Mi	Br,Cl	Cl	Br	Cl		Br
5	Re	Cl	Re	Re	Bu	Bu	Cl	Br	BW	BW
6	Vi	Bu	Cl	Bu	Re	Wh	St	BW	Fo	Fo,Ma
7	Fr	Re	Fr	Ha	Ha	Ha	Ha	Go	St	St
8	Bu	Ja	Ja	Fr	Fr	Fr	Fr	St	Ha	Ha
9	Ja	Fr	Bu				Wh	Ha		

2. Scale indices

	1	2	3	4	5	6	7	8	9	10	Avg.
S	794	695	674	674	611	690	730	766	788	760	718
R	959	888	903	925	917	954	942	932	970	900	929
R'	944	904	—	—	—	934	932	939	952	928	733
M	810	686	711	785	786	830	775	762	844	700	769
M'	717	636	—	—	—	771	775	703	782	617	714
R–M	149	202	192	140	131	124	167	170	126	200	160
N	85	79	19	25	10	49	75	90	48	49	53
Characterization	E	P+	F	F+	P	F+	G	G+	G	G+	F+ (4.3)

3. Interscale correlations: See E

W Subscale (Pro-Union)

1. Scale ranks

Respondent rank	Deck rank									
	1	2	3	4	5	6	7	8	9	10
1	Mu	Do	—	Do,Bl	—	Do	Do	Bl	Fo	Fo,Wa,Br
2	Ru,Do	Bl	—	Wa	—	Bl	Bl	Go	Wa	
3	Bl	Mi	—	Re,Bu	—	Wa	Wa	Wa,BW	Br,BW	St,Ha
4	Re	Re	—	Cl	—	Br,Bu	Br	Br	Ha	
5	Bu	Bu	—	Mi	—		Ha	St,Ha		BW
6	Vi	Cl,Vi	—	Fr,Ha	—		St		Bl,Cl,St	
7	Fr	Ja,Fr	—		—	Cl,Wh,Ha	Cl	Cl		Bl,Ma
8	Ja		—		—	Fr	Fr	Do	Do	Do
9			—		—		Wh			

2. Scale indices

	1	2	3	4	5	6	7	8	9	10	*Avg.*
S	789	643	—	833	—	929	800	757	682	792	777
R	970	911	—	962	—	982	928	897	889	871	926
R'	—	855	—	—	—	—	940	904	907	926	906
M	750	750	—	791	—	818	726	635	703	671	730
M'	—	718	—	—	—	—	667	616	642	605	650
R−M	220	161	—	171	—	164	202	262	186	226	199
N	17	13	6	10	1	18	27	22	17	9	14
Characterization	E	P	I	G+	I	G+	G+	G	P+	Q	F (3.3)

3. *Interscale correlations (W and F)*

Decks	1	2	3	4	5	6	7	8	9	10	W avg.
1		991		(947)							789
2	924			764							
3		834									
4			535								
5				703		963					
6							927				
7					673			406			
8									593		
9							804			882	
10											
F avg. 746											

F Scale (Pro Governmental Fiscal Interests)

1. Scale ranks

Respondent rank	Deck 1	2	3	4	5	6	7	8	9	10
1	Bl	Bl	Re	Re	Re,Cl	Bl,Wa	Fo	Wa	Bl	—
2	Mu	Mi	Bl,Mi	Bl,Wa	Wa	Bu,Cl	Cl	Cl,Br,BW	Cl,BW	—
3	Ru	Bu	Bu,Cl	Cl	Bl,Fr,Bu,Ha	Br	Wa,Bl			—
4	Vi	Vi,Re	Fr	Fr,Bu,Mi	Br	Do	Br	Ha,St,Go	Wa,Br,St	—
5	Re,Bu	Cl	Wa	Do	Do	Ha,Wh	Ha	Bl	Ha	—
6	Fr	Fr	Do,Ja	Ha		Fr	Wh	Do	Fo	—
7	Ja	Ja					St		Do	—
8	Do	Do					Do			—

2. Scale indices

	1	2	3	4	5	6	7	8	9	10	Avg.
S	672	713	773	683	652	644	714	552	762	—	685
R	850	892	896	845	837	819	893	852	899	—	865
R'	845	897	—	897	873	876	898	873	905	—	883
M	672	630	728	634	617	598	743	834	664	—	680
M'	609	544	—	563	587	575	730	772	659	—	630
R–M	178	262	168	211	220	221	150	018	235	—	185
N	69	53	10	13	7	17	37	20	14	5	24
Characterization	P+	P+	P+	P+	Q	M	P+	M	F	I	P
											(1.3)

3. Interscale correlations: See W

A Scale (Pro Judicial Review of Administrative,
Executive, and Legislative Policies)

1. Scale ranks

Respondent rank	Deck										Avg.
	1	2	3	4	5	6	7	8	9	10	
1	Do	Do	Re	—	—	—	Do	Do	Do	—	
2	Re	Fr	Wa	—	—	—	Bl	—	Bl,St	—	
3	Ru,Bl	Re	Bl,Cl	—	—	—	Wa	—	—	—	
4	—	Ja	—	—	—	—	Cl	Bl,Cl,Br,Go	—	—	
5	—	Bl	Do,Bu	—	—	—	St	—	Ha,BW	—	
6	Mu,Vi,Bu	Bu	Ja	—	—	—	Ha,Wh	Wa,St	—	—	
7	—	Cl	—	—	—	—	—	BW	—	—	
8	Ja,Fr	Mi	Fr,Mi	—	—	—	Fr,Br	Ha	Wa,Cl,Br,Fo	—	
9	—	Vi	—	—	—	—	—	—	—	—	

2. Scale indices

	1	2	3	4	5	6	7	8	9	10	Avg.
S	630	617	594	—	—	—	778	737	733	—	682
R	866	875	864	—	—	—	889	884	902	—	880
R'	877	870	—	—	—	—	889	937	—	—	893
M	645	722	673	—	—	—	600	694	741	—	679
M'	605	646	—	—	—	—	600	683	—	—	634
R—M	221	153	191	—	—	—	289	190	161	—	201
N	9	40	12	4	4	9	20	7	7	33*	14
Characterization	Q	M	M	I	I	I	P+	Q	Q	I	A (0.2)

*Only three computable decisions.

3. *Interscale correlations (A, N, and J*)*

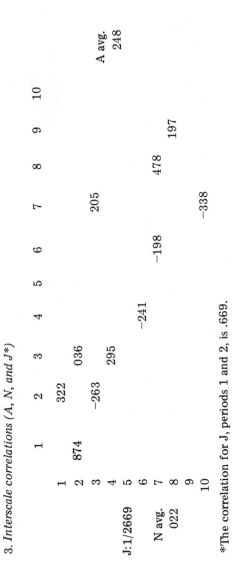

	1	2	3	4	5	6	7	8	9	10	A avg.
1											248
2	874										
3		322									
4		−263	036								
5			295	−241							
J:1/2669											
6											
7						−198	205				
N avg. 022											
8								478			
9									197		
10							−338				

*The correlation for J, periods 1 and 2, is .669.

J Scale (Pro Judicial Review of Lower Court Decisions)

1. *Scale ranks*
Respondent

Rank	Deck									
	1	2	3	4	5	6	7	8	9	10
1	Bl	Bl	—	—	—	—	Do	—	—	—
2	Bu	Bu,Ja	—	—	—	—	Br	—	—	—
3	Ja,Vi	Bu,Ja	—	—	—	—	Wa	—	—	—
4	Ja,Vi	Re,Cl	—	—	—	—	Bl	—	—	—
5	Do,Mu	Re,Cl	—	—	—	—	$\overline{Bl}$	—	—	—
6	Do,Mu	Fr	—	—	—	—	Cl,St	—	—	—
7	Re	$\overline{Vi,Mi}$	—	—	—	—	Fr,Ha	—	—	—
8	Ru	Vi,Mi	—	—	—	—	Fr,Ha	—	—	—
9	$\overline{Fr}$	Do	—	—	—	—	Wh	—	—	—

2. *Scale indices*

	1	2	3	4	5	6	7	8	9	10	Avg.
S	692	683	—	—	—	—	640	—	—	—	672
R	915	864	—	—	—	—	857	—	—	—	879
R'	926	889	—	—	—	—	889	—	—	—	901
M	744	624	—	—	—	—	643	—	—	—	670
M'	710	500	—	—	—	—	625	—	—	—	212
R–M	171	240	—	—	—	—	214	—	—	—	208
N	18	12	0	3	0	0	8	3	1	6	5
Characterization	F+	P+	I	I	I	I	Q	I	I	I	P (0.6)

3. *Interscale correlations:* See A

N Scale (Pro National Over State/Local Interests)

1. Scale ranks

Respondent rank	Deck 1	2	3	4	5	6	7	8	9	10
1	Ru	Do	Fr	Bu	—	Wh	Do	—	—	Fo,Ha
2	Do	Bl	Bl	Wa,Fr,Mi	—	Fr,Ha	Wh	—	—	Wa,Br,BW
3	Bu	Vi	Bu,Cl,Mi	Bl,Re,Cl	—	Wa	Cl	—	—	St
4	Mu,Bl	Bu	Ja	Do	—	Bl,Do,Br	Wa,Br,St	—	—	Do
5	Vi,Re	Cl	Do	Ha	—	Cl	Fr	—	—	Bl
6	Ja	Re	Wa	—	—	Bu	Bl	—	—	Ma
7	Fr	Ja	Re	—	—	—	Ha	—	—	—
8	—	Mi	—	—	—	—	—	—	—	—
9	—	Fr	—	—	—	—	—	—	—	—

2. Scale indices

	1	2	3	4	5	6	7	8	9	10	Avg.
S	571	700	714	—	—	692	737	—	—	625	673
R	853	839	902	—	—	879	883	—	—	897	876
R'	831	871	889	—	—	867	869	—	—	—	865
M	683	620	691	—	—	606	600	—	—	738	656
M'	671	584	653	—	—	593	576	—	—	—	613
R–M	170	219	211	—	—	273	283	—	—	159	219
N	25	31	8	8*	3	15	11	8	1	8	12
Characterization	M	P+	Q	I	I	P+	P+	I	I	Q	P (0.6)

3. *Interscale correlations:* See A

*Only one computable decision.

Index